The Cloud at
Your Service

The Cloud at Your Service

The when, how, and why of enterprise cloud computing

JOTHY ROSENBERG
ARTHUR MATEOS

MANNING

Greenwich
(74° w. long.)

Manning Publications Co.   Development editor: Emily Macel
Sound View Court 3B   Copyeditor: Composure Graphics
Greenwich, CT 06830   Composition: Composure Graphics
                                        Cover designer: Marija Tudor

ISBN: 9781935182528
Printed in the United States of America
1 2 3 4 5 6 7 8 9 10 – MAL – 15 14 13 12 11 10

brief contents

contents

foreword

Cloud computing is information technology (IT) offered as a service. It eliminates the need for organizations to build and maintain expensive data centers. It enables organizations to stand up new systems quickly and easily. It provides elastic resources that allow applications to scale as needed in response to market demands. Its pay-as-you-go rental model allows organizations to defer costs. It increases business continuity by providing inexpensive disaster-recovery options. It reduces the need for organizations to maintain a large IT staff.

IT is critically important: without it, most organizations can't function effectively. And yet, except in a few special cases, IT typically doesn't give its organization a competitive advantage—it isn't a core capability.

Modern economics are driving organizations to externalize noncore capabilities. If the noncore capability available from an external provider is more cost effective, then it should be externalized. By this criterion, IT is a perfect candidate for externalization.

Prior to the introduction of cloud computing, organizations externalized IT by outsourcing to IT service providers. But IT service provider relationships have never been particularly elastic. Cloud computing offers many benefits over the traditional IT outsourcing model because of the on-demand nature of the cloud business model. Organizations engage cloud-computing service providers on an application-by-application basis. It's not an all-or-nothing proposition.

Is it any wonder that cloud computing is at the center of the latest hype storm? Vendors are busy "cloud washing" their product suites and updating their *marchitecture* slide decks, hoping to capitalize on this opportunity. (It's remarkable how rapidly a terrestrial product can morph into a cloud offering.)

But moving to the cloud turns out to be more challenging than it first appears. The cloud-computing business model is still in its nascent stages, and quite a few issues remain to be worked out. *The Cloud at Your Service* is dedicated not to adding to the hype, but rather to cutting through the complexity, to aiding the decision-makers and buyers, and to helping companies develop a strategy for identifying what to move to the cloud, what not to move to the cloud, and when and how to do it.

It's easy to find one or two new noncritical applications with minimal dependencies to deploy in the cloud. But cloud adoption gets a lot trickier when you begin talking about shifting major applications to the cloud. Most cloud providers aren't willing to offer robust service-level agreements (SLAs). Can you afford to be without an application for an hour? Four hours? A day? Some cloud providers are willing to negotiate for stronger SLAs—but then the price goes up, and the compelling business case suddenly becomes much more questionable. And what happens if your chosen cloud provider goes out of business or fails to meet your requirements? How easily could you change providers or bring the application back on-premises?

What guarantees do the cloud providers give to ensure compliance with changing laws and regulations? And what about sensitive information? How damaging would it be if sensitive data leaked out? Most business applications have extensive dependencies on other applications and databases. How do you enable interoperability between cloud-based applications and the applications that remain on-premises?

These are the issues large enterprises have. It's precisely to help those enterprises that Jothy Rosenberg and Arthur Mateos wrote this book. Vendor hype, questionable business cases, and indeterminate risks increase consumer apprehension and hinder cloud adoption. But despite these issues, cloud computing is incredibly compelling. IT organizations need to understand the risks and benefits to gain the most value from cloud computing. *The Cloud at Your Service*, aimed at IT buyers (as opposed to programmers), is just what's needed.

ANNE THOMAS MANES
VICE PRESIDENT AND RESEARCH DIRECTOR
BURTON GROUP RESEARCH, A DIVISION OF GARTNER, INC.

preface

Like you, we live and work in the world of computing and computers, and we track trends and transformations as they occur. We're old enough to have witnessed mainframes and their "virtualization of time" model. We lived through the transition from minicomputers to the radical new model of client-server computing. With the same awe you had of connecting to the entire world, we witnessed the amazing change brought on by the web.

We bring that perspective to the current transformation called *cloud computing*. We've seen this movie before and know the danger of over-hyping something to death. (Literally to death—the term *artificial intelligence* had to be permanently put to rest after it made the cover of *Time* magazine.) We don't think this is hype. We see something different going on this time that isn't being exaggerated out of proportion.

We see an IT transformation that isn't primarily technology-based as the previous ones were. The same servers running the same operating systems supporting the same applications are running in corporate data centers as run in the cloud. Sure, developers have to learn a few new twists, but nothing more than they have to learn on a monthly basis anyway. Instead of technology being the basis of the change, this time it's mostly about economics and business models. That's very different, very interesting, and the reason we think this one is bigger than anything we've seen before.

We understand both small startups and big corporate IT. Our careers have been involved with both. We've lived in startups, and we've sold to and worked with large corporate IT groups for many years. As time has gone by, the ability of large IT organizations to change on a dime has diminished. We understand this trepidation about change—especially a change that may directly impact the entire organization under the corporation's CIO. That is why we wrote this book.

We had to convince Manning to publish a book that wasn't aimed squarely at programmers. When we told them the book had no source code, that didn't compute. We held firm, arguing that a huge need exists for a book that tells it like it is for the enterprise IT worker. The cloud will eventually have its greatest effect on the largest of organizations. But they're precisely the organizations that have the most trouble changing. We wanted to talk directly to you about how undertake this shift, what it will mean to you and your organization, and how to proceed in a sane and reasonable manner.

If you're in corporate IT, this book is directly written to help you. If you're in a startup, you'll find many things in this book useful as well. If you're a programmer, this may be a good addition to your bookshelf. And even if you're just curious, you'll find this book approachable, not too deeply technical, and a thorough introduction to cloud computing.

We hope the book is being published at a time that makes it helpful to the largest number of people. And we hope you find this book useful and enjoyable as you consider embarking on a journey into the clouds.

acknowledgments

Many people played a role in the long process of creating the book that you now hold in your hands, either by contributing to the body of knowledge that it contains, or by making comments and improvements to the manuscript during its writing and development.

We'd like to start with a big thank-you to the team at Manning for their support and guidance as this book evolved. They include Marjan Bace, Mike Stephens, Emily Macel, Karen Tegtmeyer, Rachel Schroeder, Tiffany Taylor, and Mary Piergies; and there were no doubt many others, through whose hands the manuscript passed on its journey from first draft to bound book.

Thanks also to the following reviewers who read the manuscript at different stages of its development, for their feedback and comments: David Sinclair, Kunal Mittal, Deiveehan Nallazhagappan, Robert Hanson, Timothy Binkley-Jones, Shreekanth Joshi, Orhan Alkan, Radhakrishna M.V., Sumit Pal, Francesco Goggi, Chad Davis, Michael Bain, Patrick Dennis, Robby O'Connor, and Christian Siegers. Also a big shout-out to the readers of Manning's Early Access Program (MEAP) for their careful reading of the early drafts of the chapters and their posts in the online forum.

Special thanks to Patrick Lightbody for contributing chapter 7, to Shawn Henry for managing the final technical review of the manuscript shortly before it went to press, and to Anne Thomas Manes for agreeing to pen the foreword to our book.

Jothy Rosenberg

First, I want to thank Dave Fachetti, a partner at Globespan Capital Venture Partners. As an entrepreneur-in-residence in his company, I had the chance to fully explore the emerging cloud market. Dave's strong vision of creating a new startup that would serve the big enterprises reflected far-sightedness. He had a rare amalgamation of CIOs from about a dozen large enterprises. They covered the gamut in their understanding and acceptance of cloud computing. The opportunity of interacting with them greatly influenced my decision about what type of book was needed for the enterprise CIO group to successfully adopt the cloud.

I would like to thank my coauthor, Arthur Mateos. Arthur was in a leadership role at Gomez, a heavy cloud user, and interacted with real users of the cloud every day. He and his team saw firsthand how the cloud was enabling new business models in exciting, transformative ways. But most important, it was Arthur who provided that extra push to make me take the plunge and agree to lead our effort to create this much-needed book.

Emily Macel is a freelance editor whom Manning brought in to work as development editor. It was her job to push and prod us to get chapters written, to stay on schedule, and to write material that was coherent, complied with Manning guidelines, and was high quality. Easy to do, I suppose, in a demanding, evil way. But Emily did it the hard way. Thank you to Emily for her kindness, patience, support, and humor. She made the hard work of creating a book fun.

My wife, Carole Hohl, thinks I am crazy because I always take on too much. When I added this book to my stack, she and my daughter Joanna, who lives with us while in graduate school, probably contemplated having me committed. Thank you, Carole and Joanna, for being incredibly supportive even when chapter deadlines sometimes robbed us of precious weekend time!

Arthur Mateos

There are several people I'd like to thank for helping us pull this book together.

First, I'd like to thank my former colleagues in the Emerging Technology group at Gomez, particularly Jason DeBettencourt, Imad Mouline, and Patrick Lightbody. In 2007, we began prototyping new SaaS products, utilizing the cloud for load-testing internet-facing load applications. It was through this early experimentation and commercialization of those products that I experienced firsthand the coming cloud revolution. A special thanks to Patrick, who also pitched in by writing chapter 7, "Testing, Deployment, and Operations in the Cloud."

I'd also like to thank Jothy Rosenberg for agreeing to join me in this project. Jothy had been pursuing a path parallel to mine, exploring cloud technologies with venture investors as potential business opportunities. The book would not have become a reality without his deep cloud expertise and boundless capacity for hard work.

Finally, I'd like to thank my wife, Grace, and our children, Arthur and Katherine, for their love and support during the writing of this book.

about this book

Cloud computing, if used properly, is a technology with tremendous promise and potential opportunity for businesses of all sizes. Yet it's a challenge for IT and business executives today to get a clear understanding of this technology while being overloaded by hype and often inaccurate information peddled by self-serving vendors and analysts.

How do you clear up the confusion; get past the fear, uncertainty, and doubt; and understand how and when the cloud best serves your organization's goals and needs?

IT organizations face numerous challenges and operate with increasingly large workloads. Severe budgetary and headcount constraints are other banes. This is why we believe it's a survival imperative to be able to appropriately harness the cloud as a potential new power tool for the IT toolbox.

The hype is more extreme than with previous IT fads or disruptions. This is because today, the industry is much bigger, and many more new vendors are chasing what is to them the next shiny new opportunity. Consequently, hype is overshadowing reality. This is making it next to impossible for responsible IT managers and business decision-makers to get a clear understanding of what the cloud really means, what it might do for them, when it's practical, and what their future with the cloud looks like. But don't let this hype discourage you from what has enormous potential benefits for your business. We aim to help cut through all this fog and help you make these critical decisions based on facts and our informed, unbiased recommendations and predictions.

The intended audience for this book

This book is for business managers, IT managers, IT architects, CIOs, CTOs, CEOs, IT strategy decision-makers, and all potential cloud services buyers. Cloud computing will be the disruptive technology of this new decade. As in the early stages of every previous major disruption of the IT industry, there is confusion, hype, fear, uncertainty, and doubt. This book aims to cut through the hype to give you a clear, unbiased view of the technology and its immense potential opportunity for you and your business. The following is a more detailed breakdown of the roles and responsibilities of the target audience.

Enterprise line of business managers

You were the first users of all previous IT disruptive technologies. You have development teams and a set of business drivers that cause you to be innovative and experimental. You get frustrated at the six-plus months it takes IT to provision new servers you request. You've discovered that you can provision what you need in the cloud in 10 minutes. This sets up conflicts with central IT, especially in these days of heightened governance and regulation. Consequently, you're hungry to learn about the cloud vis-à-vis your large enterprise issues.

Corporate IT managers and IT architects

Your budgets are down, yet your workload keeps going up. Although you constantly hear about the cloud, you know only a little about it. But you're inundated by the hype mills and can't figure out what is real. Your knee-jerk reaction toward it is doubt. You need a quick, easy way to get to the truth of what it means for you and when the time is right for you to get in.

Enterprise CEOs, CIOs, CTOs, Chief Security Officers, and Chief Risk Officers

Senior corporate officers are risk averse and have sober responsibilities to protect your organizations. But at the same time, you don't want to miss an opportunity to get an advantage before your competitors. You don't want the technical details, only the "so whats" and the truth about the cloud. This book will appeal very directly to you and arm you with critical information to assess what your staff is telling you.

Corporate IT strategy decision-makers

You work with or for the IT folks above or perhaps you're consultants brought in to help the IT organization make a strategic move to the cloud. You need a resource explaining all the facts and trends clearly without technical jargon to help you help your bosses make these hard decisions and decide the time when they need to be made.

Potential cloud services buyers

This category covers everyone else not covered earlier, if you're in the market to buy cloud services, especially if you're a small or medium-sized business. You want to learn about a new IT phenomenon that may help you. Amazon Web Services already has 600,000 small and medium-sized companies as active customers and is continuing to grow quickly. This book is different from other books on the market about cloud computing because it genuinely helps you get to the point of what the cloud may mean to you, when it may fit your IT strategy, and how you go about getting there without being loaded down with programming details you don't want or need.

Who this book is not intended for

If you're a professional programmer or a cloud expert, this book isn't designed to be your primary resource. You may still decide to add it to your bookshelf, but you'll need other books that get into details about various APIs, libraries, and frameworks you'll want to consider using.

Having said that, this book may help give you the perspective of the previously listed job descriptions. They're most likely your bosses or clients, and knowing how they think and how they're approaching the cloud will help make your job easier.

What you can expect to find in this book

This nine-chapter book covers everything you need to know about shifting some or all of your enterprise IT operations to the cloud. We've broken it into a few chapters of introduction to the cloud, how it works, and the business case for it. Going deeper into the technology, we discuss how to set up a private cloud, how to design and architect new applications that will take advantage of the cloud's unique aspects, and how the cloud changes the way you test, deploy, and operate applications. The concluding chapters include a series of practical considerations you'll want to think about before migrating to or developing for the cloud, and our take on what the future holds for cloud computing.

More specifics about what to expect from these nine chapters are outlined here.

Chapter 1, "What is cloud computing?" provides a general overview of the concepts of cloud computing. It touches briefly on the evolution of cloud computing and the growing importance of cloud computing as a boon for enterprises.

Chapter 2, "Understanding cloud computing classifications," provides an understanding of the technological underpinnings of cloud computing. It presents a framework for understanding the various types of cloud providers and gives an overview of their capabilities. It ends with a brief discussion on how to choose a cloud provider.

Chapter 3, "The business case for cloud computing," discusses the economic implications of cloud-based computing. It starts with a simplified comparison of different implementation models. Next, we look at specific examples of the cost benefit/ROI of cloud-based implementations for different sizes of organizations.

Chapter 4, "Security and the private cloud," deals with the number-one issue preventing people from adopting the cloud: security. The primary question is, "Will my data be safe?" The short answer is that security will be as much up to your policies, procedures, and careful software engineering as it ever was. Yes, in some (rare) instances, there is zero room for mistakes (for example, data related to national security), and a private cloud is warranted. As a step toward full public-cloud computing, some large enterprises are turning their existing (sunk-cost) data centers into private clouds. Why do they want to do this? Is it a good idea?

Chapter 5, "Designing and architecting for cloud scale," discusses the unique aspects of high-scale applications and how to design and architect them so they can handle the full onslaught of the entire world using your application.

Chapter 6, "Achieving high reliability at cloud scale," covers topics related to using cheap hardware in high volumes and how to deal with the expected failures of such hardware gracefully while continuing to give good service to a potentially huge number of users.

Chapter 7, "Testing, deployment, and operations in the cloud," relates to the fact that the cloud represents a different environment in which to operate from the way things are done in internal IT data centers. This chapter discusses those differences in the areas of how applications are tested, deployed, and then operated in a production scenario.

Chapter 8, "Practical considerations," looks at the practical considerations involved in running successful applications in the cloud. Beginning with the technical and business challenges that you must consider, it moves on to a discussion of the most important operational issues.

Chapter 9, "Cloud 9: the future of the cloud," discusses the future evolution of cloud computing and forecasts how the technology will evolve over the next two decades.

Author Online

Purchase of *The Cloud at Your Service* includes free access to a private web forum run by Manning Publications where you can make comments about the book, ask questions, and receive help from the authors and from other users. To access the forum and subscribe to it, point your web browser to www.manning.com/ TheCloudatYourService. This page provides information on how to get on the forum once you are registered, what kind of help is available, and the rules of conduct on the forum.

Manning's commitment to our readers is to provide a venue where a meaningful dialogue between individual readers and between readers and the authors can take place. It is not a commitment to any specific amount of participation on the part of the authors, whose contribution to the AO remains voluntary (and unpaid). We suggest you try asking the authors some challenging questions lest their interest stray! The Author Online forum and the archives of previous discussions will be accessible from the publisher's website as long as the book is in print.

About the authors

JOTHY ROSENBERG has a PhD in computer science from Duke University in the area of computer-aided design. He remained at Duke as professor of computer science until he became an entrepreneur. Jothy went on to found seven high-tech startups in areas ranging from distributed computing application management to massively parallel supercomputers to web services monitoring and security.

Most recently, Jothy was technical director for BAE Systems, running several major DARPA contracts and helping BAE develop cloud computing expertise. Before that, he ran IT investments for Angle Technology Ventures, commercializing university IP into new startups and creating two companies in that process (Aguru and Mogility). Previously, Jothy was software CTO of Ambric (semiconductor manufacturer of a teraops chip for highly compute-intensive parallel applications), founder and CEO of Service Integrity (service-oriented architecture and web services monitoring), founder and COO of GeoTrust (internet security), CEO of Novasoft (secure content management), and co-founder of WebSpective (website load-balancing and quality of service). WebSpective and GeoTrust were two companies Jothy founded that had exits greater than $100M. Jothy also held various executive positions at Borland International, including vice president and general manager of the Enterprise Tools Division, which was responsible for the Borland C++, Delphi, and JBuilder development tools.

Jothy is the author of two successful technical books: *How Debuggers Work* (Wiley, 1996) and *Securing Web Services with WS-Security* (Sams, 2004). He also holds several patents.

Throughout his career, Jothy has been involved with each computing architectural disruption (distributed computing, the internet, client-server, web services, and now the cloud) from their earliest glimmer to when they become mainstream. In many cases, he has built new companies to help make other companies' navigation through the disruption smoother. Jothy also recently published a memoir titled *Who Says I Can't* (Bascom Hill, 2010) and participates annually in athletic endeavors that have raised over $115,000 to date for charitable causes.

ARTHUR MATEOS began his career as an experimental nuclear physicist, specializing in the use of high-performance computing in the analysis of the prodigiously generated multi-terabyte data sets that are the result of colliding particles together violently at speeds close to the speed of light. Impatient at the pace of progress in high energy physics, he left that world to become a technology entrepreneur.

At WebSpective and Inktomi, he was the product manager for the web application management and content distribution product lines. Arthur was an early pioneer of the CDN space and has a patent awarded on content distribution technology. He founded Service Integrity, a company focused on web services management and providing real-time business intelligence for SOA.

Most recently, Arthur was the VP and general manager of emerging technologies at Gomez, the web performance division of Compuware. Arthur championed and led the development of a suite of innovative new SaaS offerings focused on the pre-deployment lifecycle management off web applications. The flagship offering, Reality Load, employs multiple clouds, including Gomez's own distributed worldwide cloud of over 100,000 geographically distributed measurement agents as well as those from multiple commercial cloud providers such as EC2 and GoGrid to produce the most realistic load tests possible for Internet facing applications.

Arthur holds an A.B. in physics from Princeton University and a PhD in nuclear physics from MIT.

About the foreword author

ANNE THOMAS MANES is vice president and research director with the Burton Group, a research division of Gartner, Inc., an IT research and advisory group. (See www.burtongroup.com.) She leads research on application development and delivery strategies, with a specific focus on service-oriented architecture (SOA) and cloud computing.

Anne is a widely recognized industry expert on application architecture and SOA. She is notorious for her controversial weblog post "SOA Is Dead; Long Live Services." She is one of the authors of the SOA Manifesto (www.soa-manifesto.org), the author of a forthcoming book on SOA Governance (http://soabooks.com/governance), and the author of *Web Services: A Manager's Guide* (Addison-Wesley Professional, 2003)). She is a frequent speaker at trade shows and author of numerous articles.

About the cover illustration

The figure on the cover of *The Cloud at Your Service* is captioned "Le mercier," which translates to haberdasher or a retail dealer in men's furnishings, such as shirts, ties, gloves, socks, and hats. The illustration, which is finely drawn and colored by hand, is taken from a 19th-century collection of French dress customs published in France.

The rich variety of this collection reminds us vividly of how culturally apart the world's towns and regions were just 200 years ago. Isolated from each other, people spoke different dialects and languages. In the streets or in the countryside, it was easy to identify where they lived and what their trade or station in life was just by their dress.

Dress codes have changed since then and the diversity by region, so rich at the time, has faded away. It is now hard to tell apart the inhabitants of different continents, let alone different towns or regions. Perhaps we have traded cultural diversity for a more varied personal life—certainly for a more varied and fast-paced technological life.

At a time when it's hard to tell one computer book from another, Manning celebrates the inventiveness and initiative of the computer business with book covers based on the rich diversity of regional life of two centuries ago, brought back to life by illustrations such as this one.

What is cloud computing?

This chapter covers

- Defining the five main principles of cloud computing
- Benefiting from moving to the cloud
- How evolving IT led to cloud computing
- Discussing the different layers (types) of clouds

Cloud computing is the hottest buzzword in the IT world right now. Let's understand why this is and what this cloud computing hype is all about. A growing consensus among cloud vendors, analysts, and users defines cloud computing at the highest level as computing services offered by a third party, available for use when needed, that can be scaled dynamically in response to changing needs. Cloud computing represents a departure from the norm of developing, operating, and managing IT systems. From the economic perspective, not only does adoption of cloud computing have the potential of providing enormous economic benefit, but it also provides much greater flexibility and agility. We'll continue to refine and expand our definition of cloud computing as well as your understanding of its costs and benefits throughout this book.

Not only are IT journals and IT conferences writing and talking about cloud computing, but even mainstream business magazines and the mass media are caught up in its storm. It may win the prize for the most over-hyped concept IT has ever had. Other terms in this over-hyped category include Service-Oriented Architectures (SOA), application service providers, and artificial intelligence, to name a few. Because this book is about cloud computing, we need to define it at a much more detailed level. You need to fully understand its pros and cons, and when it makes sense to adopt it, all of which we'll explain in this chapter. We hope to cut through the hype; and to do that we won't merely repeat what you've been hearing but will instead give you a framework to understand what the concept is all about and why it really is important.

You may wonder what is driving this cloud hype. And it would be easy to blame analysts and other prognosticators trying to promote their services, or vendors trying to play up their capabilities to demonstrate their thought leadership in the market, or authors trying to sell new books. But that would ignore a good deal of what is legitimately fueling the cloud mania. All of the great expectations for it are based on the facts on the ground.

Software developers around the world are beginning to use cloud services. In the first 18 months that it was open for use, the first public cloud offering from Amazon attracted over 500,000 customers. This isn't hype; these are facts. As figure 1.1 from Amazon's website shows, the bandwidth consumed by the company's cloud has quickly eclipsed that used by their online store. As the old adage goes, "where there's smoke, there must be a fire," and clearly something is driving the rapid uptake in usage from a cold start in mid-2006.

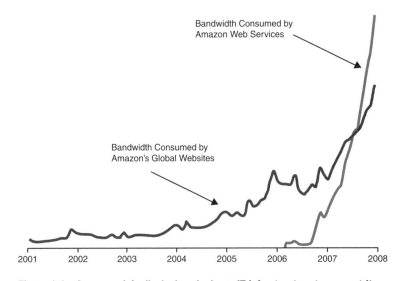

Figure 1.1   Amazon originally deployed a large IT infrastructure to support its global e-commerce platform. In less than 18 months after making the platform available as a cloud service to external users, its usage, as measured by amount of bandwidth consumed, outstripped bandwidth used internally.

Similar to the previous technology shifts—such as the move from mainframes to client-server, and then from client-server to the internet—cloud computing will have major implications on the business of IT. We hope to provide you with the background and perspective to understand how it can be effectively used as a component of your overall IT portfolio.

We'll begin by expanding on our earlier definition of cloud computing in terms of its five main principles.

1.1 Five main principles that define cloud computing

We can summarize the five main principles of cloud computing as follows:

- Pooled computing resources available to any subscribing users
- Virtualized computing resources to maximize hardware utilization
- Elastic scaling up or down according to need
- Automated creation of new virtual machines or deletion of existing ones
- Resource usage billed only as used

We assert, with very few notable exceptions called out later, that these five main principles are necessary components to call something *cloud computing*. They're summarized in table 1.1 with a brief explanation of each one for quick reference.

Table 1.1   The five main principles of cloud computing

Resource	Explanation
Pooled resources	Available to any subscribing users
Virtualization	High utilization of hardware assets
Elasticity	Dynamic scale without CAPEX
Automation	Build, deploy, configure, provision, and move, all without manual intervention
Metered billing	Per-usage business model; pay only for what you use

We'll now discuss these principles in concrete terms, making sure you understand what each one means and why it's a pillar of cloud computing.

1.1.1 Pooled computing resources

The first characteristic of cloud computing is that it utilizes pooled computing assets that may be externally purchased and controlled or may instead be internal resources that are pooled and not dedicated. We further qualify these pooled computing resources as contributing to a cloud if these resources are available to any subscribing users. This means that *anyone* with a credit card can subscribe.

If we consider a corporate website example, three basic operational deployment options are commonly employed today. The first option is the self-hosting option. Here, companies choose not to run their own data center and instead have a third party lease them a server that the third party manages. Usually, managed hosting services lease corporate clients a dedicated server that isn't shared (but shared hosting is common as well). On this single principle, cloud computing acts like a *shared managed hosting service* because the cloud provider is a third party that owns and manages the physical computing resources which are shared with other users, but there the similarity ends.

Independent of cloud computing, a shift from self-hosted IT to outsourced IT resources has been underway for years. This has important economic implications. The two primary implications are a shift of capital expenses (CAPEX) to operational expenses (OPEX), and the potential reduction in OPEX associated with operating the infrastructure. The shift from CAPEX to OPEX means a lowering of the financial barrier for the initiation of a new project. (See the definition in section 3.1.)

In the self-hosted model, companies have to allocate a budget to be spent up front for the purchase of hardware and software licenses. This is a fixed cost regardless of whether the project is successful. In an outsourced model (managed hosting), the startup fees are typically equivalent to one month's operational cost, and you must commit to one year of costs up front. Typically, the one-year cost is roughly the same or slightly lower than the CAPEX cost for an equivalent project, but this is offset by the reduced OPEX required to operate the infrastructure. In sharp contrast, in a cloud model, there are typically no initial startup fees. In fact, you can sign up, authorize a credit card, and start using cloud services literally in less time than it would take to read this chapter. Figure 1.2 showcases side by side the various application deployment models with their respective CAPEX and OPEX sizes.

The drastic difference in economics that you see between the hosting models and the cloud is due to the fact that the cost structures for cloud infrastructures are vastly better than those found in other models. The reasons for the economies of scale are severalfold, but the primary drivers are related to the simple economics of volume. Walmart and Costco can buy consumer goods at a price point much lower than you or I could because of their bulk purchases. In the world of computing, the "goods" are computing, storage, power, and network capacity.

1.1.2 *Virtualization of compute resources*

The second of the five main principles of cloud computing has to do with virtualization of compute resources. Virtualization is nothing new. Most enterprises have been shifting much of their physical compute infrastructure to virtualized for the past 5 to 10 years. Virtualization is vital to the cloud because the

Application deployment models

Figure 1.2 IT organizations have several alternatives for hosting applications. The choice of deployment model has different implications for the amount of CAPEX (up-front capital expenditure) and OPEX (ongoing operational costs). The number of $ signs represent the relative level of CAPEX and OPEX involved with the choice of deployment model.

scale of cloud infrastructures has to be enormous, based on thousands of servers. Each server takes up physical space and uses significant power and cooling. Getting high utilization out of each and every server is vital to be cost effective.

The recent technological breakthrough that enabled high utilization on commodity hardware—and which is the single biggest factor behind the cloud being a recent IT phenomenon—is virtualization where each physical server is partitioned into many virtual servers. Each one acts like a real server that can run an operating system and a full complement of applications.[1] Virtualized servers are the primary units that can be consumed as needed in the cloud. These virtualized servers constitute a large pool of resources available when required. But having such a large pool will work only if applications can use more or less of the pool as demands placed on the applications grow and shrink. As you'll see in chapter 4, the notion of a private cloud softens this first principal but keeps all the others.

1.1.3 *Elasticity as resource demands grow and shrink*

The fact that this large pool of resources exists enables a concept known as *elasticity*—the third of our five main principles. Elasticity is such a key concept in cloud computing that Amazon decided to name its cloud Amazon Elastic Compute Cloud.

Elasticity—a synonym for *dynamic scaling*—refers to the ability to dynamically change how much resource is consumed in response to how much is needed. Typical applications require a base level of resources under normal, steady-state conditions, but need more resource under peak load conditions.

In a non-cloud world, you would have to build sufficient capacity to not only perform adequately under baseline load conditions, but also handle peak load scenarios with sufficiently good performance. In the case of a self-hosted model, this means over-provisioning the amount of hardware for a given allocation. In the case of a managed hosting deployment, you can start with a small set of resources and grow as the requirements of the application grow. But provisioning for a new set of dedicated hardware resources takes weeks or, in many larger organizations, months. Having thousands of virtualized resources that can be harnessed and released in correlation to application demand would be useless if such allocation and freeing required manual intervention.

1.1.4 *Automation of new resource deployment*

The ability to automatically (via an API) provision and deploy a new virtual instance of a machine, and, equivalently, to be able to free or de-provision an instance, is our fourth principle of cloud computing. A cloud-deployed application can provision new instances on an as-needed basis, and these resources are brought online within minutes. After the peak demand ebbs, and you don't need the additional resources, these

---

[1] The rapid shift to multicore servers only strengthens the impact of virtualization. Each virtual machine with its operating system and full complement of applications can run on its own core simultaneously with all other virtual machines on the same physical server.

virtual instances can be taken offline and de-provisioned, and you will no longer be billed. Your incremental cost is only for the hours that those additional instances were in use and active.

1.1.5   *Metered billing that charges only for what you use*

The fifth distinguishing characteristic of cloud computing is a metered billing model. In the case of managed hosting, as we mentioned before, there typically is an initial startup fee and an annual contract fee. The cloud model breaks that economic barrier because it's a pay-as-you-go model. There is no annual contract and no commitment for a specific level of consumption.

Typically, you can allocate resources as needed and pay for them on an hourly basis. This economic advantage benefits not only projects being run by IT organizations, but also innumerable entrepreneurs starting new businesses. Instead of needing to raise capital as they might have in the past, they can utilize vast quantities of compute resources for pennies per hour. For them, the cloud has drastically changed the playing field and allowed the little guy to be on equal footing with the largest corporations.

1.2   *Benefits that can be garnered from moving to the cloud*

"I'll never buy another server again," said the Director of IT for a medium-sized Software-as-a-Service (SaaS) company, only partially in jest, after recently completing the deployment of a new corporate website for his organization. This website (a PHP-based application with a MySQL backend) showcased the corporate brand and the primary online lead-generation capability for the company's business.

Before the overhaul, it was run from a redundant pair of web servers hosted by one of the leading managed-hosting service providers at a total cost of roughly $2,200/month. The company replaced the infrastructure for the original website with a cloud implementation consisting of a pair of virtual server instances running for roughly $250/month—almost a 90 percent savings! Its quality of service (QoS) team monitored the performance and availability of the website before and after the change and saw no measureable difference in the service quality delivered to end users. Buoyed by the success with this initial project, this organization is looking at all future initiatives for the possibility of deployment within the cloud, including a software-build system and offsite backup.

1.2.1   *Economic benefits of the change from capital to operational expenses*

As we said when discussing the five main principles of cloud computing, the fundamental economic benefit that cloud computing brings to the table is related to the magical conversion of CAPEX to OPEX. A pay-as-you-go model for resource use reshapes the fundamental cost structure of building and operating applications. The initial barrier to starting a project is drastically reduced; and until there is dramatic uptake in the use of an application that has been developed, the costs for running it remain low.

The good news is that this isn't the only cost advantage. By harnessing the cloud, you can also take advantage of cloud providers' economic leverage because of the volume at which they can purchase hardware, power, and bandwidth resources.

In many cases, the economic benefits discussed here will pan out—but as you'll see later, there are always exceptions. For some situations and applications, it makes better economic sense not to use cloud computing. It isn't a panacea.

1.2.2 Agility benefits from not having to procure and provision servers

In addition to lowering the financial barrier to initiating new projects, the cloud approach improves an organization's agility. It comprehensively reduces the months of planning, purchasing, provisioning, and configuring.

Let's take as an example a performance-testing project launching a new consumer-facing website. In the old world, there were two ways to solve this problem, depending on your timeframes and budget. The first involved purchasing a software license for a load-testing tool like HP Mercury LoadRunner and purchasing the requisite servers to run the load-testing software. At that point, you were ready to script your tests and run your test plan. Alternatively, you could hire an outside consulting company that specialized in performance testing and have it run the tests for you. Both were time-consuming exercises, depending on how long it took to negotiate either the licensing agreement for the software or the consulting agreement with the outside firm.

Fast-forward to the new world of cloud computing. You have two new faster and more flexible ways of accomplishing the same task: use an open-source load-testing application installed on cloud instances, and use the cloud's virtual machines to perform the load test (on as many servers as you need). The time required to set up and begin applying load to a system is under half an hour. This includes signing up for an account, as the Python open source load-testing tool called Pylot demonstrates (see http://coreygoldberg.blogspot.com/2009/02/pylot-web-load-testing-from-amazon.html).

If you're looking for a more packaged approach, you can use one of the SaaS offerings that uses the cloud to generate traffic. They can automatically run tests in a coordinated fashion across multiple instances running from multiple cloud operators, all in an on-demand fashion. In either of these scenarios, the time to result is a matter of hours or days, generating time, not to mention cost efficiencies. We'll explore more about cloud-based testing in chapter 7.

1.2.3 Efficiency benefits that may lead to competitive advantages

Adopting cloud technologies presents many opportunities to those who are able to capitalize on them. As we have discussed, there are potential economic as well as time-to-market advantages in using the technology. As organizations adopt cloud computing, they will realize efficiencies that organizations that are slower to move won't realize, putting them at an advantage competitively.

1.2.4   Security stronger and better in the cloud

Surprised by the heading? Don't be: it's true. As you're aware, corporate buildings no longer have electrical generators (which they used to) because we leave electricity generation to the experts. If corporations have their own data centers, they have to develop standard security operating procedures. But it's not their core business to run a secure data center. They can and will make mistakes. A lot of mistakes. The total annual fraud and security breach tab is $1 trillion, according to cybersecurity research firm Poneman (www.nationalcybersecurity.com).

But first, as always, you must weigh the potential benefits against the potential costs. You must take into account other factors, such as reliability and performance, before making the leap into the clouds. In future chapters, we'll address these issues; but suffice it to say we believe that after you understand them and take the proper measures, they can be managed. This done, you'll be able to realize the full benefits of moving to the cloud.

In the next section, we'll look at the evolution of technology that enabled cloud computing. This short detour into history is important because you can learn from previous platform shifts to understand what is similar and what is different this time. That in turn can help you make informed decisions about your shift to this new evolution of IT—the cloud.

1.3   Evolution of IT leading to cloud computing

Cloud computing didn't sprout fully formed from the technology ether in 2005. Its technological underpinnings developed over the course of the last 40 or so years. The technological process was evolutionary, across several disparate areas. But these advances, aggregated into a bundle, represent a revolutionary change in the way IT will be conducted in the future.

Gillett and Kapor made the first known reference to cloud computing in 1996 in an MIT paper (http://ccs.mit.edu/papers/CCSWP197/CCSWP197.html). Today's common understanding of cloud computing retains the original intent. It was a mere decade later when a real-world instantiation of the cloud came into existence as Amazon repurposed its latent e-commerce resources and went into the business of providing cloud services. From there, it was only a matter of a few months until the term became commonplace in our collective consciousness and, as figure 1.3 shows, in our Google search requests (they're the same thing in today's world, right?).

1.3.1   Origin of the "cloud" metaphor

One common question people ask is, "Where did the term *cloud* come from?" The answer is that for over a decade, whenever people drew pictures of application architectures that involved the internet, they inevitably represented the internet with a cloud, as shown in figure 1.4.

The cloud in the diagram is meant to convey that anonymous people are sitting at browsers accessing the internet, and somehow their browser visits a site and begins to

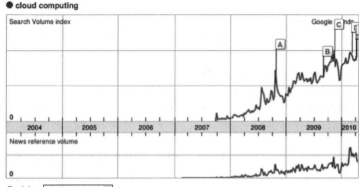

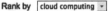

Figure 1.3   Cloud computing as a concept entered our collective consciousness in mid-2007. This figure shows the rapid rise in popularity of the search term *cloud computing* as measured by Google. The labels correspond to major cloud announcements. A: Microsoft announces it will rent cloud computing space; B: *Philadelphia Inquirer* reports, "Microsoft's cloud computing system grow is growing up"; C: *Winnipeg Free Press* reports, "Google looks to be cloud-computing rainmaker." Source: Google Trends (www.google.com/trends), on the term *cloud computing*.

access its infrastructure and applications. From "somewhere out there" you get visitors who can become users who may buy products or services from you. Unlike internal customers to whom you may provide IT applications and services, this constituency exists "somewhere else," outside of your firewall, and hence outside of your domain of control. The image of a cloud is merely a way to represent this vast potential base of anonymous users coming from the internet.

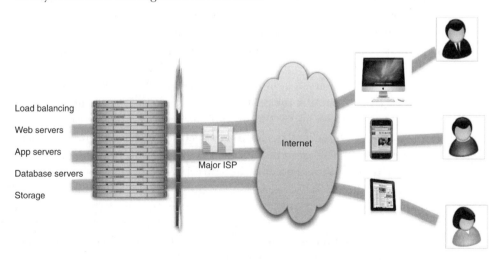

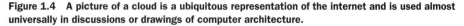

Figure 1.4   A picture of a cloud is a ubiquitous representation of the internet and is used almost universally in discussions or drawings of computer architecture.

Those users must log in from a PC to access the internet. Technically, each one needs an Internet Service Provider (ISP) that may be a telecom company, their employer, or a dedicated internet access company (such as AOL). Each ISP needs a bank of machines that people can access and that in turn has access to the internet.

Simply put, the earliest concept of the cloud consisted of large aggregations of computers with access to the internet, accessed by people through their browsers. The concept has remained surprisingly true to that early vision but has evolved and matured in important ways. We'll explore those ways in detail in this book.

1.3.2 *Major computing paradigm shifts: mainframes to client-server to web*

In the 1960s, we saw the development of the first commercial mainframes. In the beginning, these were single-user systems, but they evolved in the 1970s to systems that were time-shared. In this model, the large computing resource was *virtualized*, and a virtual machine was allocated to individual users who were sharing the system (but to each, it seemed that they had an entire dedicated machine).

Virtual instances were accessed in a thin-client model by green-screen terminals. This mode of access can be seen as a direct analog of the concept of virtualized instances in the cloud, although then a single machine was divided among users. In the cloud, it's potentially many thousands of machines. The scarcity of the computing resource in the past drove the virtualization of that resource so that it could be shared, whereas now, the desire to fully utilize physical compute resources is driving cloud virtualization.

As we evolved and entered the client-server era, the primacy of the mainframe as the computing center of the universe dissolved. As computing power increased, work gradually shifted away from centralized computing resources toward increasingly powerful distributed systems. In the era of the PC-based desktop applications, this shift was nearly complete: computing resources for many everyday computing tasks moved to the desktop and became thick client applications (such as Microsoft Office). The mainframe retained its primacy only for corporate or department-wide applications, relegating it to this role alone.

The standardization of networking technology simplified the ability to connect systems as TCP/IP became the protocol of the burgeoning internet in the 1980s. The ascendancy of the web and HTTP in the late 1990s swung the pendulum back to a world where the thin-client model reigned supreme. The world was now positioned to move into the era of *cloud computing*. The biggest stages of the evolution of IT are diagrammed vertically in a timeline in figure 1.5.

The computing evolution we are still in the midst of has had many stages. Platform shifts like mainframe to client-server and then client-server to web were one dimension of the evolution. One that may be less apparent but that is having as profound an impact is the evolution of the data center and how physical computing resources are housed, powered, maintained, and upgraded.

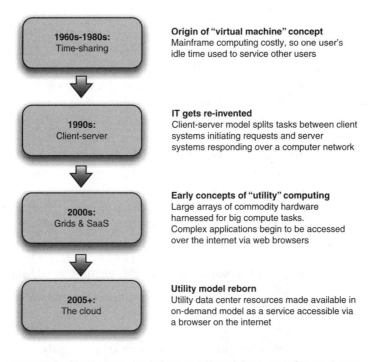

1960s-1980s:
Time-sharing

Origin of "virtual machine" concept
Mainframe computing costly, so one user's
idle time used to service other users

1990s:
Client-server

IT gets re-invented
Client-server model splits tasks between client
systems initiating requests and server
systems responding over a computer network

2000s:
Grids & SaaS

Early concepts of "utility" computing
Large arrays of commodity hardware
harnessed for big compute tasks.
Complex applications begin to be accessed
over the internet via web browsers

2005+:
The cloud

Utility model reborn
Utility data center resources made available in
on-demand model as a service accessible via
a browser on the internet

**Figure 1.5   Cloud computing is best understood as an evolutionary change.
The key elements and concepts of cloud computing emerged gradually over
several decades through the various predominant computing paradigms.**

1.3.3 Housing of physical computing resources: data center evolution

Over the past four decades, there have been tremendous changes in hardware capabilities, specifically in computing power and storage. The ability to quickly process prodigious amounts of data on inexpensive and mass-produced commodity servers means that a few inexpensive racks of servers can handle problems that were tackled on NSA-sized budgets as recently as the early 1990s.

One measure of the progress in computational power is the cost in Floating Point Operations Per Second, or FLOPS. FLOPS are simple mathematical operations (such as addition, multiplication, and division) that can be performed in a single operation by a computer. Comparing the number of operations that two computers can perform in one second allows for a rough measure of their computational strength. In 1976, the state-of-the-art Cray-1 was capable of delivering roughly 150 million FLOPS (megaFLOPS) at the price point of $5 million, or over $33,000/MegaFLOPS. A typical quad-core-processor-based PC today can be purchased for under $1,000 and can perform 50 GigaFLOPS (billion FLOPS), which comes out to about $0.02/MegaFLOPS.

Similarly, the cost of storage has decreased dramatically over the last few decades as the capacity to store data has kept pace with the ability to produce terabytes of digital content in the form of high-definition HD video and high-resolution imagery. In the early 1980s, disk space costs exceeded $200/MB; today, this cost has come down to under $0.01/MB.

Network technologies have advanced as well, with modern bandwidth rates in the 100–1000 Gbps range commonplace in data centers today. As for WAN, the turn of the millennium saw a massive build-out of dark fiber, bringing high-speed broadband to most urban areas. More rural areas have satellite coverage, and on-the-go, high-speed wireless networks mean almost ubiquitous broadband connectivity to the grid.

To support the cloud, a huge data-center build-out is now underway. Google, Microsoft, Yahoo!, Expedia, Amazon, and others are deploying massive data centers. These are the engine rooms that power the cloud, and they now account for more than 1.2 percent of the U.S.'s total electricity usage (including cooling and auxiliaries),[2] which doubled over the period from 2000 to 2005. We'll present the economies of scale and much more detail about how these mega data centers are shaping up in chapter 2.

1.3.4   *Software componentization and remote access: SOA, virtualization, and SaaS*

On the software side of the cloud evolution are three important threads of development: virtualization, SOA, and SaaS. Two of these are technological, and the third relates to the business model.

The first important thread is virtualization. As discussed previously, virtualization isn't a new concept, and it existed in mainframe environments. The new innovation that took place in the late 1990s was the extension of this idea to commodity hardware. Virtualization as pioneered by VMware and others took advantage of the capacity of modern multicore CPUs and made it possible to partition and time-slice the operation of commodity servers. Large server farms based on these commodity servers were partitioned for use across large populations of users.

SOA is the second software concept necessary for cloud computing. We see SOA as the logical extension of browser-based standardization applied to machine-to-machine communication. Things that humans did through browsers that interacted with a web server are now done machine-to-machine using the same web-based standard protocols and are called *SOA*. SOA makes practical the componentization and composition of services into applications, and hence it can serve as the architectural model for building composite applications running on multiple virtualized instances.

The final software evolution we consider most pertinent to the cloud is SaaS. Instead of being a technological innovation, this is a business model innovation. Historically, enterprise software was sold predominantly in a perpetual license model. In this model, a customer purchased the right to use a certain software application in perpetuity for a fixed, and in many cases high, price. In subsequent years, they paid for support and maintenance at typically around 18 percent of the original price. This entitled the

---

[2] Jonathan G. Koomey, Ph.D. (www.koomey.com), Lawrence Berkeley National Laboratory & Stanford University.

customer to upgrades of the software and help when they ran into difficulty. In the SaaS model, you don't purchase the software—you rent it. Typically, the fee scales with the amount of use, so the value derived from the software is proportional to the amount spent on it. The customer buys access to the software for a specified term, which may be days, weeks, months, or years, and can elect to stop paying when they no longer need the SaaS offering. Cloud computing service providers have adopted this *pay-as-you-go* or *on-demand* model.

This brings up an important point we need to consider next. SaaS is one flavor or layer in a stack of cloud types. A common mistake people make in these early days of the cloud is to make an apples-to-oranges comparison of one type of cloud to another. To avoid that, the next section will classify the different layers in the cloud stack and how they compare and contrast.

1.4   *Classifying cloud layers: different types for different uses*

First, let's learn a little more about how SaaS evolved and established itself, to set the context for discussing the other classes of clouds.

In the earliest days of commercially practicable computing, computer resources were scarce, and the primary model for their use was much like a utility. But this was different from the sense of utility that cloud computing offers today; it was more akin to the community well in a village during a drought. Members of the community had access to and were allocated a fixed amount of water. In the case of cloud computing today, we've returned to the notion of computing being available as a utility, but without the scarcity.

The cloud movement was presaged by the shift in business model toward SaaS that took over the software industry at the turn of the century. Before it was called SaaS, it was an application rented from an Application Service Provider (ASP); here, the traditional enterprise license model was turned on its head, and you purchased in a pay-as-you-go manner, with costs scaling with usage instead of having a large up-front capital investment. You didn't need to provision hardware and software; instead, the services were turned on when needed. After this approach was renamed SaaS, it evolved into several new kinds of offerings that we'll explore next.

We can classify cloud computing several ways. In this book, we present a taxonomy where cloud services are described generically as "X as a Service," where X can take on values such as Hardware, Infrastructure, Platform, Framework, Application, and even Datacenter. Vendors aren't in agreement about what these designations mean, nor are they consistent in describing themselves as belonging to these categories. Despite this, we'll reproduce one interesting hierarchy that illustrates the use of these terms, with representative vendors (some at this point only historical) populating the diagram in figure 1.6.

A more simplified representation of the cloud types shown in figure 1.7 highlights important aspects and key characteristics of different kinds of cloud offerings.

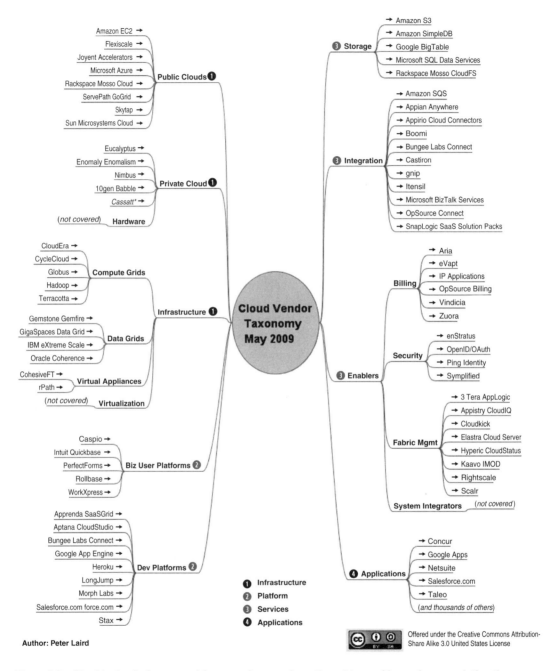

Figure 1.6   Cloud technologies are evolving as various vendors attempt to provide services populating the cloud ecosystem. These services run the gamut from the hardware systems used to build cloud infrastructure to integration services and cloud-based applications. Source: Peter Laird, http://peterlaird.blogspot.com.

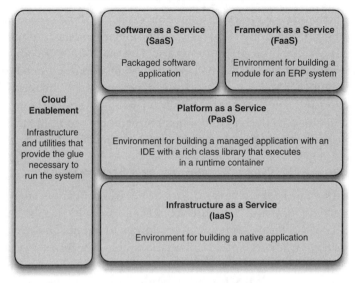

Figure 1.7   In the X-as-a-Service taxonomy, cloud services are classified by the level of prepackaging offered to the consumer of the specific service. An IaaS provides computing capabilities in the rawest form and hence offers the greatest flexibility. At the highest layers, there is less flexibility but also less complexity to be managed.

What does XaaS mean generically? It means on demand, requiring little or no capital expenditure. It means consumable remotely and across any mode of access over the internet, and in a metered billing model. Let's now go through the boxes representing the different classes of clouds in figure 1.7. First up is IaaS.

1.4.1   Infrastructure as a Service (IaaS)

The lowest level of XaaS is known as IaaS, or sometimes as Hardware as a Service (HaaS). A good example of IaaS is the Amazon Elastic Compute Cloud (EC2).

A user of IaaS is operating at the lowest level of granularity available and with the least amount of prepackaged functionality. An IaaS provider supplies virtual machine images of different operating system flavors. These images can be tailored by the developer to run any custom or packaged application. These applications can run natively on the chosen OS and can be saved for a particular purpose. The user can bring online and use instances of these virtual machine images when needed. Use of these images is typically metered and charged in hour-long increments.

Storage and bandwidth are also consumable commodities in an IaaS environment, with storage typically charged per gigabyte per month and bandwidth charged for transit into and out of the system.

IaaS provides great flexibility and control over the cloud resources being consumed, but typically more work is required of the developer to operate effectively in the environment. In chapter 2, we'll delve into IaaS and see how it works in greater detail.

1.4.2   *Platform as a Service (PaaS)*

PaaS's fundamental billing quantities are somewhat similar to those of IaaS: consumption of CPU, bandwidth, and storage operates under similar models. Examples of PaaS include Google AppEngine and Microsoft Azure. The main difference is that PaaS requires less interaction with the bare metal of the system. You don't need to directly interact with or administer the virtual OSs. Instead, you can let the platform abstract away that interaction and concentrate specifically on writing the application. This simplification generally comes at the cost of less flexibility and the requirement to code in the specific languages supported by the particular PaaS provider.

1.4.3   *Software as a Service (SaaS) and Framework as a Service (FaaS)*

SaaS, as described earlier in the chapter, refers to services and applications that are available on an on-demand basis. Salesforce.com is an example. FaaS is an environment adjunct to a SaaS offering and allows developers to extend the prebuilt functionality of the SaaS applications. Force.com is an example of a FaaS that extends the Salesforce.com SaaS offering.

FaaS offerings are useful specifically for augmenting and enhancing the capabilities of the base SaaS system. You can use FaaS for creating either custom, specialized applications for a specific organization, or general-purpose applications that can be made available to any customer of the SaaS offering. Like a PaaS environment, a developer in a FaaS environment can only use the specific languages and APIs provided by the FaaS.

1.4.4   *Private clouds as precursors of public clouds*

In addition to the classifications we discussed earlier, we should introduce some important concepts relative to the different classifications of clouds. *Private clouds* are a variant of generic cloud computing where internal data-center resources of an enterprise or organization aren't made available to the general public—that is, these pooled computing resources are actually not available to *any* subscribing users but are instead controlled by an organization for the benefit of other members of that organization. The public clouds of providers such as Amazon and Google were originally used as private clouds by those companies for other lines of business (book retailing and internet search, respectively).

If an organization has sufficient users and enough overall capacity, a private cloud implementation can behave much like a public cloud, albeit on a reduced scale. There has been a tremendous amount of capital investment in data-center resources over the past decade, and one of the important movements is the reorienting of these assets toward cloud-usage models.

Hybrid clouds combine private and public clouds. You can use them in cases where the capacity of a private cloud is exhausted and excess capacity needs to be provisioned elsewhere.

1.5 *Summary*

The cloud offers the illusion of infinite resources, available on demand. You no longer need to play the guessing game of how many users need to be supported and how scalable the application is. The cloud takes care of the peaks and troughs of utilization times. In the world of the cloud, you pay for only the resources you use, when you use them. This is the revolutionary change: the ability to handle scale without paying a premium. In this realm of true utility computing, resource utilization mirrors the way we consume electricity or water.

In this chapter, we defined the cloud as computing services that are offered by a third party, are available for use when needed, and can be scaled dynamically in response to changing need. We then touched briefly on the evolution of computing and the developments that led to where we are today. Finally, we looked at a simple cloud classification that should help you understand the various flavors of cloud offerings that are available in the market today and should prevent you from making apples-and-oranges comparisons between incompatible classes of clouds.

As we delve deeper in the next chapter and look at how the cloud works, you'll gain a better understanding of these types of clouds and when it makes sense to use each kind.

Understanding cloud computing classifications

2

This chapter covers

- Necessary technological underpinnings common to all cloud types
- Classifying the types of clouds and their capabilities
- Choosing the appropriate type of cloud and the best provider for it

Now that we've set the stage for an understanding of what cloud computing is, we can look under the hood and help you understand the different types or classifications of clouds and how they work. Keeping with the under-the-hood analogy, with cloud computing as our vehicle, the modern data center will serve as the engine and virtualization as the vehicle's suspension smoothing out the road. The cloud's API is similar to the dashboard and controls of the vehicle, allowing you to drive it; cloud storage is similar to the trunk, allowing you to transport things; cloud databases are the navigation system (specific information) you need for the trip; and elasticity is the vehicle's transmission that allows the engine's speed to be translated into low- or high-vehicle speeds, which is analogous to allowing your application to support one user and suddenly expand when it needs to support one million. Similar to the variety of vehicles available, there are a wide variety of cloud types. We'll examine the major ones in existence today. Do you need a racing car because you require the speed, or do you need a giant 18-wheeler because of its space capacity?

Let's begin by looking at the six most critical technological underpinnings of the cloud to understand what it's made of. We'll expand on our initial discussion from chapter 1 of the different types of clouds and how they compare and contrast with each other. This will prepare you to make better decisions about which type of cloud you need and how to make best use of it.

2.1 The technological underpinnings of cloud computing

Either through curiosity or because it makes us better drivers and owners, most of us learn the basics of how their car works. Similarly, let's learn about the basic technologies and infrastructure needed to build a cloud, regardless of type, to understand its workings:

- *A cloud needs servers on a network, and they need a home.* That physical home and all the gear in it make up a *data center.*
- *A cloud's servers need to be virtualized.* This is in order to use a large bank of servers effectively. Otherwise, the economics of a huge number of servers won't allow the cloud to be cost effective.
- *A cloud needs an access API.* Without an access API, the virtualized servers in the cloud would be quiet and lonely. Cloud users need a way to access the cloud, provision new virtual servers, get data in and out of storage, start and stop applications on those servers, and decommission servers that are no longer needed. All this needs to be possible remotely, because cloud users never set foot inside the data center.
- *A cloud needs some storage.* It needs to store virtual machine images, users' applications, and persistent data needed by those applications.
- *Cloud applications need a database.* Most applications also need structured data during execution. Consequently, the cloud needs some sort of database.
- *A cloud needs elasticity as a way to expand and contract applications.* A cloud must be dynamically scalable. One of the chief attractions of cloud computing is the ability to have applications that can scale up or down as per the demand the application receives.

In the following six subsections, we'll tackle each of the aforementioned aspects of technology and infrastructure that together form the technological underpinnings of cloud computing.

2.1.1 Achieving high economies of scale with cloud data centers

Revisiting the vehicle analogy, the data center is the car's engine. A *data center*—one that you might find in any large company—is a facility (usually secure) to house a large collection of computers, networking, and communications equipment. But the large internet-based companies, such as Amazon, Yahoo!, Google, Intuit, Apple, and others have, over the years, built up what have to be considered *mega* data centers with thousands of servers. These data centers are the starting point for what is being built out by the cloud providers.

It's useful to understand the structure and the economics of these massive data centers to gauge how much you can scale your operations, how reliable your cloud computing will be, how secure your data will be, and where the economics of public clouds are going. This is particularly important should you decide to build your own *private* cloud. You'll learn more about private clouds later in this chapter, and we've dedicated chapter 4 to the topics of security and private clouds.

THE STRUCTURE OF A DATA CENTER

A data center can occupy one room of a building, one or more floors, or an entire building. Most of the equipment is often in the form of servers mounted in 19-inch rack cabinets, which are usually placed in single rows with corridors between them. This allows people access to the front and rear of each cabinet. Servers differ greatly in size, from 1U servers (which occupy one of 42 slots in a standard rack) to large free-standing storage silos that occupy many tiles on the floor. Mainframe computers and storage devices may be as big as the racks themselves and are placed alongside them. Large data centers may use shipping containers packed with 1,000 or more servers each; when they need to repair or upgrade, they replace the whole container (rather than repairing individual servers).

Clean, unwavering power—and lots of it—is essential. Data centers need to keep their computers running at all times. They should be prepared to handle brownouts and even power outages. The power must be conditioned, and backup batteries and diesel generators must be available to keep power flowing no matter what.

As you can imagine, all that power generates a lot of heat. Data centers must cool their racks of equipment. The most common mode of cooling is air-conditioning; water-cooling is also an option when it's easily available, such as at some of the new data centers along the Columbia River in Washington State. Air-conditioning not only cools the environment but also controls humidity to avoid condensation or static electric buildup.

Network connectivity and ample bandwidth to and from the network backbones are vital, to handle the input and output from the entire collection of servers and storage units. All these servers will be idle if no one can access them.

Another important aspect is physical and logical security. Bigger data centers are targets for hackers all over the world. Some freestanding data centers begin with security through obscurity and disguise the fact that a data center even exists at that location. Guards, mantraps, and state-of-the-art authentication technology keep unauthorized people from physically entering. Firewalls, VPN gateways, intrusion-detection software, and so on keep unauthorized people from entering over the network. (More on all aspects of cloud security in chapter 4.)

Finally, data centers must always assume the worst and have disaster recovery contingencies in place that avoid loss of data and experience the minimum loss of service in case of disaster.

DATA CENTERS: SCALING FOR THE CLOUD

A traditional, large data center dedicated to a single large corporation costs approximately $100-200 million.[1] Contrast that to the total cost of building the largest mega data centers that provide cloud services: $500 million or more.[2,3] What is going into that much higher cost, and what can the biggest cloud data centers do that normal companies can't do with their dedicated data centers?

The largest data-center operators like Google, Amazon, and Microsoft situate their data centers in geographic proximity to heavy usage areas to keep network latency to a minimum and to provide failover options. They also choose geographies with access to cheap power. The northwest is particularly advantageous because the available hydropower is the cheapest power in the country and air-conditioning needs are low to zero. Major data centers can use a whopping amount of wattage and cost their owners upward of $30 million a year for electricity alone, which is why data-center power consumption across the U.S. represents 1.2 percent of total power consumption in the country—and it's rising. The positive side is that cloud data centers use so much power and have so much clout that they can negotiate huge power volume discounts.

Additionally, these giant data centers tend to buy so much hardware that they can negotiate huge volume discounts far beyond the reach of even the largest company that's building a dedicated data center. For example, Amazon spent about $90 million for 50,000 servers from Rackable/SGI in 2008,[4] which, without the massive volume discounts, would have cost $215 million.

Servers dominate data-center costs. This is why Google and others are trying to get cheaper servers and have taken to building their own from components. Google relies on cheap computers with conventional multicore processors. A single Google data center has tens of thousands of these inexpensive processors and disks, held together with Velcro tape in a practice that makes for easy swapping of components.

To reduce the machines' energy appetite, Google fitted them with high-efficiency power supplies and voltage regulators, variable-speed fans, and system boards stripped of all unnecessary components, such as graphics chips. Google has also experimented with a CPU power-management feature called *dynamic voltage/frequency scaling*. It reduces a processor's voltage or frequency during certain periods (for example, when you don't need the results of a computing task right away). The server executes its work more slowly, reducing power consumption. Google engineers have reported energy savings of around 20 percent on some of their tests.

In 2006, Google built two cloud computing data centers in Dalles, Oregon, each of which has the acreage of a football field with four floors and two four-story cooling

[1] http://perspectives.mvdirona.com/2008/11/28/CostOfPowerInLargeScaleDataCenters.aspx
[2] http://www.datacenterknowledge.com/archives/2007/11/05/microsoft-plans-500m-illinois-data-center
[3] http://www.theregister.co.uk/2009/09/25/microsoft_chillerless_data_center
[4] http://www.datacenterknowledge.com/archives/2009/06/23/amazon-adds-cloud-data-center-in-virginia

Figure 2.1   Photograph of Google's top-secret Dalles, OR data center, built near the Dalles Dam for access to cheap power. Note the large cooling towers on the end of each football-sized building on the left. These towers cool through evaporation rather than using more power-hungry chillers. Source: Melanie Conner, *New York Times*.

plants (see figure 2.1). The Dalles Dam is strategic for the significant energy and cooling needs of these data centers. (Some new cloud data centers rely on cooling towers, which use evaporation to remove heat from the cooling water, instead of traditional energy-intensive chillers.)

The Dalles data center also benefits from good fiber connectivity to various locations in the U.S., Asia, and Europe, thanks to a large surplus of fiber optic networking, a legacy of the dot-com boom.

In 2007, Google built at least four new data centers at an average cost of $600 million, each adding to its Googleplex: a massive global computer network estimated to span 25 locations and 450,000 servers. Amazon also chose a Dalles location down the river for its largest data center.

Yahoo! and Microsoft chose Quincy, Washington. Microsoft's new facility there has more than 477,000 square feet of space, nearly the area of 10 football fields. The company is tight-lipped about the number of servers at the site, but it does say the facility uses 3 miles of chiller piping, 600 miles of electrical wire, 1 million square feet of drywall, and 1.6 tons of batteries for backup power. And the data center consumes 48 megawatts—enough power for 40,000 homes.

World's servers surpassing Holland's emissions

The management consulting firm McKinsey & Co. reports that the world's 44 million servers consume 0.5 percent of all electricity and produce 0.2 percent of all carbon dioxide emissions, or 80 megatons a year, approaching the emissions of entire countries such as Argentina or the Netherlands.

CLOUD DATA CENTERS: BECOMING MORE EFFICIENT AND MORE FLEXIBLE THROUGH MODULARITY

Already, through volume purchasing, custom server construction, and careful geographic locality, the world's largest data-center owners can build data centers at a fraction of the cost per CPU operation of private corporations. They relentlessly work to widen that gap. The economies-of-scale trend will continue in the cloud providers' favor as they become dramatically more efficient through modular data centers. These highly modular, scalable, efficient, just-in-time data centers can provide capacity that can be delivered anywhere in the world quickly and cheaply.

Figure 2.2 is an artist's rendering of a modular data center (because photographs of such facilities are highly guarded). Corporate data centers can't compete with the myriad economic efficiencies that these mega data centers can achieve today and will fall further and further behind as time goes by.

The goal behind modular data centers is to standardize them and move away from custom designs, enabling a commoditized manufacturing approach. The most striking feature is that such data centers are roofless.

Like Google, Microsoft is driven by energy costs and environmental pressures to reduce emissions and increase efficiency. The company's goal is a power usage effectiveness (PUE) at or below 1.125 by 2012 across all its data centers.

COOLING: High-efficiency water-based cooling systems–less energy-intensive than traditional chillers–circulate cold water through the containers to remove heat, eliminating the need for air-conditioned rooms.

STRUCTURE: A 24 000-square-meter facility houses 400 containers. Delivered by trucks, the containers attach to a spine infrastructure that feeds network connectivity, power, and water. The data center has no conventional raised floors.

POWER: Two power substations feed a total of 300 megawatts to the data center, with 200 MW used for computing equipment and 100 MW for cooling and electrical losses. Batteries and generators provide backup power.

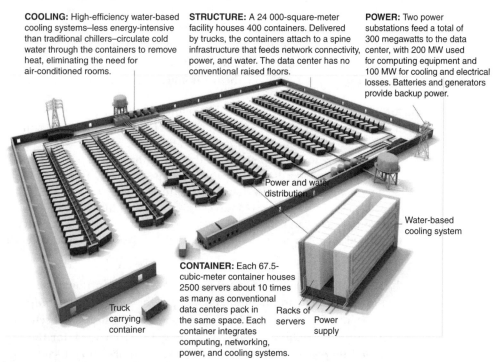

Power and water distribution

Water-based cooling system

CONTAINER: Each 67.5-cubic-meter container houses 2500 servers about 10 times as many as conventional data centers pack in the same space. Each container integrates computing, networking, power, and cooling systems.

Truck carrying container

Racks of servers

Power supply

Figure 2.2 Expandable, modular cloud data center. Notice there is no roof. New containers with servers, power, cooling and network taps can be swapped in and out as needed. Source: *IEEE Spectrum* magazine.

Power usage effectiveness (PUE)

Power usage effectiveness (PUE) is a metric used to determine the energy efficiency of a data center. PUE is determined by dividing the amount of power entering a data center by the power used to run the computer infrastructure within it. PUE is therefore expressed as a ratio, with overall efficiency improving as the quotient decreases toward 1.

According to the Uptime Institute, the typical data center has an average PUE of 2.5. This means that for every 2.5 watts in at the utility meter, only 1 watt is delivered out to the IT load. Uptime estimates that most facilities could achieve 1.6 PUE using the most efficient equipment and best practices. Google and Microsoft are both approaching 1.125, far exceeding what any corporate or cohost data center can achieve.

2.1.2 *Ensuring high server utilization in the cloud with virtualization*

Virtualization, following the car analogy, is the suspension. It provides the high server utilization you need. It smooths out the variations between applications that need barely any CPU time (they can share a CPU with other applications) and those that are compute intensive and need every CPU cycle they can get. Virtualization is the single-most revolutionary cloud technology whose broad acceptance and deployment truly enabled the cloud computing trend to begin. Without virtualization, and the 60-plus percent server utilization it allows, the economics of the cloud would not work.

> **VIRTUALIZATION** For this book, we're interested primarily in *platform* virtualization. Platform virtualization is a technique to abstract computer resources such that it separates the operating system from the underlying physical server resources. Instead of the OS running on (that is, directly using) hardware resources. The OS interacts instead with a new software layer called a *virtual machine monitor* that accesses the hardware and presents the OS with a virtual set of hardware resources. This means multiple virtual machine images or instances can run on a single physical server, and new instances can be generated and run on demand, creating the basis for elastic computing resources.

As we discussed earlier, virtualization isn't new at all. IBM mainframes used time-sharing virtualization in the '60s to enable many people to share a large computer without interacting or interfering with each other. Previously, constraints of scheduling dedicated time on these machines required you to get all your work for the day done in that scheduled time slot. The concept of virtual memory, introduced around 1962, although considered pretty radical, ultimately freed programmers from having to constantly worry about how close they were to the limits of physical memory. Today, server virtualization is proving equally dramatic for application deployment and scaling. And it's the key enabler for the cloud. How did this happen?

The average server in a corporate data center has typical utilization of only 6 percent.[5] Even at peak load, utilization is no better than 20 percent. In the best-run data centers, servers only run on average at 15 percent or less of their maximum capacity. But when these same data centers fully adopt server virtualization, their CPU utilization increases to 65 percent or higher. For this reason, in a few short years, most corporate data centers have deployed hundreds or thousands of virtual servers in place of their previous model of one server on one hardware computer box. Let's see how server virtualization works to make utilization jump this dramatically.

HOW IT WORKS

Server virtualization transforms or *virtualizes* the hardware resources of a computer—including the CPU, RAM, hard disk, and network controller—to create a fully functional virtual machine that can run its own operating system and applications like a physical computer. This is accomplished by inserting a thin layer of software directly on the computer hardware that contains a virtual machine monitor (VMM)—also called a *hypervisor*—that allocates hardware resources dynamically and transparently. Multiple guest operating systems run concurrently on a single physical computer and share hardware resources with each other. By encapsulating an entire machine, including CPU, memory, operating system, and network devices, a virtual machine becomes completely compatible with all standard operating systems, applications, and device drivers. You can see the virtual machine architecture for VMware on the x86 in figure 2.3.

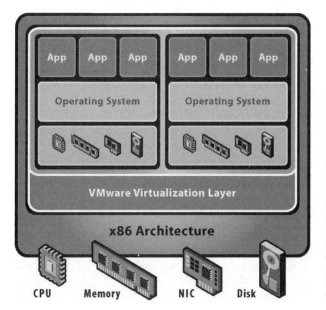

Figure 2.3 Virtual machine architecture using VMware as an example. The virtualization layer is what interfaces directly with all hardware components, including the CPU. That layer then presents each guest operating system with its own array of *virtual* hardware resources. The guest OS doesn't operate differently than it would if installed on the bare hardware, but now several instances of guest OSs with all their applications can share a single physical device and have higher effective utilization. Source: VMWare.

---

[5] McKinsey & Company, 2008 Data Center Efficiency report.

VIRTUALIZATION AS APPLIED TO THE CLOUD

When virtualization passed muster with enterprise architects and CIOs, it had arrived. It was all about saving money. Enterprises began seeing utilization of their hardware assets increase dramatically. It was easy to go from the typical 5 or 6 percent to 20 percent. They could get 65 percent utilization or better with good planning.

In addition to increased utilization and the associated cost savings, virtualization in corporate data centers set the stage for cloud computing in several interesting ways. It decoupled users from implementation; it brought speed, flexibility, and agility never before seen in corporate data centers; and it broke the old model of software pricing and licensing. Let's look at table 2.1 for more clarity.

Table 2.1   Impact of virtualization on corporate data centers

Benefit	Explanation
Decouples users from implementation	The concept of a virtual server forces users to not worry about the physical servers or their location. Instead, they focus on service-level agreements and their applications.
Decreases server provisioning from months to minutes	Getting a (physical) server requisitioned, installed, configured, and deployed takes larger organizations 60–90 days and some 120 days. In the virtual server model, it's literally minutes or hours from request to fully ready for application deployment, depending on how much automation has been put in place.
Breaks software pricing and licensing	No longer can the data center charge for an entire server or every server the software runs on. Instead, they have to charge for actual usage—a whole new model for IT.

Table 2.1 illustrates the services the cloud providers offer. We also see a growing recognition of and readiness for the cloud within the enterprise. This is because the model change that virtualization has already brought to enterprise IT has prepared companies to adapt more easily to the cloud computing model.

Let's look at a scenario that uses thousands of physical servers. Each one is virtualized and can run any number of guest OSs, can be configured and deployed in minutes, and is set up to bill by the CPU hour. The combination of cheap, abundant hardware and virtualization capability, coupled with automated provisioning and billing allows the huge economies of scale now achievable in the mega data centers to be harnessed through cloud computing. This is possible because of virtualization, much as car suspension systems enable vehicles to speed up without killing the occupants at every bump in the road.

But a powerful engine (data center) and a smooth suspension (virtualization) aren't enough. Following the vehicle analogy, you need a set of controls to start, stop, and steer the car; you need an API to control your cloud.

2.1.3   *Controlling remote servers with a cloud API*

The API is to a cloud what the dashboard and controls are to a car. You have tremendous power under that hood, but you need the dials and readouts to know what the vehicle is doing. You need the steering wheel, accelerator, and brake to control it. Remember, you'd never drive fast if you didn't have good brakes.

When you have a cloud, you need a way to access it. The highest-level clouds—those offering Software as a Service (SaaS) applications—offer a browser-based web interface. Lower-level clouds—those offering Infrastructure as a Service (IaaS)—also need a way to access applications. Each type of cloud must provide some kind of API that can be used to provision resources, configure and control them, and release them when they're no longer needed.

An API is necessary to engage the service of a cloud provider. It's a way for the vendor to expose service features and potentially enable competitive differentiation. For example, Amazon's EC2 API is a SOAP- and HTTP Query-based API used to send proprietary commands to create, store, provision, and manage Amazon Machine Images (AMIs). Sun's Project Kenai Cloud API specification is a Representational State Transfer (REST)-ful API for creating and managing cloud resources, including compute, storage, and networking components.

> **REST ARCHITECTURE AND RESTFUL APIS** Representational State Transfer (REST) is a style of software architecture for distributed hypermedia systems, such as the World Wide Web. The REST architectural style was developed in parallel with the HTTP protocol. The largest-known implementation of a system conforming to the REST architectural style is the World Wide Web. In fact, REST can be considered a post hoc description of the features of the web that made the web successful. REST-style architectures consist of clients and servers. Clients initiate requests to servers; servers process requests and return appropriate responses. Requests and responses are built around the transfer of *representations* of *resources*. A resource can be any coherent and meaningful concept that may be addressed. A representation of a resource is typically a document that captures the current or intended state of a resource. Conforming to the REST constraints is referred to as being *RESTful*.

Because your cloud applications will be the lifeblood of your company, you'll want to ensure that only authorized parties can access your applications. If an application was running in your company's secure data center protected by layers of physical and logical security you'd be certain that no unauthorized person could access it. Here, because everything having to do with your application and the server it runs on is by definition accessible over the internet, the approach Amazon and others take to security is to issue X.509 public key pairs initially and then require a key on every API call. This ensures that the caller has the credentials to access the infrastructure.

To understand a cloud API—for which there isn't yet an accepted standard—it's best to look at Amazon's cloud API as the default standard as they're the leaders. Table 2.2 outlines some of the basic definitions and operations central to the Amazon cloud API.

Table 2.2   Basic terms and operations of the Amazon EC2 API

Term	Description
AMI	An Amazon Machine Image is an encrypted and signed machine image suitable to run in a virtual server environment. For example, it may contain Linux, Apache, MySQL, or PHP, as well as the application of the AMI's owner.
	AMIs can be public (provided by Amazon), private (custom designed by its creator), paid (purchased from a third party), or shared (created by the community for free).
	AMIs can be stored in Amazon's Simple Storage Service (S3).
Instance	The result of launching an AMI is a running system called an *instance*. When an instance terminates, the data on that instance vanishes. For all intents and purposes, an Instance is identical to a traditional host computer.
Standard flow	1. Use a standard AMI by customizing an existing one.
	2. Bundle the AMI, and get an AMI ID to enable launching as many instances of the AMI as needed.
	3. Launch one or more instances of this AMI.
	4. Administer and use the running instance(s).
Connecting	From a web browser, go to http://<hostname>, where <hostname> is your instance's public hostname.
	If you want to connect to a just-launched public AMI that hasn't been modified, run the `ec2-get-console-output` command.
	The result in either case enables you to log in as root and exercise full control over this instance, just like any host computer you could walk up to in a data center.

We've barely scratched the surface of all the concepts and corresponding API calls that exist in Amazon's API. Documentation is available at http://docs.amazonwebservices.com. APIs also cover these areas:

- Using instance addressing
- Using network security
- Using regions and availability zones
- Using Amazon Elastic Block Store (EBS)
- Using auto scaling, elastic load balancing, and Amazon CloudWatch
- Using public data sets
- Using Amazon's Virtual Private Cloud

We'll revisit select aspects of the cloud API at various points throughout the book. Let's leave this now and talk about the next important layer in what it takes to set up and use a cloud: cloud storage.

2.1.4 *Saving persistent data in cloud storage*

You store your luggage in the trunk of your car. Similarly, the cloud provides a place to store your machine images, your applications, and any data your applications need.

Cloud storage has also increased in popularity recently for many of the same reasons as cloud computing. Cloud storage delivers *virtualized storage on demand* over a network based on a request for a given quality of service (QoS). Unlike the long provisioning lead times required in corporate data centers, there is no need to purchase storage or in some cases even provision it before storing data. Typically, you pay for transit of data into the cloud and, subsequently, a recurring fee based on the amount of storage consumption your data uses.

You can use cloud storage in many different ways. For example, you can back up local data (such as on a laptop) to cloud storage; a virtual disk can be synched to the cloud and distributed to other computers; and you can use it as an archive to retain (under some policy) data for regulatory or other purposes.

You can use cloud storage for applications that provide data directly to their clients via the network. The application redirects the client to a location at the cloud storage provider for the data. Media such as audio and video files are examples. The network requirements for streaming data files can be made to scale in order to meet the demand without affecting the application.

The type of interface used for this is HTTP. You can fetch the file from a browser without having to do any special coding, and the correct application is invoked automatically. But how do you get the file there in the first place, and how do you make sure the storage you use is of the right type and QoS? Again, many offerings expose an interface for these operations, and it's not surprising that many of these interfaces use REST principles. This is typically a data-object interface with operations for creating, reading, updating, and deleting the individual data objects via HTTP operations.

Keeping with Amazon's APIs as good examples to study, we've outlined a simple API dealing with Amazon's S3 in table 2.3.

A cloud storage standard

The Storage Networking Industry Association has created a technical work group to address the need for a cloud storage standard. The new Cloud Data Management Interface (CDMI) enables interoperable cloud storage and data management. In CDMI, the underlying storage space exposed by the interfaces is abstracted using the notion of a *container*. A container is not only a useful abstraction for storage space, but also serves as a grouping of the data stored in it and a point of control for applying data services in the aggregate.

Table 2.3   Basic terms and operations of Amazon S3

Terms	Description
Object	Fundamental entity stored in S3. Each object can range in size from 1 byte to 5 GB. Each object has object data and metadata. *Metadata* is a set of name-value pairs that describe the data.
Bucket	Fundamental container in S3 for data storage. Objects are uploaded into buckets. There is no limit to the number of objects you can store in a bucket. The bucket provides a unique namespace for the management of objects contained in the bucket. Bucket names are global, so each developer can own only up to 100 buckets at a time.
Key	A key is the unique identifier for an object within a bucket. A bucket name plus a key uniquely identifies an object within all of S3.
Usage	1. Create a bucket in which to store your data. 2. Upload (write) data (objects) into the bucket. 3. Download (read) the data stored in the bucket. 4. Delete some data stored in the bucket. 5. List the objects in the bucket.

In many cases, the coarse granularity and unstructured nature of cloud storage services such as S3 aren't sufficient for the type of data access required. For many applications, an alternative structured data-storage method is required. Let's explore how databases in the cloud work (and don't).

2.1.5   *Storing your application's structured data in a cloud database*

Your car's navigation system provides constant updates about your current location and destination during your journey. It guides you through the route you need to take. This data, although critical for the trip, isn't useful afterward. The navigation system is to the car what a cloud database is to an application running in the cloud: it's transactional data created and used during the running of that application. When we think of transactional data stored in databases, we usually think of relational databases.

What is a Relational Database Management System (RDBMS)? Why do we frequently hear that they don't work in the cloud? An RDBMS is a database management system in which you store data in the form of tables; the relationship among the data is also stored in the form of tables. You can see this in the simple relation in figure 2.4.

> **RDBMS** A database management system (DBMS) based on the relational model. *Relational* describes a broad class of database systems that at a minimum present the data to the user as relations (a presentation in tabular form—that is, as a collection of tables with each table consisting of a set of rows and columns—can satisfy this property) and provide relational operators to manipulate the data in tabular form. All modern commercial relational databases employ SQL as their query language, leading to a shorthand for RDBMSs as *SQL databases*.

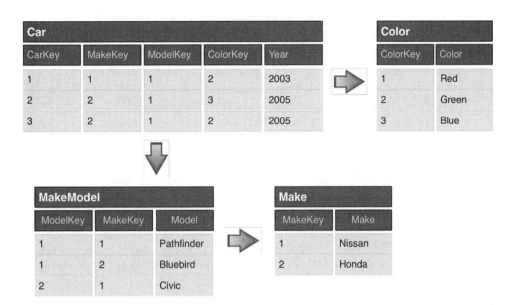

Figure 2.4 A simple example of how a relational database works. Four tables map out relationships among the data. Because a separate table lists the car manufacturers and colors, there is no need to separately list a red Nissan and a blue Nissan. But to fully understand what the car with CarKey 1 is, you must do a join of the Car, Color, MakeModel, and Make tables.

The challenge for an RDBMS in the cloud is scaling. Applications having a fixed number of users and workload requiring an RDBMS won't have any problems. Most cloud providers have an RDBMS offering for these cases. But when applications are launched in environments that have massive workloads, such as web services, their scalability requirements can change quickly and grow large. The first scenario can be difficult to manage if you have a relational database sitting on a single in-house server. For example, if your load triples overnight, how quickly can you upgrade your hardware? The second scenario can be too difficult to manage with a relational database, because it becomes a bottleneck choking the application's ability to scale. We'll cover solutions to this in depth in chapter 5.

As you've already learned, one of the core benefits of the cloud is the ability to quickly (or automatically, as we'll show) add more servers to an application as its load increases, thereby scaling it to heavier workloads. But it's hard to expand an RDBMS this way. You have to either replicate data across the new servers or partition between them. In either case, adding a machine requires data to be copied or moved to the new server. This data shipping is a time-consuming and expensive process, so databases are unable to be dynamically and efficiently provisioned on demand.

A big challenge with RDBMS partitioning or replicating is maintaining *referential integrity*. Referential integrity requires that every value of one attribute (column) of a relation (table) exist as a value of another attribute in a different (or the same) relation (table). A little less formally, any field in a table that's declared a foreign key can contain only values from a parent table's primary key or a candidate key. In practice, this means that deleting a record that contains a value referred to by a foreign key in another table break's referential integrity. When you partition or replicate a database, it becomes nearly impossible to guarantee maintenance of referential integrity across all databases. This extremely useful property of RDBMS—its ability to construct a relation out of lots of small index tables that are referred to by values in records—becomes unworkable when these databases have to scale to deal with huge workloads, but cloud applications are otherwise ideally suited for this purpose.

THE NOSQL MOVEMENT

Since 1998, there has been a small but rapidly growing movement away from SQL databases. Instead, participants in this movement promote a class of nonrelational data stores that break some of the fundamental guarantees of SQL in favor of being able to reach massive scale. This is obviously important for *some* cloud applications. These non-SQL data stores may not require fixed table schemas and usually avoid join operations. They're described as scaling *horizontally*. Some categorize them as *structured storage*.

A new non-SQL type of database, generically a key-value database, does scale well. Consequently, it's started to be used in the cloud. Key-value databases are *item-oriented*, meaning all relevant data relating to an item are stored in that item. A table can

---

NoSQL architecture

Relational databases have a limitation on handling big data volumes and typical modern workloads. Today's scale is unprecedented and can't be handled with relational SQL databases. Examples of enormous scale are synonymous with the most popular sites: Digg's 3 TB for green badges, Facebook's 50 TB for inbox search, and eBay's 2 PB overall data.

NoSQL systems often provide weak consistency guarantees, such as *eventual* consistency and transactions restricted to single data items; in most cases, you can impose full ACID (atomicity, consistency, isolation, durability) guarantees by adding a supplementary middleware layer.

Several NoSQL systems employ a distributed architecture, with the data being held in a redundant manner on several servers, often using a distributed hash table. In this way, the system can be scaled up easily by adding more servers, and failure of a server can be tolerated.

Some NoSQL advocates promote simple interfaces, such as associative arrays or key-value pairs. Other systems, such as native XML databases, promote support of the XQuery standard.

Clearly, we're in the early days of cloud evolution, with a lot of development yet to come.

Car	
Key	Attributes
1	Make:　Nissan Model:　Pathfinder Color:　Green Year:　2003
2	Make:　Nissan Model:　Pathfinder Color:　Blue Year:　2005 Trans:　Automatic

Figure 2.5 The same data as in figure 2.4, shown for a key-value type of database. Because all data for an item (row) is contained in that item, this type of database is trivial to scale because a data store can be split (by copying some of the items) or replicated (by copying all the items to an additional data store), and referential integrity is maintained.

contain vastly different items. For example, a table may contain car makes, car models, and car color items. This means data are commonly duplicated between items in a table (another item also contains Color: Green). You can see this in figure 2.5. In an RDBMS, this is anathema; here, this is accepted practice because disk space is relatively cheap. But this model allows a single item to contain all relevant data, which improves scalability by eliminating the need to join data from multiple tables. With a relational database, such data needs to be joined to be able to regroup relevant attributes. This is the key issue for scaling—if a join is needed that depends on shared tables, then replicating the data is hard and blocks easy scaling.

When companies set out to create a public computing cloud (such as Amazon) or build massively parallel, redundant, and economical data-driven applications (such as Google), relational databases became untenable. Both companies needed a way of managing data that was almost infinitely scalable, inherently reliable, and cost effective. Consequently, both came up with nonrelational database systems based on this key-value concept that can handle massive scale. Amazon calls its cloud database offering SimpleDB, and Google calls its BigTable. (Both were developed long before either company launched a cloud. They created these structures to solve their own problems. When they launched a cloud, the same structures became part of their cloud offerings.)

Google's BigTable solution was to develop a relatively simple storage management system that could provide fast access to petabytes of data, potentially redundantly distributed across thousands of machines. Physically, BigTable resembles a B-tree index-organized table in which branch and leaf nodes are distributed across multiple machines. Like a B-tree, nodes split as they grow, and—because nodes are distributed—this allows for high scalability across large numbers of machines. Data elements in BigTable are identified by a primary key, column name, and, optionally, a timestamp. Lookups via primary key are predictable and relatively fast. BigTable provides the data storage mechanism for Google App Engine. You'll learn about this PaaS cloud-based application environment in detail later in this chapter.

Google charges $180 per terabyte per month for BigTable storage. Here are some examples of BigTable usage (in Python):

This code declares a data store class:

```
class Patient(db.Modal);
    firstName = db.UserProperty()
    lastName = db.UserProperty()
    dateOfBirth = db.DateTimeProperty()
    sex = db.UserProperty()
```

This code creates and stores an object:

```
patient = Patient()

patient.firstName = "George"
patient.lastName = "James"
dateOfBirth = "2008-01-01"
sex = "M"

patient.put()
```

This code queries a class:

```
patients = Patient.all()

for patient in patients:
    self.response.out.write('Name %s %s. ',
            patient.firstName, patient.lastName)
```

And this code selects the 100 youngest male patients:

```
allPatients = Patient.all()
allPatients.filter('sex=', 'Male')
allPatients.order('dateOfBirth')
patients = allPatients.fetch(100)
```

Amazon's SimpleDB is conceptually similar to BigTable and forms a key part of the Amazon Web Services (AWS) cloud computing environment. (Microsoft's SQL Server Data Services [SSDS] provides a similar capability in their Azure cloud.) Like BigTable, this is a key-value type of database. The basic organizing entity is a *domain*. Domains are collections of items that are described by attribute-value pairs. You can see an abbreviated list of the SimpleDB API calls with their functional description in table 2.4.

Table 2.4   Amazon's SimpleDB API summary

API call	API functional description
CreateDomain	Creates a domain that contains your dataset.
DeleteDomain	Deletes a domain.
ListDomains	Lists all domains.
DomainMetadata	Retrieves information about creation time for the domain, storage information both as counts of item names and attributes, and total size in bytes.
PutAttributes	Adds or updates an item and its attributes, or adds attribute-value pairs to items that exist already. Items are automatically indexed as they're received.
BatchPutAttributes	For greater overall throughput of bulk writes, performs up to 25 PutAttribute operations in a single call.

Table 2.4   Amazon's SimpleDB API summary (*continued*)

API call	API functional description
DeleteAttributes	Deletes an item, an attribute, or an attribute value.
GetAttributes	Retrieves an item and all or a subset of its attributes and values.
Select	Queries the data set in the familiar "Select target from *domain_name* where *query_expression*" syntax. Supported value tests are =, !=, <, >, <=, >=, like, not like, between, is null, isn't null, and every(). Example: select * from mydomain where every(keyword) = "Book". Orders results using the SORT operator, and counts items that meet the condition(s) specified by the predicate(s) in a query using the Count operator.

Converting an existing application to use one of these cloud-based databases is somewhere between difficult and not worth the trouble; but for applications already using the Object-Relational Mapping (ORM)-based frameworks, these cloud databases can easily provide core data-management functionality. They can do it with compelling scalability and the same economic benefits of cloud computing in general. But as table 2.5 illustrates, there are definite drawbacks to these new types of cloud databases that you must take into account when contemplating a shift to the cloud.

Table 2.5   Cloud database drawbacks

Database use	Challenges faced with a cloud database
Transactional support and referential integrity	Applications using cloud databases are largely responsible for maintaining the integrity of transactions and relationships between tables.
Complex data access	Cloud databases (and ORM in general) excel at single-row transactions: get a row, save a row, and so on. But most nontrivial applications have to perform joins and other operations that cloud databases can't.
Business Intelligence	Application data has value not only in terms of powering applications but also as information that drives business intelligence. The dilemma of the pre-relational database, in which valuable business data was locked inside impenetrable application data stores, isn't something to which business will willingly return.

Cloud databases could displace the relational database for a significant segment of next-generation, cloud-enabled applications. But business is unlikely to be enthusiastic about an architecture that prevents application data from being used for business intelligence and decision-support purposes, which fundamentally require a relational database. An architecture that delivered the scalability and other advantages of cloud databases without sacrificing information management would fit the bill. We can expect a lot of innovation and advancements in these database models over the next few years.

The last technological underpinning you need to learn about is elasticity, the transmission in the ongoing vehicle analogy.

2.1.6   Elasticity: scaling your application as demand rises and falls

The transmission smoothly adapts the speed of a car's wheels to the engine speed as you vary the accelerator position. Similarly, *elasticity* enables an application running in a cloud to smoothly expand and contract according to demand. More precisely, elasticity is the ability to have capacity as demand increases and to release that capacity when you're done with it. Many big organizations have been close to disaster or faced it because of scalability failures in times of need.

Elasticity and celebrity deaths

In July 2009, two celebrity deaths occurred on the same day. First, *Charlie's Angels* star Farrah Fawcett died, which resulted in a minor news flurry. Then, later in the afternoon, a major web storm erupted when news of Michael Jackson's death hit the social web. Unexpectedly, Twitter had major scaling issues dealing with the sudden influx of hundreds of thousands of tweets as news of Jackson's death spread. But Twitter wasn't alone.

According to TechCrunch, "Various reports had the AOL-owned TMZ, which broke the story, being down at multiple points throughout the ordeal. As a result, Perez Hilton's hugely popular blog may have failed as people rushed there to try and confirm the news. Then the *LA Times* had a report saying Jackson was only in a coma rather than dead, so people rushed there, and that site went down. (The *LA Times* eventually confirmed his passing.)"

Numerous examples exist of a news story, a product announcement, or even the infamous Victoria's Secret Super Bowl commercial, sending people directly to a web site that then crashes. Too much traffic meets with insufficient capacity and results in catastrophe. When people are directed to a site and it then breaks down, their reaction is to not try that again. These issues severely hurt a company's business. This illustrates the criticality of being able to scale as capacity dynamically grows.

Scalability is about the cloud platform being able to handle an increased load of users working on a cloud application. *Elasticity* is the ability of the cloud platform to scale up or down based on need without disrupting the business. Without this, the economies of moving a business/application to the cloud don't make sense.

The example code snippets that follow set up an EC2 application to be load balanced and auto-scaled (that is, elastic) with a minimum of 2 instances and a maximum of 20 instances. Auto-scaling in this example is configured to scale out by 1 instance when the application's average CPU utilization exceeds a threshold of 80 percent and scale in by 1 instance when it drops below 40 percent for 10 minutes.

Call `CreateLoadBalancer` with the following parameters:

```
AvailabilityZones = us-east-1a
```

```
LoadBalancerName = MyLoadBalancer
Listeners = lb-port=80,instance-port=8080,protocol=HTTP
```

Call `CreateLaunchConfiguration` with the following parameters:

```
ImageId = myAMI
LaunchConfigurationName = MyLaunchConfiguration
InstanceType = m1.small
```

Call `CreateAutoScalingGroup` with the following parameters:

```
AutoScalingGroupName = MyAutoScalingGroup
AvailabilityZones = us-east-1a
LaunchConfigurationName = MyLaunchConfiguration
LoadBalancerNames = MyLoadBalancer
MaxSize = 20
MinSize = 2
```

Call `CreateOrUpdateScalingTrigger` with the following parameters:

```
AutoScalingGroupName = MyAutoScalingGroup
MeasureName = CPUUtilization
Statistic = Average
TriggerName = MyTrigger1a
Namespace = AWS/EC2
Period = 60
LowerThreshold = 40
LowerBreachScaleIncrement = -1
UpperThreshold = 80
UpperBreachScaleIncrement = 1
BreachDuration = 600
```

You learned in chapter 1 that there is more than one flavor of cloud computing. Let's combine what you learned in chapter 1 about the different types of clouds with what you now know about the six critical enabling technologies in clouds to better understand how these different flavors of clouds work, what they offer, and how they differ. The next section will help you better understand which is best for you.

2.2   *Understanding the different classifications of clouds*

Now that you've learned about the technological underpinnings of cloud computing, such as virtualization, elasticity, storage, and databases, it's useful to understand how those concepts are employed in the different types (classifications) of cloud computing services being offered. Let's go back to the taxonomy of cloud types from chapter 1—IaaS, PaaS, and DaaS—to classify the clouds from the most prominent providers in the industry.

2.2.1   *Amazon EC2: Infrastructure as a Service*

Amazon EC2 is categorized as IaaS (some cloud observers call it HaaS, but Amazon has added so many additional services that Hardware as a Service would now be a misnomer). It was the first and is by far the biggest in this category. Amazon opened its service in 2006 after initially using excess capacity from its retail operation. The company claimed to have over 500,000 users by the end of 2008.

Amazon EC2 is the most general purpose of the major clouds but has the least support for automatic scaling or failover, both of which have to be programmed into the application. This is in contrast to the automatic and invisible scaling that occurs in the PaaS types of clouds, such as Google's AppEngine, which we'll discuss in section 2.2.3. In IaaS-type clouds, such as EC2, elasticity requires careful programming using their APIs. On the other hand, you can use any programming language, and you have complete control over your application in an IaaS cloud. Sure, it requires more manual work, but you get something that has the appearance of being physical hardware that you have control over from the operating system outward. The LAMP stack is the easiest and most common EC2 configuration (see table 2.6).

Table 2.6   The components of the LAMP stack in an IaaS cloud

L	Linux	Operating system
A	Apache	Web server
M	MySQL	Relational database
P	PHP	Server side of website

Amazon EC2 and Xen paravirtualization

Amazon EC2 utilizes a customized version of the open source Xen hypervisor, taking advantage of paravirtualization. Because paravirtualized guest OSs rely on the hypervisor to provide support for operations that normally require privileged access, the guest OS runs with no elevated access to the CPU.

Paravirtualization is more efficient than a virtualized environment where the guest OS runs unmodified. But the OS must be ported to the paravirtualized environment so that certain OS tasks that would have to be performed by the VMM and run more slowly can be directly executed by the guest OS. This is why Amazon doesn't run any OS you may desire—it runs only OSs that it or the original vendor has ported and fully tested.

Amazon has an extensive API for all its services, some of which are described in table 2.7. It has a SOAP as well as a simple HTML (GET, POST) form for its APIs. The company needs only a dozen and a half calls to request and configure virtualized hardware in the cloud.

Table 2.7   Other Amazon cloud services (effectively providing some PaaS capabilities)

Service	Description
Simple Storage Service (S3)	Cloud storage used to store and retrieve large amounts of data from anywhere on the web through a simple API. Well integrated with EC2: AMIs are stored in S3, and data transferred from S3 to EC2 doesn't invoke separate charges.

Table 2.7 Other Amazon cloud services (effectively providing some PaaS capabilities) (*continued*)

Service	Description
SimpleDB	Provides the core database functions of indexing (special organizational entities for faster lookups) and querying. Avoids the big expense of relational database licensing, the requisite DBA, and the complex setup. But it isn't a relational database, has no schema, and doesn't work with SQL.
CloudFront	A web service for content delivery that competes with Akamai. Provides an easy way to distribute content to end users with low latency and high data-transfer speeds in a pay-as-you-go model.
Simple Queue Service (SQS)	A hosted queue for storing messages as they travel between computers. Useful for moving data between distributed components of applications that perform different tasks, without losing messages or requiring each component to be always available.

EC2 pricing starts at roughly a nickel per small Linux-based instance (CPU) hour, up to about half a dollar on a high-end Linux instance.[6] S3 pricing is about $0.15 per GB per month, scaling downward as more storage is used.

2.2.2 *Microsoft Azure: Infrastructure as a Service*

Microsoft's Azure is IaaS in the same way as Amazon EC2, but it also has other services that operate more at the PaaS level. Many of Microsoft's end-user applications are being recast to run in the cloud. As a result, increasingly, this overall platform is trying to reach the SaaS level to head off Google's thrust against Microsoft Office with the Google Docs and Google Apps SaaS offerings.

The box labeled Windows Azure in figure 2.6 is Windows Server 2008 modified to run in the cloud environment. This means it was paravirtualized to make it run efficiently in the virtualized environment created by running Microsoft's Hypervisor on bare hardware in Microsoft's cloud data centers.

Internally, the OS layer—derived from Windows Server 2008—consists of four pillars: storage (like a file system); the fabric controller, which is a management system for modeling/deploying and provisioning; virtualized computation/VM; and a development environment, which allows developers to emulate Windows Azure on their desktop and plug in Visual Studio, Eclipse, or other tools to write cloud applications against it. Because of this architecture, you merely have to deploy Azure on a single machine; then, you can duplicate multiple instances of it on the rest of the servers in the cloud using virtualization technology.

---

[6] http://aws.amazon.com/ec2/pricing/

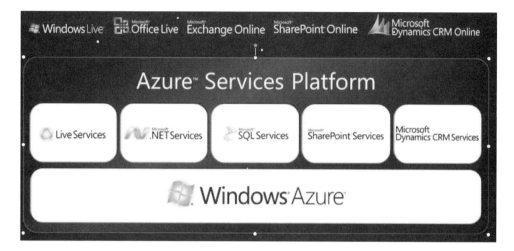

Figure 2.6   The Windows Azure architecture and framework. At the bottom level is the Windows Azure operating system. This runs in the virtualization environment created by Microsoft's Hypervisor running on bare hardware. At the top layer are end-user applications, which Microsoft is recasting to be delivered as SaaS. Source: Microsoft.

Applications for Microsoft's Azure are written in proprietary programming environments like Visual Studio using the .NET libraries, and compiled to the Common Language Runtime, Microsoft's language-independent managed environment.

WINDOWS AZURE API

The Windows Azure API is a REST-based API that uses X.509 client certificates for authentication. Table 2.8 lists a portion of the API, giving you an idea of how applications running in the Azure cloud are manipulated and controlled. This is the set of calls related to performing operations on hosted services.

Similar to Amazon, a set of building-block services run on top of Azure creating Microsoft's PaaS capabilities. The initial set of services includes the following:

- Live Services
- SQL Services
- .Net Services
- SharePoint Services
- CRM Services

You can treat these lower-level services as APIs—they have no user interface elements—when constructing cloud applications.

Azure pricing is comparable to Amazon with computing time set at $0.12 per hour, storage at $0.15 per GB, and storage transactions at $0.01 per 10 KB. For the structured database, fees for the web edition are set at up to 1 GB relational database at $9.99 per month and for the business edition up to 10 GB relational database at $99.99 per month. A tiered, all-you-can-eat (within limits) model is said to be coming.

Table 2.8   A portion of the RESTful Windows Azure API

Service	Description
List Hosted Services	Lists the hosted services available under the current subscription.

```
GET
https://management.core.windows.net/<subscription-id>/services/
    hostedservices
```

Service	Description
Get Hosted Service Properties	Retrieves system properties for the specified hosted service. These properties include the service name and service type; the name of the affinity group to which the service belongs, or its location if it isn't part of an affinity group; and, optionally, information about the service's deployments.

```
GET
https://management.core.windows.net/<subscription-id>/services/
    hostedservices/
        <service-name>
```

Service	Description
Create Deployment	Uploads a new service package and creates a new deployment on staging or production.

```
POST
https://management.core.windows.net/<subscription-id>/services/
    hostedservices/
        <service-name>/deploymentslots/<deployment-slot-name>
```

Service	Description
Get Deployment	May be specified as follows. Note that you can delete a deployment either by specifying the deployment slot (staging or production) or by specifying the deployment's unique name.

```
GET
https://management.core.windows.net/<subscription-id>/services/
    hostedservices/
        <service-name>/deploymentslots/<deployment-slot>/
GET
https://management.core.windows.net/<subscription-id>/services/
    hostedservices/
        <service-name>/deployments/<deployment-name>/
```

Service	Description
Swap Deployment	Initiates a virtual IP swap between the staging and production deployment slots for a service. If the service is currently running in the staging environment, it's swapped to the production environment. If it's running in the production environment, it's swapped to staging. This is an asynchronous operation whose status must be checked using Get Operation Status.

```
POST
https://management.core.windows.net/<subscription-id>/hostedservices/
    <service-name>
```

Table 2.8   A portion of the RESTful Windows Azure API (*continued*)

Service	Description
Delete Deployment	Deletes the specified deployment. This is an asynchronous operation.

```
DELETE
https://management.core.windows.net/<subscription-id>/services/
   hostedservices/
     <service-name>/deploymentslots/<deployment-slot>
DELETE
https://management.core.windows.net/<subscription-id>/services/
   hostedservices/
     <service-name>/deployments/<deployment-name>
```

2.2.3   *Google App Engine: Platform as a Service*

App Engine is a pure PaaS cloud targeted exclusively at traditional web applications, enforcing an application structure of clean separation between a stateless computation tier and a stateful storage tier. The virtualization and the elasticity that are so visible in the IaaS model are almost completely invisible here. But they're a big part of the picture behind the scenes. One of the selling propositions of this model is its *automatic* elasticity in the face of capacity requirement changes.

The App Engine programming languages are Python and Java. App Engine isn't suitable for general-purpose computing. It works best for web applications and relies on the assumption of a request-reply structure, which assumes long periods of no CPU utilization (such as, human think time). Consequently, Google can and does severely ration CPU time for each request.

App Engine's automatic scaling and high-availability mechanisms, and the proprietary MegaStore data storage (built on BigTable) available to App Engine applications, all rely on these constraints. But if your application fits within those constraints, there is probably no faster and cheaper way to build an application that scales automatically and runs on the largest cloud on the planet.

APP ENGINE DEVELOPMENT ENVIRONMENT

The App Engine development environment consists of these elements:

- *Sandbox*—Applications run in a secure environment that provides limited access to the underlying operating system. These limitations allow App Engine to distribute web requests for the application across multiple servers and to start and stop servers to meet traffic demands. The sandbox isolates your application in its own secure, reliable environment independent of the hardware, operating system, and physical location of the web server.

- *Java runtime environment*—You can develop applications for the Java 6 runtime environment using common Java web development tools and API standards. An app interacts with the environment using the Java Servlet standard and can use common web application technologies, such as JavaServer Pages (JSPs). Apps access most App Engine services using Java standard APIs. The environment includes the Java SE Runtime Environment (JRE) 6 platform and libraries. The restrictions of the sandbox environment are implemented in the JVM. An app can use any JVM bytecode or library feature, as long as it doesn't exceed the sandbox restrictions.

- *Python runtime environment*—You can develop applications using the Python 2.5 programming language and run it on a Python interpreter. App Engine includes APIs and tools for Python web application development, including a data-modeling API, a web application framework, and tools for managing and accessing the App's data. The Python environment includes the Python standard library within the limitations of the sandbox environment. Application code written for the Python environment must be written exclusively in Python. The Python environment provides APIs for the datastore, Google Accounts, URL fetch, and email services.

- *Datastore*—App Engine provides a distributed data-storage service that features a query engine and transactions. This distributed datastore scales with the application's needs automatically. As we discussed previously regarding cloud databases, the App Engine datastore isn't like a traditional relational database. Data objects, or *entities*, have a kind and a set of properties. Queries can retrieve entities of a given kind filtered and sorted by the values of the properties. Property values can be of any of the supported property value types. Datastore entities are *schemaless*. The application code enforces and provides the structure of data entities. The Java JDO/JPA interfaces and the Python datastore interface include features for applying and enforcing this structure.

App Engine is free under these daily thresholds: 6.5 hours of CPU time, and 1 GB of data transferred in and out of the application. Beyond this, outgoing bandwidth costs $0.12 per GB, incoming bandwidth costs $0.10 per GB, CPU time is $0.10 per hour, stored data is $0.15 per GB per month, and recipients emailed are $0.0001 per recipient.

2.2.4 *Ruby on Rails in a cloud: Platform as a Service*

Ruby on Rails (RoR) is an open-source web application framework for the Ruby programming language. It's intended to be used with an agile development methodology, often used by web developers due to its suitability for short, client-driven projects. Similar to Google's App Engine, RoR applications are limited to request-response architecture web applications.

OPEN SOURCE SOFTWARE Computer software available in source code form for which the source code and certain other rights normally reserved for copyright holders are provided under a software license that permits users to study, change, and improve the software. Some consider open source a philosophy; others consider it a pragmatic methodology. Before the term *open source* became widely adopted, developers and producers used a variety of phrases to describe the concept; *open source* gained hold with the rise of the internet and the attendant need for massive retooling of the computing source code. Open-source software is most often developed in a public, collaborative manner.

The Ruby language was designed to combine Smalltalk's conceptual elegance, Python's ease of use and learning, and Perl's pragmatism. Many teams experience 10X faster development of web applications using RoR. But many have reported significant challenges getting RoR to scale massively, which probably has to do with architecture and design choices made in the application as opposed to something endemic to RoR itself.

Many small companies jumped in early to offer RoR stacks that run on top of Amazon's EC2, including Heroku, Aptana, EngineYard, and others.

2.2.5 *Salesforce.com's Force.com: Platform as a Service*

Salesforce.com is the most successful SaaS application used in the enterprise. It's a customer-relationship-management (CRM) application that has run strictly as a cloud application since 1999.

Force.com is the company's PaaS capability, where developers use the Apex programming language to create add-on applications that integrate into the main Salesforce application and are hosted on Salesforce.com's cloud infrastructure.

Google and Salesforce have created an integration between App Engine and Force.com such that applications can be built using either environment and still access the stored repository of corporate data on Salesforce's site.

Force.com also runs an exchange called AppExchange; it's a directory of applications built for Salesforce by third-party developers, which users can purchase and add to their Salesforce environment. More than 800 applications are available from over 450 ISVs.

The Force.com list price is $5.00 per login with a maximum of five logins per user per month. According to the company's website, "Force.com cloud pricing is for occasional-use, widely-deployed apps and is available for platform use only and not for CRM applications."

Our last classification is a strange one—strange because it's not about a different type of application environment but instead is about a different ownership structure. So-called Datacenter as a Service is about private companies creating a *private* cloud just for their use.

2.2.6 *Private clouds: Datacenter as a Service (DaaS)*

Private cloud (also *internal cloud* and *corporate cloud*) is a term for a computing architecture that provides hosted services to a limited number of people behind a firewall. The same advances in virtualization, automation, and distributed computing that enable the cloud for Amazon, Microsoft, and Google have allowed corporate network and data-center administrators to effectively become service providers that meet the needs of their customers within the corporation.

The concept of a private cloud is designed to appeal to an organization that needs or wants more control over its data than it can get by using a third-party hosted service, such as Amazon's EC2 or S3. Internal IT providers that build private clouds have to make fundamental changes in their operations so they behave and provide benefits (on a smaller scale) similar to those of cloud computing providers. In addition to economic gains through higher utilization and a pay-for-what-you-use model, an enterprise, to enable the private cloud model, implements changes in operations which, at the very least, makes an organization better equipped to shift to or overflow to a public cloud when appropriate.

The contrarian view

Here's the rub: some say private clouds are expensive data centers with a fancy name. Pundits predict that within the next year or so, we'll have seen the rise and fall of this concept. Whereas everyone agrees that virtualization, service-oriented architectures, and open standards are all great things for companies operating a data center to consider, critics argue that all this talk about private clouds is a distraction from the real news: the vast majority of companies shouldn't need to worry about operating any sort of data center anymore, cloud-like or not.

SOME CONCERNS FOR THOSE THINKING ABOUT PRIVATE CLOUDS

If you're considering implementing a private cloud, keep the following in mind:

- *Private clouds are small scale.*   There's a reason why most innovative cloud computing providers have their roots in powering consumer web technology—that's where the numbers are. Few corporate data centers will see anything close to the type of volume seen by these vendors. And volume drives cost savings through the huge economies of scale we've discussed.
- *Legacy applications don't cloudify easily.*   Legacy applications moved to a private cloud will see marginal improvements at best. You can achieve only so much without re-architecting these applications to a cloud infrastructure.
- *On-premises doesn't mean more secure.*   The biggest drivers toward private clouds have been fear, uncertainty, and doubt about security. For many, it feels more secure to have your data behind your firewall in a data center that you control. But unless your company spends more money and energy thinking about security than Amazon, Google, and Salesforce, that is a fallacy.
- *Do what you do best.*   There's no simple set of tricks that an operator of a data center can borrow from Amazon or Google. These companies make their living operating the world's largest data centers. They're constantly optimizing how

they operate based on real-time performance feedback from millions of transactions. You can try to learn from and emulate them, but your rate of innovation will never be the same—private clouds will always be many steps behind the public clouds.

AMAZON VIRTUAL PRIVATE CLOUD

Amazon Virtual Private Cloud (Amazon VPC) is a secure and seamless bridge between a company's existing IT infrastructure and the AWS cloud. Although it isn't a private cloud as we defined it, this approach offers corporations a hybrid model merging aspects of their data center with Amazon's cloud.

Amazon VPC enables an enterprise to connect its existing infrastructure to a set of isolated AWS compute resources via a Virtual Private Network (VPN) connection and to extend existing management capabilities, such as security services, firewalls, and intrusion-detection systems, to include AWS resources. You'll learn much more about cloud security, private clouds, and VPC in chapter 4.

Until now, we've explored the technological underpinnings of clouds to understand how they work, and we've applied that knowledge to a few of the most prominent clouds in a variety of categories to understand how they compare and contrast. You're now informed enough to ask this question: What type of cloud do I need?

2.3 *Matching cloud providers to your needs*

We've looked under the hood of a lot of different cloud types, their APIs, their other service offerings, and the technologies that underpin them. Which of them is appropriate for you? How can you prevent lock-in when you do make the choice? We'll try to answer those questions by going back through the major cloud providers and applying a framework of decision criteria by which you can evaluate each one for your projects.

2.3.1 *Amazon web services IaaS cloud*

Summarizing what we've explored so far, AWS is a flexible, lower-level offering (closer to hardware), which means you have more possibilities. And in general, it will be higher performing at the cost of "everything is left up to you," including how and when to scale, move or replicate your data, and more.

Amazon EC2 runs the platform you provide, supports all major programming languages, and offers a set of industry-standard services (getting more standard as standards groups and the open source Eucalyptus seeks to formalize theirs as the standard cloud API). But Amazon, being an IaaS, requires much more work, which means a longer time-to-market for your applications.

Use AWS if you

- Want to use third-party open-source software
- Have existing code
- Want to transfer a web app to your own machine/servers later
- Port code to another language

- Want complete control
- Need to stress/load test an app (for example, load up 1,000 instances)

And as for avoiding lock-in, Amazon EC2 is good because Amazon-compatible services can and will be easily provided by other companies as well as an open-source initiative. The leader always gets to set the standards. EC2 is practically the closest to zero lock-in of any choice you can make today.

2.3.2 Microsoft Windows Azure IaaS and PaaS cloud

Azure is intermediate between application frameworks, such as App Engine, and hardware virtual machines, such as EC2. Microsoft is trying to make the transition from desktop (data center) to its cloud as seamless as possible. The company suggests that you can build and test an application locally and then deploy to its cloud. But Microsoft does admit that all UI and any data-extraction logic must be rewritten to deal with low-bandwidth internet connections. Note that we said *its cloud*. In that sense, Microsoft is similar to App Engine and Force.com in terms of locking you in to its cloud, run by the company.

Use Windows Azure if you

- Already use the .NET and SQL Server portions of the Microsoft stack
- Have existing code developed to those Microsoft APIs
- Have teams that normally develop in Visual Studio using C#
- Want to blend development from desk top to cloud
- Have no issue with lock-in to Microsoft

As for lock-in, Windows Azure isn't looking as bad as Google App Engine. Although it will still be hosted exclusively by Microsoft, it may be possible for other companies to come up with (almost) compatible cloud service because core pieces of Windows Azure are based on the well-known SQL Server, IIS, and .NET framework stacks.

2.3.3 Google App Engine PaaS cloud

Google App Engine is a tightly controlled environment—a decision Google made to enable automatic scaling of application threads as well as the datastore. The environment supports only Python and Java, and no installation of any open source software is possible.

Use App Engine if you

- Have no preexisting code
- Are building request-response web apps or mashups
- Consider time-to-market the most important thing
- Aren't doing anything fancy (installing software)
- Aren't worried about lock-in to Google

App Engine is high on the lock-in scale. It's hard to imagine any compatible products from any other company for a long time, if ever. It's proprietary, and Google doesn't plan to release its technology. Automatic scale and time-to-market have many advantages, but almost complete lock-in will most likely be the price you pay for those benefits.

2.3.4 Ruby on Rails PaaS cloud

Ruby is slightly more computationally expensive than other languages, but having easy resource expansion available can cure a lot of the "what if I get mentioned on Oprah?" scares that business people experience. Rails is a particularly good match for cloud computing because of its shared-nothing architecture. This means you can generate new instances of an application, and they will begin to run. And developers love Ruby because of their much higher productivity. Many small companies are now providing RoR clouds (many layered on top of Amazon).

Use Ruby on Rails if you

- Are building request-response web apps with existing Ruby expertise
- Consider time-to-market critical
- Aren't doing anything fancy (installing software)
- Don't care about lock-in

Lock-in isn't a big concern with RoR because, as we've said, there are many choices of RoR vendors and probably more to come.

2.3.5 Force.com PaaS cloud

Force.com is an extension of the SaaS service Salesforce.com. Many companies have been using Salesforce for a long time. They have rich, sophisticated databases of sales contacts, history of sales cycles, information about their products, and a lot of other sales-process related information. This information forms the crown jewels of any company's sales team, and companies want many applications that aren't built into Salesforce.com. For this reason, Salesforce.com created a framework using many of the same back-end services used by the company's main SaaS application, operating on the same back-end data, and made it accessible and programmable to end users. Force.com is ideal for building applications that tie into your existing Salesforce.com databases, such as sales contacts, the internal sales team, your products, and so on.

Use Force.com if you

- Are already a customer of Salesforce.com's SaaS customer-resource-management product
- Have a requirement for a simple mashup style of web application
- Are willing to use Force.com's specialized programming language
- Don't care about lock-in

We didn't include a section about when to use private cloud because it's a much more complex discussion. We'll deal with the subject in chapter 4.

2.4   *Summary*

This chapter built on your understanding from chapter 1 of the types of clouds and the reasons—technical and economic—for this step in the evolution of computing. We've focused on how the cloud works by looking under the hood and examining the technological underpinnings. Cloud providers are making phenomenal economies of scale. Their costs keep getting lower while their specialized expertise in operating these massive data centers gets better.

This chapter examined some of the core enabling technologies of cloud computing. First and foremost is virtualization, which even most corporate data centers have embraced as a way to increase server utilization and thereby lower costs. Because a cloud is a virtualized server environment where you can quickly crate new instances of machines or applications and then control them over the network, both automation and network access are also vital in cloud computing. An API to create, operate, expand elastically, and destroy instances is also required. Trends seem to be leading in the direction of Amazon's API becoming an industry standard. We looked at cloud storage, focusing on Amazon's S3 API as an example.

You saw how relational databases don't scale because they have to be shared. This has led to the emergence of new key-value types of databases as the norm in the cloud. One of the biggest benefits of moving to the cloud is the ability to scale almost infinitely as application demand grows. You learned how this elasticity works with the example of the calls required in Amazon EC2 to create an automatically scaled, load-balanced EC2 application. We compared Amazon's SimpleDB to Google's BigTable.

This chapter also compared and contrasted the major flavors of cloud computing. Amazon EC2 is the most prominent example of IaaS. Microsoft Azure is mostly IaaS as well but has many PaaS offerings. Google is the most prominent of the PaaS with its App Engine. The plethora of Ruby on Rails offerings (such as Force.com from Salesforce) are highly specialized types of platforms.

Somewhat tongue in cheek, we expanded the taxonomy of cloud terms to include data center as a service and examined the concept of private clouds to see if this is something that will stick or is just a fad. This understanding of the cloud classifications should help you avoid the all-too-common "apples to oranges" comparisons between, say, an IaaS and a PaaS cloud. You're now in a position to distinguish between them. More important, you're in a better position to make an informed decision about what's best for you, depending on what you're trying to do.

You've learned that a major driver behind this IT evolution isn't technology but economics. Consequently, we'll spend the next chapter looking closely at the business case for cloud computing.

The business case for cloud computing

Chapter 1 gave you the "what" of cloud computing. Delving into the technology behind cloud computing in chapter 2, you learned the "how." Let's now look at the "why" and "when." These two questions have to do with the economics and the broader business issues that you need to examine when and if you consider moving to the cloud. You'll need to know how to make the transition, the type of cloud that makes sense, and when is the right time to make the move.

In looking at the economics of cloud computing, first we'll examine the most common models for setting up and managing IT infrastructure including internal IT, colocated, managed services, and the cloud. A good way of doing this is to compare the detailed costs of deployment in the different models—comparing apples to apples. Next, we'll explore what application characteristics do and don't make sense for deploying to the cloud. Zero-capital startups are a new and interesting phenomenon made possible by the cloud. But many of the parameters that make a zero-capital startup using the cloud compelling don't apply to medium or large businesses; still, it's illustrative to see why many startups getting funded today don't purchase a single server.

We'll analyze case studies that are fresh startups as well as established small and medium-sized businesses. At the end of this chapter, we'll discuss a few large enterprises that have found a way to use the cloud for high-value business benefits. As we discussed in the last chapter, cloud providers are actively buying servers, power, and bandwidth to provision data centers at an enormous scale. Let's now focus on the implications of this large-scale build-out as we look at the economics for the consumers of cloud computing.

3.1 The economics of cloud computing

Cloud computing has the ability to change the economics of IT. It changes the ratio between capital expenses (CAPEX) and operational expenses (OPEX) because of its pay-only-for-what-you-use principles. Let's start with an overview of various IT deployment models and then apply them to the specific example of a small-scale e-commerce application. This will provide you with a baseline understanding of the costs and trade-offs that may make one solution better than another for a given situation.

CAPEX and OPEX

CAPEX are expenses that create future benefits. When a business spends money to buy fixed assets, it incurs a capital expenditure. Accounting adds a capital expenditure to an asset account (capitalizing it). Typically, CAPEX requires a large up-front investment to be amortized (written down) as its value decreases over time. The initial CAPEX purchase can require a large cash outlay—one reason startups are avoiding these purchases altogether.

OPEX is an ongoing cost for running a product, business, or system. It's a day-to-day expense akin to costs, such as sales and marketing, and as such, it can much more easily be increased or decreased as business needs dictate. This isn't possible with CAPEX because you've already purchased the equipment.

3.1.1 Traditional internal IT vs. colocation vs. managed service vs. cloud model

In this section, we'll compare and contrast the economics of the four common models for setting up and managing IT for an enterprise: traditional internally managed IT, colocation, managed service, and the newest—the public cloud model.

TRADITIONAL INTERNAL IT

In the traditional internal IT model, or *zero-outsource model,* all aspects that constitute an IT application or service are purchased and managed using internal resources.

The most common form is office IT infrastructure. In many offices, an internet connection is provisioned from an ISP and connected to the internal network via a router. This internal network is then provisioned with firewalls, switches, central file and print servers, desktop computers, and perhaps a wireless network and laptops. Internal IT purchases, installs, and operates all this equipment as well as general office software. IT for more specialized business applications can be handled in the same manner, with custom or packaged applications that are loaded onto hardware provisioned for that purpose.

You can also deploy applications for external audiences, such as a corporate website in a traditional IT model. Depending on the scale of such an application, it can either share the network connection (typically on a separate VLAN to isolate it from internal traffic for security reasons) or be provisioned with its own dedicated internet connectivity and an isolated network.

COLOCATION

Another possible model for deploying an application is within a third-party data center, otherwise known as a *colocation facility*. In this model, the company is still responsible for purchasing the server hardware and developing or purchasing the required software for running the application. The colocation facility provides that third party with power, cooling, rack space, and network connectivity for their hardware. The colocation facility typically also provides redundant network connectivity, backup power, and physical security.

Colocation services are typically purchased as annual contracts with an initial service fee and monthly charges based on the amount of rack space (usually bundled with a specified allocation of power) and committed bandwidth. For hardware housed in facilities that aren't in close proximity to a company's IT resources, you can purchase what some call "remote-hands" capability in case a manual intervention is required on your behalf.

MANAGED SERVICE

In the managed-service model, in addition to outsourcing the core infrastructure, such as power and network connectivity, the company no longer purchases server and networking hardware. The managed-service provider rents these to the company and also takes on the responsibility of managing the hardware systems and base operating system software. In some cases, the provider also rents standard software such as databases and rudimentary DB management services as part of their service offering.

Similar to the colocation scenario, contracting with a managed-service provider typically involves at minimum an annual commit, with an initial setup fee followed by a recurring monthly charge based on the configuration of hardware and software being rented. In this model, bandwidth isn't typically charged for separately; instead, you get a standard allotment based on the number of servers for which you contracted. You can also contract for ancillary services, such as backups. Typically, the charge is based on the amount of storage required on a monthly basis.

CLOUD MODEL

Finally we get to the cloud model. In this model, as in the managed-service model, the company outsources the infrastructure and hardware, but in an entirely different way. Instead of dedicated hardware resources, the company utilizes virtualized resources that are dynamically allocated only at the time of need.

You can think of this as the analog of just-in-time manufacturing, which brought tremendous efficiencies to the production of goods. Instead of stockpiling large inventories, manufacturers can reduce their carrying costs by having inventory delivered just as it's needed in manufacturing. Similarly, the dynamic allocation of resources in a cloud service allows a customer to use computing resources only when necessary. Servers don't have to sit idle during slack periods.

The billing model for cloud services is aligned with this sort of usage profile, with service provisioning often requiring no up-front cost and monthly billing based on the actual amount of resources consumed that month. This may translate into significant cost advantages over traditional deployment models.

3.1.2 *A detailed comparison of the cost of deploying in different models*

To get a clear idea of what drives costs in each deployment model, let's study a specific example. Let's run a cost analysis of deployment for each of the models we described in the last section and get a quantitative picture of what makes up the total bill. By looking in detail at where the dollars and cents go, you'll be in a position to understand the kinds of applications for which a cloud model makes the most sense.

For our hypothetical example, let's look at a small-scale e-commerce application. For this discussion, let's assume it has been designed as a three-tier system, with a front-end web server, a middle-tier application server, and a back-end database. Because it's a small-scale system, let's assume that one server of each flavor will suffice for handling the web traffic you anticipate receiving; but for reliability reasons, because you wish to minimize downtime, you'll deploy a redundant pair of each infrastructure component (physical or virtual; see figure 3.1). In the non-cloud deployment models, you'll deal with physical infrastructure that you either purchase (in the cases of an internal IT or colocation model) or rent (in the case of the managed-service model). The main hardware components of the system and their approximate purchase costs are as follows:

- 2 firewalls: 2 x $1,500 = $3,000
- 2 load-balancers: 2 x $5,000 = $10,000
- 6 commodity servers: 6 x $3,000 = $18,000

For simplicity, let's ignore the various other ancillary pieces of the hardware infrastructure. Let's also assume that you're running using open-source software; we'll ignore the costs of such things as the operating system, the application server, and database software.

Small E-commerce Configuration

Linux/MySQL
DB Replicated
w/ hot standby

Linux/Jboss
Business Rules
Active/Active

Linux/Apache
Presentation
Active/Active

Cisco LB
Active/Active

Cisco VPN
Active/Active

Figure 3.1   For redundancy, the e-commerce example configuration consists of a pair of each functional component required to operate the application. The hardware chosen for the configuration is rack mountable, commodity servers, and network gear. Except for the database, each component is active; the DB is replicated with a hot standby. We chose a LAMP open source stack to simplify the treatment of software costs.

INTERNAL IT DEPLOYMENT

As we discussed in chapter 1, a good way to look at the costs of a specific deployment model is to examine the CAPEX and OPEX components separately. CAPEX is the primary driver for the up-front cost of the application; but for financial planning purposes (cash considerations aside), these costs depreciate over the lifetime of the equipment. OPEX, as you'll see here, are the operational costs related directly to the infrastructure. Generally, there are also operational costs related to the human resources required to maintain and operate the infrastructure.

The CAPEX in this internal IT example for your e-commerce application is the cost of the hardware listed earlier: $31,000. Assuming a three-year lifetime for this gear, you can calculate the attributed monthly cost by dividing the total by 36, giving a monthly cost of $861. This is the monthly depreciated cost of the internal IT scenario. Table 3.1 summarizes this example.

Table 3.1   Internal IT cost calculation: assumes the existing data center, power, and bandwidth cost nothing extra

		Hardware
	$3,000	Two firewalls
+	$10,000	Two load-balancers
+	$18,000	Six servers
=	$31,000	Total CAPEX cost of hardware
÷	36	Depreciated over three years (36 months)
=	$861	per month

In the internal IT model, if there is adequate power, cooling, rack space, and bandwidth to house the new gear for the application, there is no additional incremental cost to be taken into account. But note that the boxes in the end do consume power, produce heat, and require bandwidth to do work; you're not getting something for nothing.

COLOCATION DEPLOYMENT

In the colocation case, you can assume the same CAPEX expense as in the internal IT model. In the internal IT model, you ignore the ongoing OPEX cost associated with running the application because you assume the cost is absorbed somewhere else. In a colocation deployment, there is an ongoing OPEX cost for the rack space and the bandwidth.

For this deployment, you should be able to get by with half a rack and, let's say, 10 Mbits of bandwidth. You should be able to purchase this on an annual contract for about $1,000/month. This yields a total monthly cost of $1,861/month for the colocation model (see table 3.2).

Table 3.2 Colocation cost calculation: assumes CAPEX for hardware plus OPEX for the colocation contract

Hardware		Bandwidth
$31,000	Total cost of HW	10 Mbit contract
÷ 36	Months	
= $861	per month +	$1,000 per month
	= $1,861 per month	

You can think of the colocation example as a proxy for a cost-allocation model and treat the two models as the same. This overestimates the cost for the internal IT case when facilities exist to house it. But on the other hand, when new facilities need to be provisioned, this model can be more financially advantageous.

MANAGED-SERVICE DEPLOYMENT

Next, let's turn to the managed-service model. In this case, you're in a pure rental model. All of your costs are OPEX. A typical rental cost for the pair of firewalls is $300/month and for the load-balancer pair is approximately $1,500/month. Each of the six servers will cost approximately $1,000 per month, or $6,000/month combined. This yields a total cost of $7,800/month. In a managed model, there is typically a bandwidth utilization allocation of 500 GB/month per server. This is enough for your e-commerce application, so there should be no additional charge for bandwidth. There is also typically a one-time initialization fee equal to approximately one month of service. Spreading that out over three years yields an effective monthly cost of $8,017/month (see table 3.3).

Table 3.3   Managed-service cost calculation: a pure OPEX expenditure for hardware rental and contract

Hardware		Bandwidth	
$300/month	Firewalls	500 GB/server included	
+ $1,500/month	Load balancers	$0	Additional charge
+ $6,000/month	Six servers +	$7,800 ÷ 36	Installation (once)
= $7,800 per month		+ $217 per month	
= $8,017 per month			

You can see a large disparity in the cost of a colocation deployment and managed service deployment—approximately $6,200/month. The general argument for managed hosting revolves around a value proposition that a savings in the model is inherent because the $6,200/month difference is related to the savings realized from reduced human resources to manage the infrastructure, which you don't take into account in these scenarios.

CLOUD DEPLOYMENT

Now that we're finished discussing the traditional models, let's press on and turn our attention to the cloud. We'll run through this model in more detail. As you'll see, it's trickier and more challenging to run the analysis for a cloud deployment because there are quite a few more moving parts. But running through this scenario will help you understand the key factors that you must take into account to get a good estimate of the cost of a cloud deployment.

As with the managed-service model, you're now in a pure rental model, with the primary difference being that you're renting virtual capacity instead of dedicated capacity. The first thing you need to do is figure out the configuration that's analogous to what you've been modeling in the world of physical infrastructure.

To calculate the cost of the deployment, let's take a specific cloud provider—Amazon—and use its pricing structure to provide a point of comparison. First, you model the six servers that represent the (doubled) web servers, the application servers, and the database servers. Server capacity is measured in terms of compute units, which they define in terms of an equivalent physical hardware unit (see table 3.4).

Table 3.4   Amazon EC2 instance size equivalents

Size	Memory	Num EC2 compute units (1 = 1.0-1.2 GHz 2007 Opteron CPU)	Storage	Platform
Small	1.7 GB	1	160 GB	32-bit
Large	7.5 GB	4	850 GB	64-bit
Extra large	15 GB	8	1690 GB	64-bit

To model your $3,000-server boxes, choose Amazon's Large Instance option. Large instances can be used in a pure on-demand model with no up-front fee for $0.34/hr. More economical options are available if you elect to pay an up-front fee. Because you're making calculations based on a three-year time horizon, choose an option that allows you to lock down a price per large instance of $0.12/hr for three years; Amazon's reserved instance one-time fee is $1,400 but then gives you the per-hour charge of only $0.12. If you plan to run the application 24 x 7, the monthly charge will be $87.65 based on the average hours in a month being 730.48. When you add this to the $38.88/month for the initial one-time fee amortized over 36 months, you arrive at a total of $126.53/month for each large instance. Because you need six of these for your deployment, that works out to about $759/month for the compute resources.

You also need to pay for bandwidth. In the colocation example, you purchased an allocation of 10 Mb/s. Colocation bandwidth is typically charged in what is called a 95th percentile billing model. Usage is measured in five-minute buckets over the course of the month, and the bucket representing the 95th largest usage in Mb/s is taken as the measured utilization for the month.

95th percentile billing model

Many providers of network bandwidth have adopted a method for charging known as the *95th percentile billing model.* Unlike most metered models, in which a certain quantity of usage is measured over the billing interval (say, a month), in this model, the charge corresponds to a measurement of usage near the peak for the month, with the top 5 percent thrown out to remove extreme outliers.

To understand exactly how this works, let's consider a 30-day month. To calculate the monthly bandwidth usage, the network provider measures the amount of bandwidth (in megabits consumed in each of the 8,640 five-minute intervals that make up the month) and then identifies the 432nd largest (the 95th percentile of 8,640). It then divides the Mb consumed by 300 seconds to find the megabits per second value. The monthly bill is based on this quantity.

Cloud bandwidth is typically charged by counting the number of bytes transferred in a given time interval and not by using a percentile billing method. To calculate the consumption equivalent to the 10 Mb/s in a transit (pay-as-you-go) billing model, assume that the 10 Mb/s was chosen as 4 times the average sustained bandwidth utilization, meaning that the e-commerce application runs at an average bandwidth utilization of 2.5 Mb/s. This translates to 320 Kb/sec, which, over a month, translates to around 780 GB of transit. Inbound and outbound transits have different fees, with inbound transit being much cheaper than outbound. Web traffic tends to be asymmetric, with requests that are generally much smaller than responses. From the server perspective, the response is outbound traffic. Again, for simplicity, model all the traffic use as outbound, which means your result overestimates the cost. For outbound transit of less than 10 TB, the per-GB transit cost is $0.17/GB, yielding a cost of about $135/month.

The physical infrastructure for your e-commerce application includes a pair of load-balancers. In a cloud service, load balancing is provided as a service, again in a consumption model. The charge includes two components: enabling the service ($0.025/hr) and a bandwidth-related cost for the amount of data transferred ($0.008/GB). The cost, including bandwidth for load-balancing services, is approximately an incremental $25/month.

The redundant firewalls in the colocation example allow for VPN access into the e-commerce infrastructure for secure remote management of the application. Virtual VPNs are also available from Amazon as part of the cloud service offering. The virtual VPN allows for the creation of IPSec tunnels between your corporate infrastructure and the application running in the cloud. The billing model includes a per-VPN tunnel charge of $0.05/hr whenever the VPN tunnel is active, and an inbound and outbound bandwidth charge at the same rates as regular bandwidth usage. In this example, let's assume that the bandwidth used in management is negligible in comparison to the traffic coming into the e-commerce site. Additionally, for simplicity, let's assume you keep a VPN tunnel open to each of the six instances all the time, yielding an additional $0.30/hr or an incremental $216/month.

Finally, you'd probably like to keep copies of your instances, of which you have three flavors (the web server, the application server, and the database server) stored in Amazon, and perhaps some additional backup storage, which you can generously size at 2 TB. The monthly cost for storage in Amazon's Elastic Block Store (EBS) is $0.10/GB, yielding an additional cost of $200/month. The fees for I/O into the EBS of $0.10 per 1 million I/O requests are additional. Let's be conservative and add $100/month related to I/O, bringing the total cost to $300/month for storage-related services.

Adding up all the monthly costs (the instances, the load balancer, the VPN, and the associated bandwidth charges and storage), you get a grand total of approximately $1,435/month (see table 3.5).

Table 3.5   Public cloud cost calculation: pure OPEX, based on resource consumption

Hardware + storage		Bandwidth
	$216/month Virtual VPN (firewall)	10 TB max outbound
+	$25/month Load-balancing service	
+	$300/month Storage	
+	$759/month Six large instances	$135/month @ $0.17/GB
=	$1,300/month	+ $135/month
	= $1,435 per month	

Now, let's see how this compares to the other possible models. If you recall, the three other models—internal IT (assuming existing space and power), colocation, and managed services—yielded monthly costs of $861, $1,861, and $8,017, respectively. The costs for the cloud deployment model sit roughly halfway between the internal IT and colocation models. The managed model is clearly in a different realm of cost. Note that this is related to the additional management services provided in these types of offerings.

You may wonder about all the purported savings the cloud is supposed to offer. Wasn't this supposed to be the magic bullet, the super-cost-savings alternative? The answer lies in how you set up the example. For a reasonably small application with a fixed workload that needs to run 24 x 7 for three years, there is no compelling reason today to use the cloud. If you have excess data-center resources you can use, it's more cost effective to run the application in an internal IT model—again, noting that the example doesn't count human resource costs. It turns out that the assumptions used to build the model are suboptimal for a cloud deployment. It's interesting that even in this case, you achieve something near cost parity. One of the key advantages of the cloud is the fact that you can use resources dynamically in an on-demand fashion.

Several application characteristics tilt the economics in favor of the cloud model; we'll look at them in greater detail in the next section.

3.2 Where does the cloud make sense?

As you saw in the preceding example, a fixed-load model may have limited economic advantage over a cloud deployment. In figure 3.2, you see the total cost for deploying the original e-commerce example in each of the four models over time. The flat line represents the internal IT model, meaning an initial spend. Let's assume no ongoing monthly costs, because in this model you're consuming preallocated resources that already exist and are accounted for. In comparison, the cloud model requires less initial cash outlay than the CAPEX in the internal IT case, and a full 18 months pass before it catches up to the cost of the internal IT deployment.

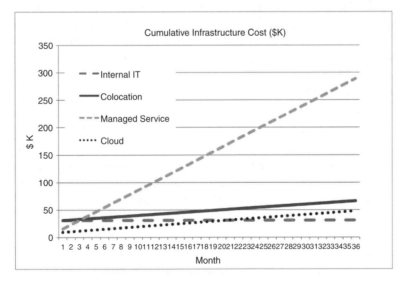

Figure 3.2 The total cumulative infrastructure cost for the example e-commerce application deployed in four different models. The internal IT model depicts a fixed initial cost due to capital equipment purchase and the implicit assumption that the organization is able to use existing operational resources allocated elsewhere, including the human resources to manage the infrastructure.

But certain application types are practically begging to be deployed in a cloud. Let's examine several of these and look at specific case studies for companies of different sizes.

3.2.1 Limited lifetime requirement/short-term need

Applications needed for a short, well-defined period of time are good candidates for a cloud deployment model. The main reason for this is the large up-front fixed capital cost for the hardware needed to run the application. Recalling the e-commerce application, let's assume you have an application that must run at exactly the same scale as the original application, but which has a fixed lifetime of six months. You require the same hardware resources and initial expenditure, but instead of realizing value for it over the three-year depreciation cycle, you should calculate the cost of the hardware for only that half-year interval, yielding an effective cost due to hardware of $5,167/month.

A six-month term for colocation is somewhat harder to negotiate than a standard one-year term, but let's suppose you can negotiate a $1,500/month fee with an initial $1,500 setup fee. Over the six-month term, this will translate into $1,750/month for hosting. In this example, you have, for both the internal IT and colocation models, an effective total cost of $5,167/month and $6,917/month, respectively.

What will it cost you in the cloud model? In the original example, you pay a one-time charge of $1,400 to lock in a price of $0.12/hour per large instance for three years. For an application you need for only six months, you can instead contract to lock in the same price of $0.12/hour for only one year at $910 per large instance. Over the six-month period, that amounts to a cost of $1,428/month for the instances plus the same costs as the original example for the bandwidth, load-balancer, VPN, and storage. This adds up to $580/month. The total cost becomes $2,008/month, which is clearly a substantial savings compared to either the internal IT or colocation models.

3.2.2 Scale variability/volatility

In the last section, what drove the cost savings for the cloud deployment was the finite time interval for which the application was needed. Let's look at another application characteristic where the scale and load variability requirement can make it advantageous to deploy using a cloud model. Scale requirements for an application may vary in several ways. Some types of capacity variability are predictable, and you can anticipate them. For example, the daily variations for financial or online trading applications that see the most traffic and hence require the largest amount of capacity are at the open and close of the market. These applications typically see variations in traffic load of 4X between the open and close and the low point of the day.

Another example is the seasonal variation seen by online e-commerce sites in the days immediately following Thanksgiving, the traditional start of the Christmas shopping season. For these e-commerce applications, peak capacity requirements can be as much as 20X normal capacity requirements, as you can see in figure 3.3 for Target.com.

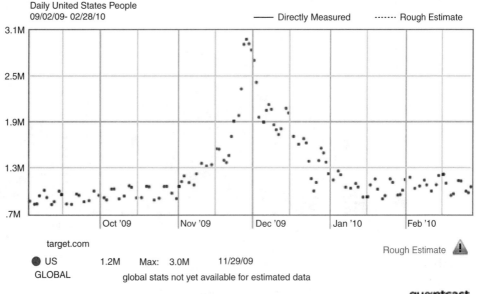

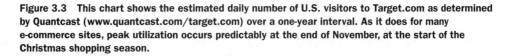

Figure 3.3 **This chart shows the estimated daily number of U.S. visitors to Target.com as determined by Quantcast (www.quantcast.com/target.com) over a one-year interval. As it does for many e-commerce sites, peak utilization occurs predictably at the end of November, at the start of the Christmas shopping season.**

If you consider designing and building infrastructure in an internal IT or colocation deployment model to handle peak capacity 4X or 20X normal capacity, you're looking at increasing the cost of the deployment by roughly the same factors. Granted, you'll gain some efficiency by purchasing larger volumes, but these gains are minimal compared to the overall size of the difference in required investment to scale. At peak utilization times, the entire infrastructure will be maximally taxed servicing the application. At other times, it will be severely underutilized.

In the cloud model, you can manage predictable traffic peaks in a much more cost-effective manner. You can bring additional instances online to handle the increased load during the hours or days of the increased capacity. For example, if you require 4X the normal capacity at 9:00 A.M., and at other times of the day only four instances are needed, you can spin up 12 additional instances for the hour they're needed and only pay for the additional instances when they're active.

Other scale variations are less predictable. Event-driven spikes in scale requirements can hit with as little warning as a tsunami and have devastating effects on the operation of the application. One example illustrated in figure 3.4 is the spike in traffic on the TMZ.com website after they were the first to report the death of Michael Jackson on June 25, 2009.

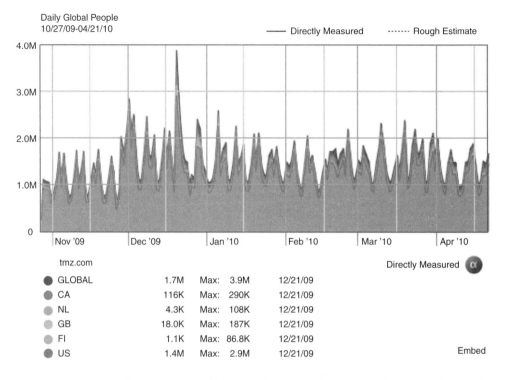

Figure 3.4   This chart shows the estimated daily number of U.S. visitors to TMZ.com as determined by Quantcast (www.quantcast.com/tmz.com) between 6/03/09 and 8/31/09. This is an example of an event-driven spike in demand on 6/25/09, when TMZ.com was the first to report the death of Michael Jackson.

If you have to rely solely on resources deployed in either an internal IT model or a colocation model, you literally have no recourse but to try to weather out high-demand periods. If you have the ability to use the cloud and can dynamically spin up capacity, handling all the unexpected traffic will happen seamlessly.

3.2.3   *Nonstrategic applications/low organizational value*

The final example of a situation in which it may be economically advantageous to deploy in a cloud model is when you're dealing with applications that are commodities and aren't strategic to the business. Many tactical applications serve internal constituents within an organization that could be moved to a cloud deployment, resulting in savings of scarce IT resources in an organization. A classic example is backup data storage. Instead of wasting internal IT resources on maintaining a backup system, you can use a cloud-based backup service. Because this is a core competency of the company providing the cloud backup service, it can be done more efficiently and economically by them than it can be by using internal IT resources. This can free up these resources to work on projects that are generally more strategic to the business.

3.3 Where does the cloud not make sense?

Although many application types make a good case for deployment to the cloud, in several cases you should pause before running down a cloud path. This isn't to say that these scenarios should never consider a cloud computing paradigm, but serious consideration and planning are certainly wise if you want to proceed down this path.

3.3.1 Legacy systems

Cloud service providers have put together large data-center infrastructures built on commodity hardware running commodity software. The sweet spot for deployment on the cloud is applications designed to run on these sorts of hardware and software platforms. Standard virtual instances are available loaded with operating systems such as Linux and Windows, not HP-UX or VMS.

Legacy applications built some time ago on legacy or proprietary hardware and software platforms would take an inordinate amount of effort to convert onto a cloud platform. Instead of conversion, if the systems are near end-of-life and are good candidates for the cloud, you should redesign and rewrite the applications from scratch.

3.3.2 Applications involving real-time/mission-critical scenarios

One of the strengths of the cloud is access to a tremendous amount of computing capacity without the carrying cost of all that hardware on your books. Real-time image processing, as is necessary for processing MRI brain scans, is an example of this type of application. This sort of real-time view of the brain is incredibly useful as a guide for surgeons during an operation. But a cloud deployment for this type of application is probably not the way to go.

Cloud services are at this time delivered on a best-effort basis, and the only recourse for poor service availability is a refund of the service fee. Even assuming the cloud service could perform flawlessly and deliver 100 percent uptime, the fact that the application must rely on connectivity over the public internet makes it a questionable proposition to try to run an application with extreme mission criticality (such as life and death) and with stringent real-time constraints.

If you look at the sectors where SaaS businesses thrive, you'll see that they're successful in providing services such as customer relationship management (CRM) that are important to a business and need to be highly available, but where a glitch that requires a browser refresh isn't catastrophic. These classes of application too aren't amenable for an organization to attempt to deploy in a cloud model yet.

3.3.3 Applications dealing with confidential data

Another genre of application that requires caution when thinking about cloud deployment models deals with highly sensitive or confidential data. For example, the healthcare industry is careful about complying with privacy, as mandated by the Health

Insurance Portability and Accountability Act (HIPAA). IT organizations have over the years developed best practices, such as classifying the level of security required for different classes of data. If you're contemplating migrating potentially sensitive information, you must make sure you take as much care protecting that data as you do with data in the internal IT infrastructure.

Let's consider the problem of deleting confidential data. Typically, when data is deleted from a disk it isn't truly deleted, but only marked for deletion. When another process needs to write data to the disk, it has the opportunity to write over the location marked for deletion, thereby destroying the data. In the case of a disk that you own or have direct control over, if simple deletion isn't good enough, you can choose to reformat the disk; or if that is insufficient, you can take an axe to the disk drive and then throw it into an incinerator. But data stored in a cloud infrastructure is sitting on a shared disk drive. You lose a degree of control over the disposition of the data. You can attempt to delete a file, but you have no way to be certain the data is truly destroyed.

3.4   Zero-capital startups

The emergence of the cloud has greatly impacted entrepreneurs (and their investors) eager to start a new business. It has lowered the barrier of entry for innovation and has leveled the playing field for new entrants who can now bring new software services to market with little up-front investment. By unleashing large amounts of computing capacity, it has enabled new classes of applications that previously only companies with deep pockets could afford.

3.4.1   Then and now: setting up shop as startup ca. 2000 vs. startup ca. 2010

Entrepreneurs today face a different set of challenges than they did a decade ago, particularly those trying to set up a software service or online business. The main difference is how far a startup can get today without obtaining a large amount of capital to fund their business compared to how far they could get in the past. Formerly, without an external source of funding, a couple of founders might be able to dream up a new application or service and start prototyping it on their desktop computers and then load it up on a laptop to take in to demo to some angels or venture capitalists. If they had a little more capital resource available, they might be able to purchase a handful of servers, sign an annual contract for some colocation space, and then hope for the best. If they either ran into a tough patch or had extreme success, they were severely constrained: they had to look to external resources for capital to either keep the business afloat or keep up with growing demand.

Today, the picture is entirely different. Entrepreneurs don't have to stop at a prototype or a demo application because they lack the capital necessary to launch the offering. They can much more easily bootstrap the operation because the availability of cloud services means there are no up-front costs such as hardware to buy or data-center space to rent. They can have fully functional and operational businesses online generating value. If the business idea isn't that great after all, nothing is lost except the sweat equity that went into putting the idea into practice. If, on the other hand, the business takes off, the on-demand nature of provisioning cloud services means that more instances can be brought online as needed so that costs only ramp as usage (and, we hope, revenue) ramps. As a small organization, the startup has the advantage of being nimble and able to react quickly to changing needs of the market. Because of the availability of the cloud, some of the advantages a larger company may have, because of its better access to capital, are reduced.

But the leveling of the playing field cuts both ways. The barrier to starting and operating a business has not only been lowered for one, it has been lowered for all. Many small competitors can enter a space; and without sustainable differentiation, such as superior technology, better distribution, or service, the only means of competing ultimately is price. For example, let's explore the concept of load testing using the cloud by looking at the open-source project Pylot. In a matter of minutes, you can launch an instance, point it at a website, and run a load test. It isn't a particularly big stretch from that exercise to putting together a service for load-testing in the cloud by writing some software for coordinating several instances and collecting and summarizing the results. Several startups are trying to make a go of this, some with little or no external funding and others with traditional venture backing. These startups face the challenge of differentiating themselves with almost no intrinsic defensibility in their offering. They must rely on better technology, service, or distribution to come out on top.

3.4.2   Is venture capital funding a necessity?

With the barrier to starting a software service or online business so greatly reduced, you may ask whether all this leveling of the playing field has obviated the need for entrepreneurs to get funding from venture capitalists. As discussed previously, the main change brought about by the cloud is the ability to get farther along before requiring large amounts of capital. The cloud may obviate the need for some companies to achieve scale without taking on external capital. But you must remember that the capital cost of running an application infrastructure is only one of many aspects required to scale a business. To cite one example, the availability of cloud services hasn't reduced the costs of hiring people to market and sell products and services. In many cases, in order to scale a business, you still need external funding.

The availability of cloud services as a possible deployment model allows an entrepreneur to go farther in developing a business than was possible before. From the venture capitalists' perspective, this has the desirable effect that they can evaluate a fully formed and realized idea that should theoretically reduce the risk for the investor. After the idea has been executed and the business model demonstrated, it becomes less of a risk. You may guess that such a reduction in risk means better terms and higher valuations for prospective entrepreneurs looking for backing; but alas, this generally isn't the case. Other entrepreneurs are maturing their businesses in the same environment, meaning the bar is raised for all uniformly to obtain financial backing as the market for available capital adjusts to the changing quality of deals.

In the next two sections, we'll look at a couple of startups that are using the cloud in new ventures. We've selected them for discussion from the finalists in the Amazon AWS Start-Up Challenge as thematic representations of the kinds of new businesses being launched using the cloud. The first is a business that uses the large on-demand compute capacity to enable a business that previously wasn't possible for a new market entrant because of the capital outlay that formerly would have been necessary. The second is a service utilizing the on-demand flexibility of the cloud to build a SaaS application for a specific targeted niche.

Amazon AWS Start-Up Challenge

The Amazon AWS Start-Up challenge is an annual competition that has been held since 2007 by Amazon to promote innovation on the company's cloud. Entry to the competition is open between July and September, with several finalists chosen in November. The final round is held in December, with each finalist presenting to a judging panel that includes representatives from venture capital firms. The winner of the contest gets $50,000 in cash and $50,000 worth of credit for Amazon AWS cloud services.

3.4.3   *Example 1: FlightCaster—airline flight-delay prediction*

FlightCaster was one of seven finalists in the AWS Start-Up Challenge in 2009. Flight-Caster is a startup whose service targets business travelers. The FlightCaster service predicts whether a flight will be delayed by comparing real-time conditions with historical data.

Users of the service enter flight numbers for upcoming flights using the FlightCaster Blackberry or iPhone application on their smartphone. It uses a patent-pending algorithm and processes large volumes of data consisting of information about the weather and statistics on the departure and arrival times of all flights over that time frame. FlightCaster updates the probability for delay continuously for the flight selected and assesses the likelihood that the flight will be on time or will be delayed for an hour or more, by matching current conditions to situations in the past. Advance warning allows travelers to anticipate and plan around delays by reserving alternative itineraries before delays are officially announced. This gives travelers the potential for more available options.

Without the cloud as a deployment option, this business would be difficult to start up, because it would need a large amount of capital to store the data for analysis and to make the calculations to provide the service.

3.4.4   *Example 2: business intelligence SaaS*

The Grand Prize winner of the 2009 AWS Start-Up Challenge was GoodData, which is a business intelligence (BI) SaaS provider. GoodData is an easy-to-use service for businesses that need BI to help understand data about their business, so they can make better decisions.

The deployment of a traditional BI solution in an enterprise can run in the millions of dollars for software and hardware and can take several months to implement. Several business services (CRM, payroll, and travel and expense [T&E] management) have been offered in a SaaS model. But BI as SaaS is a relatively new concept, perhaps because, before the cloud, it wasn't economically feasible. BI as SaaS requires more storage and processing than other, more traditional, SaaS businesses.

Using the cloud to run its BI service allows GoodData to support large-scale compute and data-intensive analytics without the need to scale up its own internal infrastructure. Elasticity allows GoodData to use resources only when customers need them to support their BI needs. GoodData can in turn pass these savings on to its customers by offering a relatively inexpensive alternative. As a SaaS solution, potential customers can evaluate GoodData for free immediately after signing up for the service, via a web interface. The service can be purchased in an on-demand model for $500/month.

3.5 *Small and medium businesses*

In the case of a startup venture, the discussion of cloud utilization revolves around companies and applications that are technology-oriented, because those are the kinds of companies for which the cloud has particular relevance. When we turn to small and medium businesses, millions of different companies fit this description. Unlike the startups discussed earlier, a cloud implementation isn't necessarily core to their operation. For many of these businesses, running an application in the cloud may be as relevant as landing a spaceship on the moon.

Let's focus on three specific examples, each with a varying degree of technical complexity and varying applicability to small and medium businesses in general. A general theme will emerge: such businesses can use cloud services to give a company greater flexibility and position the company for growth through more efficient use of capital and IT resources.

3.5.1 *Low-tech example: corporate website*

Nearly all businesses today have a corporate website. It may be as simple as a handful of pages with basic corporate information, or it may be an elaborate application designed to market a company's products and services and generate leads for its sales force. Corporate websites typically begin their lives on a shared hosting service, where they may reside on a simple Linux server alongside hundreds or thousands of other corporate websites for a modest fee around $20/month.

As the corporate website grows in popularity, traffic increases, and the importance of the website to the business grows commensurately until it needs to migrate elsewhere. Before the advent of cloud computing, you could go to a colocation type scenario with a dedicated server for the website (typically about $200/month) and manage it yourself. Alternatively, you could use a managed-service offering (typically around $800/month). In the beginning, this was overkill because of wasted capacity—the website's volume could be handled safely on a shared server and hardly taxed the dedicated servers. At the other extreme, when the site started growing and exceeded the capacity of the single server, more servers were needed, each at an incremental cost of $200/month or $800/month, depending on the chosen deployment model.

The cloud model provides a more economical choice, because you can rent a small virtual CPU for about a nickel an hour or $36.50/month. When a company exceeds this capacity, it can add and scale capacity as needed, dynamically. The system deployed in the cloud is able to start small, at an affordable price, while still having the flexibility to grow as and when needed at a moment's notice.

3.5.2 Medium-tech example: backup and file-storage systems

A slightly more ambitious approach a small to medium business can take is to begin moving some of its traditional IT services to the cloud. One common IT task is the backing up of the corporate file-share systems. Organizations often do this using a tape backup system at regular intervals. They can move these backup tapes to a remote location so that if the office location that contains the original is destroyed, the data on the backup can be recovered. The importance of remote backups for organizations of any size can't be overemphasized. In the event of a disaster, it can mean the difference between staying in business and going out of business.

Because the cloud is remote and located in an offsite third-party location, it's naturally suited to offsite backups. An initial copy of the data to be backed up can be sent to the cloud provider on physical media. From then on, differentials can be sent over the internet, providing a safe, offsite copy of the data.

From using the cloud as a storage location for backups, it's only a small step to using it as the primary file-storage system for a corporate document-management system. As mentioned in section 3.3.3, you must take care if the data is extremely sensitive or subject to compliance or regulatory controls; but otherwise it's possible to store confidential corporate data in this matter. More than one million users in corporations of all sizes are storing confidential CRM data on the cloud using Salesforce.com.

3.5.3 High-tech example: new product development

The final example relates to a small to medium business that develops software, either as a product (an independent software vendor [ISV]) or a service (a SaaS provider). These types of companies can use cloud services as a part of a cost-effective and flexible product-development process.

The fact that cloud services can be provisioned on an on-demand basis means that companies can develop and test products without the capital expense of provisioning new hardware. For an ISV developing enterprise software, for example, the cost of a quality assurance (QA) test lab to verify the functionality of the solution can be greatly reduced by using the Amazon cloud. A virtual test lab running in both Windows and

Linux environments, and testing compatibility with different web and application servers, and different database environments, such as Microsoft SQL Server, MySQL, Oracle, and even DB2, is possible with zero up-front expense. Once the testing cycle is complete, there's no ongoing expense associated with the QA environment, and it can be fired up when needed on the next development cycle.

For SaaS providers, where the ultimate offering being developed is a service, gains aren't limited to the development and testing cycle. After a new product is fully developed and tested, the provider can directly launch it on the cloud with much less financial exposure than was previously possible. When the new product has proved itself, the company can decide whether it's advantageous to continue to serve it for the cloud, or whether it should be brought in-house for more control.

3.6   *Cloud computing in the enterprise*

As you've seen in the last two sections, startups and small and medium businesses are using cloud computing to great advantage. In many cases, these smaller organizations either have no other feasible choice to deploy their applications other than on the cloud, or to do so doesn't make business sense because of the clear cost advantage of the cloud solution. Smaller organizations tend to be less fettered by constraints and requirements around security, availability, and reliability. They also usually have less formalized processes and procedures in place to govern the deployment of applications.

It's probably not surprising that larger enterprises have been less aggressive in moving to the cloud. Unlike in smaller organizations, their IT departments must operate under stricter rules, guidelines, and procedures. Many of the applications they deploy and operate are mission critical in nature and hence have stringent security and performance requirements. Furthermore, because of the size of the organizations, they often have more resources available and hence more choices. Some larger and more advanced organizations may be evolving toward a cloud-like deployment model after several years of experience virtualizing their data-center resources. We'll look at these internal or private clouds in more detail later. For now, let's look at a few case studies of successful initiatives by large enterprises using public cloud services.

3.6.1   *Eli Lilly: large data set, high-compute scenarios*

As discussed earlier, cloud services offer a new capability to access large amounts of computing capacity in an on-demand fashion. It's therefore not surprising that one of the first tangible scenarios of successful use of public cloud services comes in this form.

Eli Lilly is a global pharmaceutical company that requires vast amounts of computing resources as part of its drug development R&D process. In late 2007, the IT organization within Eli Lilly was frustrated at its inability to provision computing capacity for its scientists. According to David Powers, a long-time associate information consultant at Eli Lilly, it took more than 50 days to get a new machine up and running within existing corporate processes.

For a pharmaceutical company, time literally is money. When it files a new drug patent, the 20-year clock begins ticking. During that time, the drug must pass through several stages of clinical trials before being approved by the FDA. The faster the company can get a drug through that process, the longer it can market the drug exclusively and hence enjoy significant margins. The Eli Lilly IT team took the plunge and decided to use the Amazon AWS cloud as a platform for high-performance computing. They were able to set up a 64-node Linux cluster that could be brought online in only 5 minutes; formerly, it took 100 days for them to bring such a cluster online. The IT team made this resource available to hundreds of scientists within Eli Lilly and in the future hopes to extend its use to research partners for other projects.

3.6.2 *Washington Post: deadline-driven, large compute problems*

The next example is similar to the last in that it involves a problem that requires a vast computing infrastructure to perform. In this case, *The Washington Post* was looking for a fast way to make public the contents of Hillary Clinton's daily activity record from 1993–2001, the period that President Bill Clinton was in office. In response to a Freedom of Information Act request, the National Archives released this data at 10:00 A.M. on March 19, 2008, in the form of a 17,481-page low-quality, nonsearchable PDF. Peter Harkins, a senior engineer working at *The Washington Post*, used PDF-reading OCR software and devised a procedure to process the document at a rate of 1 page every 30 minutes. He moved his procedure over to the cloud, fired up 200 EC2 instances, and was able to process the entire document in 9 hours.

Harkins immediately made the data available to reporters, and *The Washington Post* made the entire searchable document available to the public 26 hours after its release.[1] The speed of accomplishing this task was phenomenal; but perhaps even more impressive is the fact that the 1,407 hours of virtual machine time cost the princely sum of $144.62. As a point of comparison, photocopying those pages at $0.05 a page would cost more than six times more: $874.05.

3.6.3 *Virgin Atlantic: online web presence and community*

The last enterprise example is somewhat different from the previous two; it's more similar to the cloud usage we discussed in section 3.5. It represents a shift from project-oriented enterprise usage models to one in which the enterprise relies on the cloud infrastructure day in and day out to provide services.

Virgin Atlantic launched a new travel portal called Vtravelled.com and deployed it completely on a cloud infrastructure. It's a conventional website application that takes advantage of load balancing for improved reliability, performance, and scalability, as well as content delivery network (CDN) services provided by Amazon CloudFront to improve global service delivery. Because it's deployed in a cloud model, there was no

---

[1] Available at http://projects.washingtonpost.com/2008/clinton-schedule.

up-front capital expenditure, and the number of resources can be dialed up or dialed down in response to traffic patterns that may be driven by promotional campaigns. This deployment of a mainstream application by a large enterprise serves as a portent for the general adoption of cloud services by enterprises for everyday computing applications.

3.7 Summary

Cloud computing represents both a technology and an economic shift. This chapter introduced four common deployment models and examined the costs associated with operating a hypothetical e-commerce application in each. You saw that when the application workload is constant and an organization has existing internal data-center resources that can be used at no additional incremental cost, it can be more economical to deploy an application that way. The balance tips in favor of a cloud deployment model in cases where there are variations in the expected workload that the application must handle, or in cases where the application is needed for a short, fixed amount of time. We also looked at the application of the cloud by organizations of various sizes, from startups to large Fortune 500 enterprises.

Having reviewed the business and economic implications of cloud computing, and when utilizing such an approach may be appropriate, we're now ready to look at issues of security in cloud computing. In the next chapter, we'll explore why this and other factors are driving some organizations toward private clouds. We'll also discuss how the trend toward a new concept called a virtual private cloud—that runs on top of the public cloud—may bring the best of both worlds together into a secure cloud computing solution.

Security and the private cloud

In the previous chapter, you learned about the economics of cloud computing—or, more specifically, the economics of public cloud computing. You saw that for startups, the use of the cloud can often be game-changing, enabling entrepreneurs to launch services that were never before possible. They can create new businesses with very little capital. Small and medium-size enterprises can use the public cloud for applications that aren't necessarily strategic to their business. These can be moved into the cloud to great advantage. Large enterprises—with a few notable exceptions, and mostly for their nonstrategic uses—are much more reticent to move to the cloud, due to security concerns. In this chapter, you'll learn how they can overcome these issues and still benefit. You'll see two alternatives to public clouds: private clouds and virtual private clouds.

Private clouds (and virtual private clouds) are a hot topic in IT; a wide range of opinions exists about whether private clouds fit into today's corporate IT strategy. Cloud computing technologies, in general, are evolving rapidly with private cloud computing in particular undergoing a rapid metamorphosis. A classic (and humorous) example is our research for this chapter. We spent a couple of days experimenting and putting together a private cloud implementation from open source. When we got around to writing the chapter several weeks later, we found that some folks had put together an even simpler procedure. What took us two days only a couple of weeks earlier could now be done in a matter of hours!

Some industry analysts, such as the Gartner Group, predict that private cloud spending will soon exceed public cloud spending. Consultancy McKinsey, on the other hand, goes as far as saying that there's no such thing as a private cloud and that by focusing on virtualization, you can improve the efficiency of internal IT operations and increase the utilization of existing resources to the point where you can beat the economics of the public cloud. We disagree with this extreme view.

Security concerns and the economics of existing data centers are the two drivers toward private clouds. Both will eventually go away; the tenure of real (versus virtual) private clouds is temporary. Security is the hot-button *du jour*, so you need to know the facts about information security. If you aren't familiar with the technical underpinnings of information security, please refer to this book's appendix, which provides a review of the key concepts.[1]

4.1 Information security in the public cloud

Information security is about keeping data secret. If you want to keep data perfectly secret, you must never let it out of a vault. But you need to process the data in some way, and that means it has to come out of the vault and be used by some application and combined with other data to produce useful results. Security has a funny way of making people issue dogmatic statements. You'll hear declarations such as "My sensitive corporate data will never be in the cloud" repeated all the time. Let's begin this section with an examination of why security concerns are slowing cloud adoption.

4.1.1 Security concerns slowing cloud adoption

The most significant difference between cloud security and traditional infrastructure security stems from the sharing of infrastructure on a massive scale. Users spanning different corporations and trust levels often interact with the same set of compute resources. Layer on top of that the dynamic and transient aspects endemic to a public cloud, the desire to continually load-balance and optimize for performance, energy, availability, and other SLA-level goals, and the problem becomes further complicated, creating more opportunities for misconfiguration and malicious conduct. When IDC

---

[1] One of the authors has an authoritative book on this topic: *Securing Web Services with WS-Security* by Jothy Rosenberg and Dave Remy, Sams, 2004.

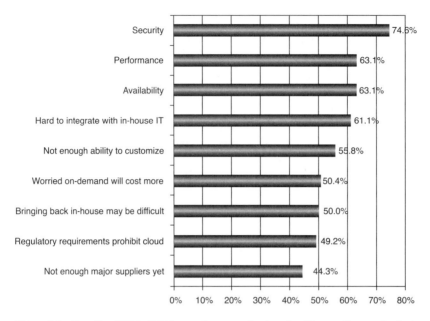

Figure 4.1   Results of IDC's 2009 annual survey of enterprise IT executives regarding concerns about adopting cloud computing for their core applications. Security has remained the top concern for the past three years.

polls enterprise IT executives about their concerns about cloud computing, security continues to be their number-one concern and impediment toward moving to the cloud. You can see the IDC survey's results from 2009 in figure 4.1.

Current cloud offerings are public (rather than private) networks, exposing the system to more attacks. You also have requirements for auditability from regulations like Sarbanes-Oxley (SOX) and the Health Insurance Portability and Accountability Act (HIPAA) for affected data to be moved to the cloud.

We believe that no fundamental obstacles exist to making a cloud-computing environment as secure as the vast majority of in-house IT environments. You can overcome many of the obstacles immediately with well-understood technologies, such as encrypted storage, virtual local area networks (VLANs), and standard network security tools, such as firewalls and packet filters. For example, encrypting data before placing it in a cloud may be even more secure than using unencrypted data in a local data center. A healthcare company with access to sensitive patient records and healthcare claims successfully used this approach when moving its HIPAA-compliant application to a public cloud.

Similarly, auditability can be added as an additional layer beyond the reach of the virtualized guest operating system (OS), providing facilities more secure than those built into the applications themselves and centralizing the software responsibilities related to confidentiality and auditability into a single logical layer. Such a new feature reinforces the argument that cloud computing can and will provide more security than any one corporation will know how to implement or can afford.

A related concern is that many nations have laws requiring SaaS providers to keep customer data and copyrighted material within national boundaries. Similarly, some businesses may not like the ability of a country to get access to their data via the court system; for example, a European customer may be concerned about using SaaS in the United States, given the USA PATRIOT Act.

Let's begin by examining current state-of-the-art public cloud data-center security. In the next three sections, you'll learn about data-center security, access-control measures, and network and data security applied to public clouds.

4.1.2 *Major cloud data center security*

Security of the major cloud data centers begins with the physical security of the data centers that providers use to house their computing equipment.

PHYSICAL SECURITY

Companies such as Google, Microsoft, Intuit, Yahoo!, Amazon, and many other huge data-center operators have years of experience in designing, constructing, and operating large-scale data centers. They have applied this experience to their companies' cloud platforms and infrastructure. The state of the art in physical security is to house these data centers in nondescript facilities (*security by obscurity*) with extensive setback and military-grade perimeter control berms as well as other natural boundary protection. Frequently, these buildings are in residential neighborhoods with no signage or markings, making them extra obscure. Physical access is strictly controlled both at the perimeter and at building ingress points by professional security staff utilizing video surveillance, state-of-the-art intrusion detection systems, and other electronic means. Authorized staff have to use two-factor authentication no fewer than three times to access data-center floors. Typically, all visitors and contractors have to present identification and sign in. They're continually escorted by authorized staff.

Cloud companies are going way beyond what even financial services company data centers do by putting their servers into fortified bunkers that easily outdo anything seen in spy movies. Salesforce.com's Fort Knox data center boasts round-the-clock security patrols, five levels of biometric hand-geometry scanners, and even man-trap cages designed to spring on those without the proper clearances. Figure 4.2 shows some of these physical security measures.

Figure 4.2 Physical security at state-of-the-art data centers includes perimeter security (razor wire), biometric authentication (palm reader), and access control (man trap).

Another important policy, employed to avoid the kind of internal attacks that have become a problem in many large organizations, is to provide data-center access and information to employees only if and when they have a legitimate business need for such privileges. They also routinely log and audit all physical and electronic access to data centers by employees. Although all these measures could easily be employed by any organization, the point is that they aren't typical and yet they matter as SAS 70 certification asserts.

SAS 70 CERTIFICATION

Most public cloud providers have achieved the Statement on Auditing Standards No. 70: Service Organizations, Type II (SAS 70 Type II) certification. This and similar certifications provide outside affirmation defined by the American Institute of Certified Public Accountants (AICPA) that the provider has established adequate internal controls and that those controls are operating efficiently.

The SAS 70 audit isn't a spot check: it requires six months of evidence collection in a steady state before the actual audit process may begin. The audits can take up to six months and are typically done once per year. They're expensive and intrusive and can be a big problem for any but the largest data center operators.

Many recent regulations require SAS 70 audits on the managed services and facilities where applications affected by those regulations run. For example, the Gramm-Leach-Bliley Act (GLBA), SOX, and HIPAA all now require SAS 70 audits. SOX in particular has heightened the focus placed on understanding the controls over financial reporting and identified a Type II SAS 70 report as the only acceptable method for a third party to assure a service organization's controls.

Physical security is strictly the domain of the cloud provider, which can vouch for its compliance through the continuous maintenance of a certification like SAS 70. Access control is the joint responsibility of the provider and its users. Let's examine this area of information security next.

4.1.3 *Public cloud access control measures*

After physical security, the next most important security measure is to control who can access the cloud, particularly your portion of the cloud. If this breaks down, not much else can protect you. If the bad guys can access your servers, spin up new servers, and start up applications, you've pretty much lost. To understand how cloud access control works, let's walk through the process Amazon Web Services (AWS) uses to set up access control at the initial sign-up. Their process is almost identical to that of Microsoft Azure and the other cloud providers. As with most identification and authentication procedures, this depends on a multilevel process that layers one type of shared-secret question/answer interaction on top of another. Your credit card used for payment is the first shared secret information.

BILLING VALIDATION

E-commerce sites and others commonly use billing validation for authentication to make sure you're the legitimate holder of the credit card you're trying to use for a transaction. Because the billing address isn't printed on a credit card, entering the correct billing address is using a shared secret. This is the first step in making sure you're an authorized individual setting up cloud services.

IDENTITY VERIFICATION VIA PHONE (OUT OF BAND)

Using a completely separate database for the next level of verification goes a long way toward making sure you are who you say you are. An *out of band* (meaning not using the same browser interface being used for sign-up) mechanism makes this a strong form of verification because it requires that you use something you possess (the physical phone). The shared secret is the phone number. By asking you to enter a PIN generated randomly through your browser, the cloud provider can verify that the individual sitting at the browser is the same one who is on the phone. Figure 4.3 shows the AWS screen before you enter the PIN.

Credentials used to sign in must be provided next.

SIGN-IN CREDENTIALS

You're in complete control of your sign-in credentials, and the password needs to be strong. Alternatively, you can use multifactor authentication, such as RSA's SecurID. This is highly recommended because it has been shown that multifactor authentication is much stronger than single-factor, particularly when the single factor is password-based. You can see the specification of sign-in credentials using a simple password in figure 4.4.

You use sign-in credentials each time you want to access the web services for the cloud. But on every interaction with the service through its API, you have to provide an authentication key.

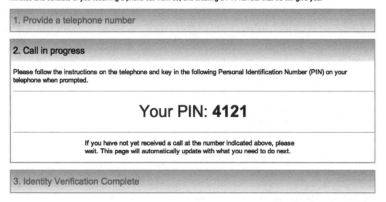

Identity Verification by Telephone

A simple identity verification by telephone is required to complete the sign up process. This process takes only a couple minutes and consists of you receiving a phone call from us, and entering a PIN number that we will give you.

1. Provide a telephone number

2. Call in progress

Please follow the instructions on the telephone and key in the following Personal Identification Number (PIN) on your telephone when prompted.

Your PIN: **4121**

If you have not yet received a call at the number indicated above, please wait. This page will automatically update with what you need to do next.

3. Identity Verification Complete

Figure 4.3   The AWS screen during the identity verification out-of-band phone call asking the user to enter a PIN. This mechanism verifies that the user of the browser doing sign-up and the user receiving the phone call are one and the same individual whose billing validation has already been completed.

Sign-In Credentials

To sign in to AWS web sites and applications, AWS requires your Amazon e-mail address and password. Additionally, it supports the AWS Multi-Factor Authentication option. Each sign-in credential is explained below.

Amazon E-mail Address and Password

To sign in to secure pages on the AWS web site, the AWS Management Console, the AWS Discussion Forums, and the AWS Premium Support site, you need to provide your Amazon e-mail address and password.

E-mail Address: jothy@whosaysicant.net
Password: ••••••••

If you'd like to change your e-mail address or password now, click here.

For your protection, do not share your password with anyone. Industry best practice recommends frequent change of passwords, and passwords that have a mixture of letters, numbers, and special characters.

Figure 4.4   The AWS step of providing sign-in credentials. In this case, it's single-factor, password-based. But multifactor authentication is highly recommended, such as using a time-based hardware token (something you have) in addition to a password (something you know).

ACCESS KEYS

Every API call to do anything with the cloud requires an access key. As part of the initiation process, you're given a generated secret key. (Actually, it's better to generate the key pair locally on your machine and provide the public key half of that pair back to the cloud providers, thus protecting the private key half all the more.) This key is then used in each API call to indicate that the initiator is legitimate. It's critical that you don't share this secret key. As the screen in figure 4.5 says, frequent rotation of this secret key is considered best practice.

X.509 CERTIFICATES

X.509 certificates are based on the idea of *public key cryptography*, which we discuss in the appendix to this book. Specifically, X.509 certificates consist of a certificate file and a companion private key file. In the X.509 certificate itself is the public key and related metadata. The X.509 and its incorporated public key aren't secret; they're included in each service request. The private key is used to calculate the digital signature to include in a request to the service. The private key is a secret and must never be shared.

Access Keys	X.509 Certificates	Key Pairs

Use access keys to make secure REST or Query protocol requests to any AWS service API. We create one for you when your account is created — see your access key below.

Your Access Keys

Created	Access Key ID	Secret Access Key	Status
May 14, 2010	AKIAJAD7W33WFPG364ZQ	Show	Active (Make Inactive)

Create a new Access Key

For your protection, you should never share your secret access keys with anyone. In addition, industry best practice recommends frequent key rotation.

Figure 4.5   A secret key is generated by the service for your use in all API calls. Each call requires that this key be included so the service can validate that the call is from a legitimate user.

The cloud provider typically has a way to generate a certificate for you. This is never the most secure approach because they possess your private key, if only for a moment. Despite assurances that they never retain the key, you can't be 100 percent sure.

Let's see how to use the X.509 in service requests. When you create a request, you create a digital signature with your private key and include it in the request, along with your certificate. When the provider gets the request, it uses the public key in the certificate to decrypt the signature and confirm that you're the request sender. The provider also verifies that the certificate you provide matches the one on file. Figure 4.6 shows the results of the process where we had AWS generate the certificate (again, not recommended for best security).

The third and final type of access credentials is the key pair.

KEY PAIRS

The key pair constitutes the most important access credential for dealing with instances in the cloud. You have to use different key pairs for each service. You use a specifically assigned key pair each time you launch an instance. The key pair ensures that only you have access to the instance. You can't replace a particular key pair, but you can have as many as you like. You can use one key pair for all your instances or one pair for a particular type of instance—you get to decide how you want to organize access. You must not lose the private key for an instance because then you could no longer access it.

Amazon will create the EC2 key pair through the AWS Management Console if you chose not to generate them yourself on the local machine where the private key will reside. Figure 4.7 shows the fingerprint for the public key retained at AWS after a key pair is generated. AWS doesn't retain the private key—it's to be kept secret by you.

Access Credentials

There are three types of access credentials used to authenticate your requests to AWS services: (a) access keys, (b) X.509 certificates, and (c) key pairs. Each access credential type is explained below.

Access Keys	**X.509 Certificates**	Key Pairs

Use X.509 certificates to make secure SOAP protocol requests to AWS service APIs.

Exceptions: Amazon S3 and Amazon Mechanical Turk instead require your Access Keys for SOAP requests.

Created	X.509 Certificate	Status
May 18, 2010	cert-64SA47JVIUPYJLTIBTFL74UMSCDJN3SH.pem (Download)	Active (Make Inactive)

Create a new Certificate | Upload Your Own Certificate

For your protection, AWS doesn't ask for your private key or retain it on file. You should also never share your private key with anyone. In addition, industry best practice recommends frequent certificate rotation.

Learn more about X.509 Certificates

Figure 4.6   The results of having the provider generate the X.509 certificate. A private key file was downloaded, and then the certificate file was as well. The provider doesn't retain the private key. But the provider does have it for a moment, and it's downloaded over the public internet to the browser, making this an insecure process. It's better to get a certificate from a Certificate Authority and *upload* the private key back to the cloud provider while retaining complete control over the private key.

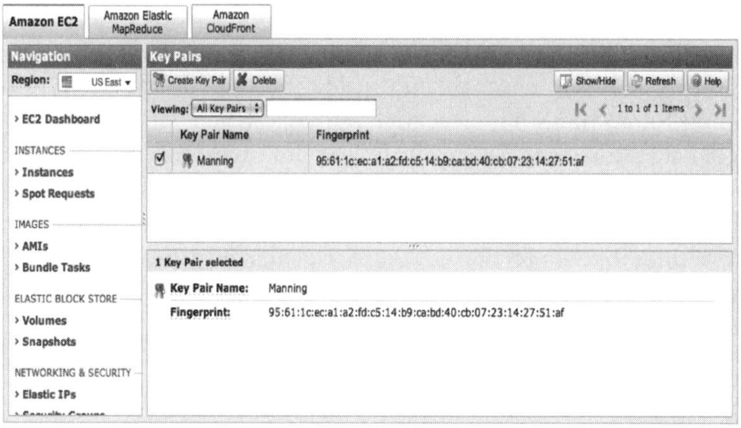

Figure 4.7   The ways key pairs are generated and managed through AWS's Management Console. The public key is retained at AWS, whereas the private key isn't. You can download it to your machine for secret storage.

Public cloud access-control measures such as those you've seen outlined for Amazon's AWS (which are almost identical to those used at Microsoft's Azure and other public clouds) are of vital importance to maintain the identity, authentication, and authorization of the users of the cloud at all times. As long you keep the secret key strictly secret and your passwords are of high strength and follow all other best practices, this provides a high level of security and control over the creation of instances and other cloud services. Now, let's look at how network and data security work in public clouds.

4.1.4 *Major cloud network and data security*

Of high concern to most potential cloud users is protection of their data. The recent announcements of virtual private clouds (see section 4.3) and the ability of cloud providers to segregate data are already allaying many fears. But the secret is that already, the *cloud is more secure than most data centers*—and again, this gap will widen over time.

   Using the cloud already has security benefits. Centralizing data in the cloud as opposed to having it distributed all over the organization means less leakage because there's less data on people's laptops. When data is centralized, it's easier to monitor access and usage. On the other hand, if there is a breach, having data centralized can mean a much more comprehensive and damaging data theft. With the number of data thefts of significant size and publicity at an all-time high, turning over the means to protect data to the cloud experts is still a much safer bet as thieves become more sophisticated.

   If an incident occurs, the cloud provides a faster and more comprehensive means of response. Acquisition time of forensic data is low. Downtime during the investigation is low due to the availability of so many resources not tainted by the breach. Finally, cloud providers are providing more and better built-in verification. For example, Amazon's S3 does an MD5 hash (a fast cryptographic algorithm to validate that the original data is intact and unmodified) on all stored S3 objects.

All of this leads to the conclusion that data centers run by individual corporations for their use will become even more expensive and less reliable compared to the biggest cloud providers. Meanwhile, the cloud will become cheaper, more secure, and more reliable. Corporations will finally get over their reticence and will move project after project to the cloud, keeping fewer in their own data centers. It will take a full generation before most corporations completely give up their proprietary data centers, but within half that time most of their critical systems and all of their new projects will be cloud-based.

OPERATING SYSTEM SECURITY

System-level security within a public cloud is provided on multiple levels: the OS of the host system, the virtual instance operating system or guest OS, a stateful firewall, and signed API calls. Each of these items builds on the capabilities of the others. The ultimate goal is to ensure that data contained in the public cloud can't be intercepted by non-authorized systems or users and that virtual machine instances in the cloud are secure.

For instance, to maintain security of the host OSs, Amazon requires AWS administrators with a business need to use their individual cryptographically strong SSH keys to gain access to a *bastion* host. Bastion hosts are specifically built systems designed and configured to protect Amazon's management plane of the cloud and are inaccessible by cloud users. Once connected to the bastion, authorized administrators are able to use a privilege escalation command to gain access to an individual host. Amazon routinely logs and audits all such accesses. When an AWS employee no longer has a business need to administer EC2 hosts, their privileges on and access to the bastion hosts are revoked.

NETWORK SECURITY

The public clouds all provide a firewall; ideally (but not true in all public clouds), the inbound firewall is configured in a default *deny* mode for safety, and the user must explicitly open any ports to allow inbound traffic. Like any good firewall, the traffic may be restricted by protocol, by service port, as well as by source IP address (individual IP or Classless Inter-Domain Routing [CIDR] block).

Paravirtualization's role in security

Most public clouds (such as Amazon's EC2) are based on a type of virtualization called *paravirtualization*. In paravirtualization, a software interface to virtual machines similar but not identical to that of the underlying hardware is presented. The intent is to reduce the portion of the guest's execution time spent performing operations that are substantially more difficult to run in a virtual environment compared to a nonvirtualized environment. A paravirtualized platform allows the virtual machine monitor (VMM) to be simpler (by relocating execution of critical tasks from the virtual domain to the host domain), and/or reduces the overall performance degradation of machine-execution inside the virtual guest. More important, for this security discussion, the guest OS has no elevated access to the CPU. This leads to a clear separation between guest and hypervisor, which, in theory, provides strong security.

Control of and changes to the firewall aren't controlled by the host/instance itself, but require the customer's X.509 certificate and key to authorize changes, thus adding an extra layer of security. Within EC2, the host administrator and cloud administrator can be separate people, permitting two-man-rule security policies to be enforced. In addition, AWS encourages customers to apply additional per-instance filters with host-based firewalls such as IPtables. This can restrict both inbound and outbound traffic on each instance.

The level of security afforded by the firewall is a function of which ports are opened by you, and for what duration and purpose. The default state is to deny all incoming traffic, and developers should plan carefully what they'll open when building and securing their applications. It still requires well-informed traffic management and security design on a per-instance basis.

The fact that the prominent public cloud providers were first and foremost major internet destination sites has enormous benefits. Their e-commerce operations were and are subject to incoming attacks, such as Distributed Denial of Service (DDoS) attacks. Their prowess in preventing such attacks bleeds over to their public clouds. To wit, public cloud control API endpoints are hosted on the same internet-scale, world-class infrastructure that supports the public cloud provider's other business sites. They use standard DDoS mitigation techniques, such as SYN cookies and connection limiting. To further mitigate the effect of potential DDoS attacks, providers maintain internal bandwidth that exceeds their provider-supplied internet bandwidth. This prevents bandwidth saturation from an external attack agent.

Amazon EC2 instances aren't permitted to send spoofed traffic (including to another Amazon customer). The Amazon-controlled, host-based firewall infrastructure won't permit an instance to send traffic with a source IP or MAC address other than its own.

CO-MINGLING SECURITY

It isn't possible for a virtual instance running in promiscuous mode to receive or *sniff* traffic intended for a different virtual instance anywhere in Amazon's cloud. Although customers can place their interfaces into promiscuous mode, the hypervisor won't deliver any traffic to them not addressed to them. This includes two virtual instances owned by the same customer, even if they're located on the same physical host. Attacks such as ARP cache poisoning don't work in EC2. Although Amazon EC2 provides ample protection against one customer inadvertently or maliciously attempting to view another's data, as a standard practice customers should encrypt sensitive traffic.

Cloud providers are already providing stored data verification. They do this efficiently by performing an MD5 hash on all stored data objects. Your machine instances have no access to raw disk devices but instead are presented with virtualized disks. The cloud provider's disk virtualization layer automatically wipes every block of storage you use and guarantees that your data is never exposed to another. Vigilance is still important, and best practice is to also run an encrypted file system on top of the virtualized disk device.

SYSTEM CONTROL SECURITY

Calls to launch and terminate instances, change firewall parameters, and perform other functions are all signed by an X.509 certificate or your Amazon Secret Access

Key (described in the appendix). Without access to your Secret Access Key or X.509 certificate, Amazon's EC2 API can't make calls on your behalf. In addition, API calls can be encrypted in transit with SSL to maintain confidentiality. It's best practice to always use SSL-protected API endpoints.

DATA STORAGE SECURITY

An *access control list* (ACL) associated with the large-granularity storage containers provided by each cloud storage service controls the write and delete permissions. An ACL controls the permission to modify the bucket, and it defaults to creator-only access. In this way, you maintain full control over who has access to your data; you can still grant access to whomever you want.

Another potential concern is whether data can be intercepted while in transit from one node on the internet to the cloud storage you're using. As with all cloud service APIs, storage APIs are accessible via SSL-encrypted endpoints. You can access the encrypted endpoints from both the internet and your instances in the cloud, ensuring that data is transferred securely both within the cloud and to and from sources outside of the cloud.

Best practice is to secure data even when it's being stored in cloud storage. You should encrypt your data before it's uploaded to the cloud so the data can't be accessed or tampered with by unauthorized parties either in transit or at rest.

4.1.5 *Application owner's roles and responsibilities*

Individual users are responsible for the security of the guest OSs running in the virtualized environment. You have full root access and all administrative control over additional accounts, services, and applications. This makes it vitally important to keep account passwords and access to secret keys strong and secret, and to rotate them frequently. As with all security, social engineering[2] always remains the weakest link in the information security chain.

Public cloud administrators never have access to customer instances and can't log in to the guest OS. It's considered good practice to disable password-based access to hosts and utilize token or key-based authentication to gain access to unprivileged accounts. It's also standard best practice to employ a privilege escalation mechanism with logging on a per-user basis. For example, if the guest OS is Linux, use SSH with keys to access the virtual instance, enable shell command-line logging, and use the sudo utility for privilege escalation. You should generate your own key pairs in order to guarantee that they're unique (not have the provider generate them) and not shared with anyone else, particularly the cloud provider. The good news is that all the practices we're describing are nothing new to system administrators—they already do these things in corporate data centers all over the world.

You've been reading about the various types of security measures used to make public clouds as secure as corporate data centers. But it's now time to talk about the concept of private clouds.

---

[2] *Social engineering* is the act of manipulating (tricking) people into performing security functions or divulging confidential information.

4.2   Rationale for a private cloud

It may be useful to step back and recall what exactly a *cloud* is. This is necessary in the context of the discussion of private clouds because you can lose clarity in understanding: IT vendors, knowing how attractive the moniker is, often try to cast any and every solution as a cloud solution. Many vendors with products and services that involve virtualization, storage, or data-center automation claim that they have a private cloud offering.

4.2.1   Defining a private cloud

A private cloud comprises a subset of the five main principles we've been using as our definition of cloud computing:

- *Pooled resources*—Available to any subscribing users
- *Virtualization*—High utilization of assets
- *Elasticity*—Dynamic scale without CAPEX
- *Automation*—Building, deploying, configuring, provisioning, and moving, all without manual intervention
- *Metered billing*—Per-usage business model: pay for what you use

For private clouds, the three principles associated with the technical attributes still hold true—virtualization, elasticity, and automation—and translate directly from public clouds to private clouds. The other two—pooled resources and metered billing—relate more specifically to the business attributes of public clouds and are less directly applicable to the private cloud. Private clouds by definition aren't a pool of computing resources accessible to subscribing users on demand. Not just anyone with a credit card can access the resources in a private cloud; these resources are reserved for the exclusive use of the organization which owns the resources. They may implement metered billing in certain cases for private clouds within large organizations, but not necessarily.

> **PRIVATE CLOUD (OR INTERNAL CLOUD OR CORPORATE CLOUD)** A computing architecture that provides hosted services to a specific group of people behind a firewall. A private cloud uses virtualization, automation, and distributed computing to provide on-demand elastic computing capacity to internal users.

As you saw earlier in chapter 3, public cloud providers are spending a great deal of money in new data centers to power their cloud initiatives, with Google investing approximately $2.3 billion in 2008 for its buildout.[3] At first glance, in the face of this massive investment, it may seem like a foolhardy proposition to attempt to go it alone and build your own private cloud. But remember that large IT organizations have a long history of providing data-center services, many with longer track records of doing so than most if not all of today's incumbent cloud providers (Amazon, Google, and Microsoft). They have tremendous amounts of resources and past investment in hardware and data center assets. They can certainly put these to good use.

---

[3] Rich Miller, "Facebook: $20 Million a Year on Data Centers," www.datacenterknowledge.com/archives/2009/05/18/facebook-20-million-a-year-on-data-centers/.

Public cloud spending in perspective

Before you get too carried away with the thought that public cloud providers have economies of scale beyond the reach of anyone else because of the amount they spend on hardware and data centers, you should ground yourself with a few facts. Let's assume that Google, Amazon, and Microsoft each spend $10 billion per year next year on cloud infrastructure. That amount is only a drop in the bucket compared to the total amount of money spent annually on IT worldwide. The financial services industry alone will spend over 50 times that much on IT in 2010 (~$500 billion).

Over the last decade, many large enterprises have launched virtualization projects and initiatives and have reaped the benefit of increased resource utilization and efficiencies. Those that have done so are one step closer toward having a private cloud. As described earlier, this is one of the three key technology principles for private cloud computing. The only incremental changes needed to have a private cloud are the addition of elasticity and cloud-automation technologies.

Four primary considerations—security, availability, user community (size), and economies of scale—drive the choice of a private cloud as a deployment strategy. You can see this in table 4.1.

The security and availability constraints of target applications and data, and the degree to which they must be under direct control, may dictate whether a public cloud option is viable or whether you should consider a private cloud solution. For a private cloud deployment to make sense, your company's size and needs should be sufficiently large to have economies of scale when purchasing capital equipment.

Table 4.1   The four primary private cloud considerations

Consideration	Rationale
Security	Applications that require direct control and custody over data for security or privacy reasons
Availability	Applications that require certain access to a defined set of computing resources that can't be guaranteed in a shared resource pool environment
User community	Organization with a large number of users, perhaps geographically distributed, who need access to utility computing resources
Economies of scale	Existing data center and hardware resources that can be used, and the ability to purchase capital equipment at favorable pricing levels

If your organization's security and availability requirements are high at the same time, the scope of the user base to be supported and the purchasing power of your organization must be sufficiently strong for a private cloud to be a good option.

4.2.2   Security considerations

Although as you saw earlier in this chapter, security within the public cloud can often be comparable or superior to data security in a corporate data center, public cloud computing isn't always an option. For example, many government organizations have applications that deal with confidential or classified data that under no circumstances may be put at risk, such as those dealing with national security. Other applications in other industries have regulatory requirements that make them think twice before deploying to a public cloud. The main distinction that makes private clouds more secure and more appropriate for compliance concerns is simply this: they can physically and logically segregate resources more thoroughly and thereby remove more doubts among users that their data is safe and secure.

Public cloud providers are aware that security is a main blocking or gating factor for many enterprises and have devoted significant resources to designing and proving their ability to deal with secure data. As mentioned previously, Amazon has achieved SAS 70 Type II certification for AWS, which ensures that it has the appropriate processes and infrastructure in place to handle data securely and with high availability for customers. Amazon has also made claims that its infrastructure has been designed such that it can support the requirements of regulatory frameworks, such as HIPAA. HIPAA spells out the measures that organizations in the healthcare industry must adhere to in order to ensure the privacy of their patient's data. Having the hooks to enable HIPAA compliance and implementing a HIPAA-compliant application are two different things. Providers must develop best practices and gain experience in supporting HIPAA-compliant applications in the public cloud before most enterprises will be comfortable with this mode of deployment.

4.2.3   *Certainty of resource availability*

Although you may think of the cloud as an infinite resource pool from which resources can be drawn, this isn't always the case. For example, consider an application that requires a huge number of resources for massive processing in a short time window. As of late 2009, Amazon has advised its users that it can't guarantee the availability of 500 XL instances (where XL instances are high-compute resources with 8 CPU virtuals) at any given time from a specific availability zone. For cases requiring resources in excess of 1,000 XL instances, Amazon requests a week's prior notice to improve the chances of the resources being available.

Resource constraints are a much more serious matter in smaller cloud providers. Rackspace, also in late 2009, imposed a limit of 50 virtual instances being run in its environment per day for any given user. Overall total capacity in these systems should improve going forward; but even so, there is still the caveat related to variations in demand caused by overlapping requirements from multiple different public cloud customers. By comparison, electric utilities, which have been running for more than a century, still have capacity issues in the heat of the summer when demand for electricity to power air-conditioning can cause brownouts due to a mismatch of available supply and demand. You can easily imagine the same thing happening in the cloud context if all e-commerce sites were public cloud consumers and witnessed 10X traffic spikes on Black Friday as the shopping season began or if there were another terrorist incident. At some point, cloud pricing will take into account this type of variability in demand, and providers will introduce variable pricing.

4.2.4 *Large utility-computing community*

If you have a relatively small requirement for utility computing resources, having a good virtualized infrastructure can probably suffice. But if your organization has many constituents that can take advantage of a generalized infrastructure for their needs, then the added complexity and sophistication of a cloud infrastructure may make sense. By implementing a private cloud, you'll introduce the concept of multitenancy and, hence, the ability to segment and isolate individual groups and users.

4.2.5 *Economies of scale*

A public cloud provider has two potential primary advantages from an economic perspective over a company interested in running its own private cloud. The first relates to the physical resources required to run a cloud. In chapter 2, you saw how the public cloud providers' buying power is harnessed to purchase large quantities of hardware for servers and build data centers with good network connectivity and low-cost power. In chapter 3, you saw how that translated in terms of a business case for deploying applications. These arguments are based on the ability to purchase servers and hosting resources at small scale. For a large multinational or government, the economics may be much different given the long-term relationships and volumes that are purchased annually from their sources. On top of this, consider that these organizations may already have large quantities of hardware and pipe available. In addition, if a company is already in the midst of executing a virtualization strategy, the existing investments may be well positioned to be converted into a cloud.

The second aspect relates to the expertise required to run and maintain a cloud infrastructure. The public cloud providers, as they've been designing for scale, have been creating infrastructure where one of the primary objectives is the reduction of the number of resources required to operate a data center. In most cases, conventional IT organizations require more engineers and technicians to run a smaller data center. By migrating to a cloud-style deployment, they may save money over their existing deployment. But this may require a retooling of their current resources or hiring a smaller number of more skilled resources.

4.2.6 *Some concerns about deploying a private cloud*

Before you or anyone jumps to deploying a private cloud, let's assess a quick set of four major concerns.

PRIVATE CLOUDS ARE SMALL SCALE

Why do most innovative cloud-computing providers have their roots in powering consumer web technology? Because that's where the big numbers of users are. Few corporate data centers see anything close to the type of volume seen by these vendors. And, as you've seen, volume drives costs down through the huge economies of scale.

LEGACY APPLICATION DON'T CLOUDIFY EASILY

Legacy applications moved to a private cloud will see marginal improvements at best.

You can achieve only so much without rearchitecting these applications to a cloud infrastructure.

ON-PREMISES DOESN'T NECESSARILY MEAN MORE SECURE
The biggest drivers toward private clouds have been fear, uncertainty, and doubt about security. For many, it feels more secure to have your data behind your firewall in a data center that you control. But unless your company spends more money and energy thinking about security than Amazon, Google, and Salesforce, that isn't true.

DO WHAT YOU DO BEST
Do you think there's a simple set of tricks that an operator of a data center can borrow from Amazon or Google? No way. These companies make their living operating the world's largest data centers. They're constantly optimizing how they operate based on real-time performance feedback from millions of transactions. Although you can try to learn from and emulate them (hard to do because they protect their trade secrets as if national security depended on it!), your rate of innovation will never be the same—private clouds will always be many steps behind the public clouds.

4.2.7   *Private cloud deployment options*

If, despite these concerns, you plan to proceed down the private cloud path, you have several options available for building your private cloud. As discussed earlier, for companies and organizations that can acquire and provision hardware and data-center resources efficiently enough, a private cloud may make sense. In addition to the capital costs for hardware, an organization needs to determine its strategy with respect to the software infrastructure it'll use to operate and manage the cloud. The costs involved vary substantially and can range from free if you adopt an open source approach to over $1 million for a full-service offering that includes proprietary software and architecture, design, and implementation services. Table 4.2 summarizes the possible private cloud implementation categories and example vendors/solutions.

Table 4.2   Private cloud deployment options by type

Provider type	Example vendors	Description
Open source	Eucalyptus, OpenNebula	Free software for creating a private cloud implementation, primarily on UNIX-based systems
Proprietary software	VMware, Enomaly, Appistry	Proprietary private cloud solutions open with a specific strength in a core cloud technology, such as virtualization, storage, or management
Hosted offering	Savvis, OpSource, SunGard	Dedicated hardware hosted in a cloud model for a single customer, built using either open source or a proprietary solution
System integrator	Appirio, Accenture, Infosys	Specialty providers or practice areas in large firms dedicated to architecture, design, and deployment of private clouds

DO-IT-YOURSELF PRIVATE CLOUDS/OPEN SOURCE

The public cloud providers have primarily implemented their solutions with a combination of open source and homegrown software. Their user-facing APIs are publicly visible, but they haven't released the core technologies for operating and managing their clouds. Eucalyptus and OpenNebula are two open source initiatives, both offshoots of university research projects, that have created software to replicate the homegrown software of the large public cloud providers. They provide a software capability for provisioning and managing a multiuser private cloud built on top of commodity hardware. They've also made their solutions compatible with the APIs provided by Amazon.

Using these software solutions allows you to create an interoperable infrastructure that can work as a hybrid cloud. They're open source initiatives and, unlike proprietary approaches, there's no specific incentive (such as having you buy more of their software) to create lock-in; and you have unlimited flexibility as usual and with the same regular caveats around support and usability. Constructing a private cloud using open-source technologies requires a high degree of technical sophistication and probably works best in organizations that have a history of working with open source on other projects.

PROPRIETARY SOFTWARE CLOUD SOLUTIONS

Several vendors offer commercial packages to enable private clouds. Best-of-breed startups, such as Appistry, focus specifically on this problem. Like the open-source solutions described previously, they're designed to enable the creation of a private cloud on multiple commodity hardware resources. Some providers, such as ParaScale, focus specifically on the aspects of cloud computing related to storage. Large IT vendors, such as EMC, Oracle, IBM, and Unisys, are positioning themselves as being able to provide an entire private cloud stack, including hardware systems, virtualization technology, and software applications for operating and managing the private cloud. These systems can be as small as a handful of rack-mounted appliances or as large as data centers filled with thousands of servers housed in modular container pods. Additionally, these providers offer provide consulting services for the architecture, design, and implementation of clouds.

PRIVATIZATION OF PUBLIC CLOUDS

Public cloud service providers also provide services that are moving closer to the concept of private clouds. The Amazon Virtual Private Cloud (VPC) offering allows you to connect resources in the public cloud from within its firewall via an IPSec VPN. This isn't the same as a private cloud—merely the ability to connect and communicate securely with public cloud resources. You'll read much more about the VPC concept in section 4.3.

The next logical step for hosting and public cloud providers is to deliver dedicated private cloud services. In this model, a service provider reserves or dedicates a specific portion of the cloud infrastructure to a specific customer. Some example providers of dedicated private cloud hosting include Savvis, which provides cloud services as a horizontal solution; and SunGard, which provides dedicated cloud services for financial services customers. Dedicated cloud services are much more costly than public cloud services; the difference in cost is similar to the difference in cost between shared commodity hosting, which can be had for under $100/year, and traditional dedicated hosting, which can cost as much as $1,000/month per server.

Up to this point in the chapter, you've read about the merits and drawbacks of pursuing a private cloud strategy and have looked at some of the options for creating a private cloud. Now, let's switch gears and look practically at how to build a private cloud system using open source. It turns out that putting together a private cloud, at least a small-scale proof-of-concept system, is straightforward. Building such a system can help you understand the software components that make up a cloud. Because the open-source private cloud systems have been designed for interoperability with Amazon EC2, they can also provide a playpen environment for experimenting with a hybrid cloud (part private, part public).

IMPLEMENTING AN OPEN-SOURCE PRIVATE CLOUD

It's becoming increasingly easy to put together a private cloud using open source as major Linux distributions start bundling cloud software in their standard packages. Ubuntu 9.10 Server, for example, has an option to deploy a configuration called Ubuntu Enterprise Cloud (UEC). On a clean install of the OS, UEC is provided as an option. When you choose this option, Eucalyptus cloud software is installed on the system.

The Eucalyptus system consists of several software components that run the private cloud. The first component is called the Node Controller (NC); it resides on each computer that consists of the pool of available resources for creating virtual instances. The NC is responsible for managing the virtual instances started and stopped on an individual computer. One or more computers with NCs on them constitute a cluster, which is managed by another process called the Cluster Controller (CC). The CC is responsible for managing the NCs in its cluster and farms out work orders it receives to the NCs to start and stop virtual instances. A single Cloud Controller (CLC) manages one or more CCs. The CLC is the central management point for the entire system. It's the system of record that contains data tables that describe the overall system and keeps track of the users of the system. The administrator of the system can connect to the CLC to add users and set overall system parameters, such as the sizes and allocations of instances within the system. The CLC also handles authenticating users and processing their requests to do things, such as start and stop instances. The Eucalyptus components talk to each other, but only the CLC need be exposed to a public address space to enhance the security of the system. The network communication between the CLC and the CC and between the NC can all be isolated in private network space.

The smallest possible cloud system would consist of two computers: one that served as the CLC and the CC, and another with a NC managing all the available virtual instances. The default virtualization technology used by Eucalyptus is Xen, although you can use other virtualization technologies, such as VMware and VirtualBox. Xen as the virtualization technology has the advantage of being interoperable and migratable

Clusters within a Eucalyptus System

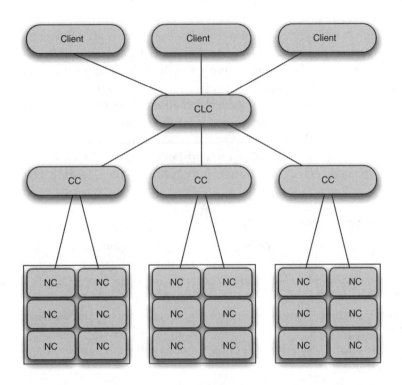

Figure 4.8   Architectural model for a Eucalyptus private cloud implementation. The Node Controllers (NCs) manage virtual instances on each physical server. These are controlled up in the hierarchy by Cluster Controllers (CCs) that manage an availability zone. At the top level, the Cloud Controller (CLC) manages the entire private cloud system and takes commands from both administrator and user client systems.

to the Amazon cloud. Much larger configurations are also possible with multiple CCs managing virtuals on multiple NCs.

The clusters in a Eucalyptus system are analogous to the availability zones within Amazon. You can see an architecture diagram depicting the topology in figure 4.8.

As mentioned earlier, a plus point of the open-source cloud implementations is the fact that they have been built to interoperate with the Amazon cloud. The CLC exposes SOAP-based client interfaces that conform to the WSDL documentation provided by Amazon. Because Amazon publishes its user-facing APIs, open-source cloud software providers are able to provide client interfaces that are compatible. Administration interfaces used by Amazon to run EC2 aren't publicly available, so Eucalyptus implemented its own interfaces. The administrator, either through a web-based interface or via command line, accesses these Eucalyptus-specific interfaces. For registration, to use the Amazon cloud, automatic approval is granted using credit-card verification. In the Eucalyptus system, you can request access via a web-based interface that sends an email to the administrator who manually grants access. The administrator can start or terminate your instances and is able to add disk images. The administrator is also in charge of adding clusters and nodes to the cloud configuration.

The open-source private cloud implementations provide a simple way to begin experimenting with private cloud technologies. Both Eucalyptus and Open Nebula were developed as academic research projects; both were built to help elucidate the functionality of private clouds. They were also built with extensibility in mind, meaning that the prebuilt functionality was designed to allow additional capabilities to be layered on. Proprietary cloud software offers greater functionality out of the box. You'll find some examples of this in load-balancing and fault-tolerance functionality as well as more extensive management and monitoring capabilities for effectively administering the cloud.

4.3   A virtual private cloud

Amazon is the first to have created a virtual private cloud (VPC) that connects your data center to Amazon's EC2. The idea is to use Amazon EC2 instances within VPC to add additional web-facing servers to your application when the traffic exceeds your on-premise capacity. The back-end of your application, database servers, authentication servers, and so forth, remains within the walls of your data center. When demand subsides, you can terminate the Amazon EC2 instances that you no longer require. Amazon has chosen not to call this cloudbursting, but that's precisely what it is.

4.3.1   How it works

A VPC is a secure and seamless bridge between an organization's existing IT infrastructure and a provider's public cloud. You can see this in a high-level simplistic fashion in

A virtual private cloud

Amazon Virtual Private Cloud is a secure and seamless bridge between a company's existing IT infrastructure and the public cloud. Although not a private cloud as you've read about earlier, this approach offers corporations a hybrid model merging aspects of the company's data center with a major cloud provider's public cloud.

Amazon's VPC enables enterprises to connect their existing infrastructure to a set of isolated AWS compute resources via a Virtual Private Network (VPN) connection, and to extend their existing management capabilities, such as security services, firewalls, and intrusion-detection systems to include their AWS resources.

Google has a similar structure called Secure Data Connector, which connects legacy infrastructure to Google's AppEngine Platform as a Service (PaaS) public cloud.

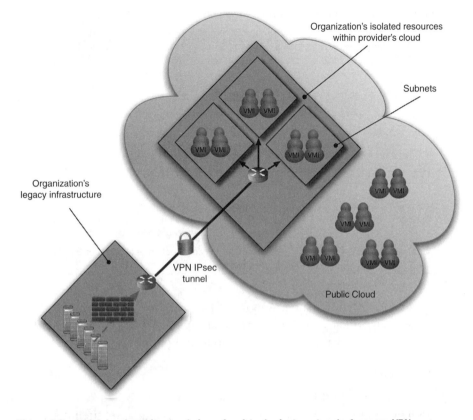

Figure 4.9 A high-level architectural view of a virtual private network. A secure VPN connection connects an organization's existing infrastructure—including all its security components, such as firewalls and intrusion-detection systems—to a portion of the public cloud isolated for the organization.

figure 4.9. The idea is to connect an organization's existing infrastructure to a set of isolated cloud-compute resources via a VPN connection.

In this way, an organization can extend its existing management capabilities and security services, such as firewalls and intrusion-detection systems, to include the cloud resources that have been dedicated to the organization, and protect the information there the same as is done now.

4.3.2 The API

The operation of a VPC when there's an existing mature public cloud is fairly simple. You launch standard instances, such as for Amazon EC2, into a new VPC, and then EC2 API calls are used to dictate the IP address range from which this new instance will receive its IP address. Then, you use your preexisting security infrastructure, such as firewalls, intrusion-detection systems, and management systems, to enforce policies based on these IP address ranges and control who and what has access to resources running inside your VPC. Table 4.3 briefly outlines the steps.

Table 4.3 Basic steps to create a virtual private cloud using EC2 API calls

API call	Function
CreateVpc	Creates your VPC, within which you define the IP address space you wish to use. Create one or more subnets where your isolated resources, such as Amazon EC2 instances, are placed. You need at least one subnet, but you can have more.
CreateCustomerGateway	Creates a Customer Gateway, providing information about your devices such as IP address and other networking-related information. CreateCustomerGateway returns a Customer Gateway ID that you can use to represent your device when interacting with the service.
CreateVpnGateway	Creates a VPN Gateway, which anchors the VPC side of your VPN connection and encrypts/decrypts messages to/from the Customer Gateway via the VPN connection.
CreateVpnConnection	Creates a VPN connection between your Customer and VPN Gateways.

In addition to cloudbursting, Amazon's VPC tries to offer a solution that addresses cloud security, which, as we've said, remains the single biggest impediment most enterprises cite as their reason not to adopt cloud computing.

4.3.3 Implications

A virtual private cloud has many usage scenarios. Let's briefly discuss three here: expanding corporate applications into the cloud, scaling a website into the cloud, and setting up a disaster-recovery site.

EXPANDING CORPORATE APPLICATIONS INTO THE CLOUD

Moving your corporate applications into the cloud to reduce the total cost of ownership can realistically be achieved using a VPC. Applications such as email systems, financial systems, trouble-ticketing systems, CRM applications, and others are standard fare for all large organizations. These corporate applications can be logically grouped by IP address range according to existing deployment policies; and because the VPC you set up exists behind your corporate firewall, users can access the applications moved into the VPC the same way they do today.

ELASTICALLY SCALING YOUR WEBSITE IN THE CLOUD

Corporate websites can be an embarrassing place for failure due to sudden spikes in traffic. Any new ad or a news story can set this in motion. You can use VPC to add web servers. When the traffic load exceeds your on-premises capacity, you have room to expand dynamically (and quickly). The back-end of your website, database servers, authentication servers, and so on, can remain within the walls of your data center. When demand subsides, you terminate the Amazon EC2 instances you no longer require, and you don't have to pay for the excess capacity you'd normally have.

DISASTER RECOVERY

Disaster recovery is vitally important but expensive and can be difficult because you have to use a different data-center location. Using VPC, you can periodically back up mission-critical data from your data center to a small number of virtual instances in conjunction with large cloud storage volumes. In the event of a disaster, you can quickly launch replacement compute capacity to ensure business continuity. When the disaster is over, you send your mission-critical data back to your data center and terminate the cloud instances you no longer require.

That's the theory. Now, let's look at several real-world case studies to further illuminate how private clouds can be used effectively.

4.4 Private clouds in practice

Let's look at three specific private cloud initiatives and implementations as a way to understand how attributes such as the security constraints of the application and requirements of specific organizations caused the implementation to take a private cloud route.

4.4.1 Sprint: private cloud for fraud-detection application

The first example comes from the telecommunications industry and involves Sprint. Sprint is the third largest provider of wireless voice and communications in the U.S. It has roughly 50 million subscribers and needs to process the operational events generated by these users across a nationally distributed network in real time. Sprint chose to deploy a private cloud to process this data for the purposes of fraud detection.

A fraud application deals with private information of the wireless carrier's subscribers; using a private cloud makes good sense. In addition to private data related to your identity, such as your credit card information, a wireless carrier also has access to data relating to your geographic location in real time. Not only can it determine your location from the cell tower your phone is using during a call, but often, if the cell phone is on, it can determine your location at all times.

Sprint could have chosen to deploy the fraud application in a traditional manner, utilizing a few expensive, high-performance computing servers. Instead, the company chose a cloud-like approach of developing the application for deployment on many commodity x86 servers. The Sprint private cloud is small scale in comparison to a public cloud, using on the order of 100 commodity servers as opposed to the thousands or more that are involved in a public cloud deployment. It uses software from Appistry as the cloud technology to provide management infrastructure for these servers. Appistry also provides the middleware layer that allows the application to be distributed and load-balanced across multiple servers so that it can run reliably and in a fault-tolerant manner across the infrastructure.

The cheap, commodity-server strategy allows an organization to deploy incrementally and dynamically as load increases. Deploying as a private cloud, as opposed to a public cloud, allows for greater control and a guarantee that all available resources can be allocated to the task. This example, although it's small scale, demonstrates many of the aspects of a successful private cloud deployment.

One aspect of a private cloud, although not present in this example, is that it isn't strictly speaking a utility platform for general computing, and it isn't shared across multiple constituencies for various purposes. In the next example, we'll look at a deployment that does have this characteristic.

4.4.2 *Bechtel Project Services Network (PSN)*

Bechtel is a large construction and engineering company with over 40,000 employees. The company runs projects in 50 countries worldwide. Its CIO, Geir Ramleth, set out in 2006 to transform the traditional IT infrastructure into one that was state of the art. His basic premise was that in the last decade, most IT innovation was being performed in consumer-oriented companies. He studied 18 of them to see how he could improve the way his organization operated. He found there were drastic differences in the cost and efficiency of his organization when compared with these best-in-class operations. In his keynote address at the 2008 IT Roadmap Conference and Expo, Ramleth cited some of these differences:

- *Bandwidth*—YouTube pays $10-15/megabit for its WAN bandwidth, whereas Bechtel paid $500/megabit.
- *Storage*—Amazon charges its cloud customers $0.15/GB/month, compared to the $3.75/GB/month Bechtel pays.
- *IT server maintenance*—Google can maintain 20,000 servers with one systems administrator, whereas Bechtel needed 1 for every 100 servers.
- *Software applications*—Salesforce.com has only one version of its application servicing 1 million users, which it upgrades four times a year with little downtime and few training requirements. In comparison, Bechtel used 230 different applications with up to 5 versions each, amounting to almost 800 different versions of applications servicing 40,000 employees. These applications required ongoing training and frequent maintenance upgrades.

Bechtel transformed its IT infrastructure into a private cloud by standardizing its hardware and software infrastructure. It consolidated its data-center assets, closing seven data centers and consolidating its core computational assets into three retooled and standardized centers. It virtualized its infrastructure, resulting in improved server and storage utilization. From the application perspective, it moved to a more standardized overall portal with modules for customized applications. The result of the transformation was a savings of 25 to 30 percent in overall IT costs.

4.4.3 *Government private clouds*

As our final private cloud example, let's look at the government sector. In September 2009, the federal CIO, Vivek Kunda, announced the launch of a government cloud initiative. The aim of this initiative was to save money by reducing the cost of government data centers while simultaneously maintaining a high level of security.

The federal government has an annual IT budget of over $75 billion. Kunda stated, "We need a new model to lower costs and innovate. The government should solve problems, not run data centers." For nonsecret applications, there's a push toward using public-cloud-powered solutions to reduce cost. The Apps.gov website (http://apps.gov) allows sourcing of cloud-provided technologies by government agencies (see figure 4.10).

In the case of applications that require secrecy, private clouds are also under development. In October 2008, the Defense Information Systems Agency (DISA), which operates under the Department of Defense (DoD), launched a private cloud military application called the Rapid Access Computing Environment (RACE). The RACE platform is the military version of Amazon's AWS. It streamlines the acquisition, customization, and provisioning of computing resources, bringing up test and development environments in 24 hours and true production environments in 72 hours.

Figure 4.10 The federal government is proceeding headlong into using public cloud services as a means of reducing costs. On the Apps.gov website, SaaS and cloud-based offerings can be purchased with a government credit card and the appropriate approvals.

Computing resources run on a LAMP stack (Linux, Apache, MySQL, PHP) and are available in both Linux and Windows environments, with configurations of 1–4 CPUs, 1–8 GB RAM, and 60 GB to 1 TB of SAN storage. As in the case of a public cloud, these resources are offered in a pay-as-you-go model on a monthly basis, with pricing starting at $500/instance/month, and can be purchased with a government credit card.

4.5   *The long-term viability of private clouds*

As you've seen throughout this chapter, private cloud computing is a burgeoning area, and in some cases deployments of this kind make sense today. Such a deployment requires a lot of existing investment in data centers. Also, best IT practices as they relate to security in the public cloud haven't been entirely worked out. As these best practices are worked out over the next several years, it remains an open question whether the private cloud will become a pervasive phenomenon.

It may be useful to think of cloud computing in the context of the way electric power is generated and consumed today. In his book *The Big Switch*, Nicholas Carr describes how in the 18th century, companies used waterwheels to generate their own electricity. Waterwheels and expertise in generating electricity for factories *were* considered competitive differentiators.

As public utilities reached scale, it was no longer a competitive differentiator to maintain your own waterwheel. In fact, doing so became a potential liability as electricity provided through the electric grid by dedicated electric utilities became more cost-effective than generators.

Electric power generation outside of public electric utilities didn't disappear entirely: companies and governments maintain their own power-generation capabilities as necessary in the form of backup generators in hospitals and factories as well as generators in field operations on the battlefield or to power cruise ships or nuclear submarines. In the same way, you might expect that in a decade or so, there will still be instances of private clouds, but they will become less and less prevalent. The challenge for companies that have private clouds is to understand whether it continues to make sense to have them or whether ultimately they should migrate to a public cloud.

4.6   *Summary*

Security remains the single biggest fear factor for larger organizations considering a major move to the cloud. This chapter delved into security in general, discussed how it's being practiced by major cloud providers, and examined the case for and against private clouds.

Private cloud computing is a potential alternative deployment option available and may make sense for large enterprises and organizations. For organizations with enough scale, buying power, and expertise, private clouds offer the advantages of increased control, predictability, and security. You have many options available, including building a private cloud from open-source technologies, using proprietary purpose-built solutions, and partnering with service providers willing to allocate or partition dedicated resources for a private cloud. We also discussed a variant of the private cloud—the virtual private cloud—and explained how it works, what it's good for, and how to use it.

We finished with a survey of private clouds in practice. Looking at things from the perspective of the cloud provider, let's return to examining the cloud from the perspective of a cloud user. In chapter 5, you'll learn how applications should be designed and architected for the cloud (either public or private).

Designing and architecting
for cloud scale

In this chapter, you'll learn how to design and architect applications that can handle the potentially massive scale possible when you're using the cloud and are exposed to the entire internet. You're now prepared for an in-depth discussion of designing and architecting applications specifically for the cloud. This is important because you may have applications that scale to large numbers of users—a number so large that we call it *cloud scale*. Although this chapter doesn't require a programmer's background, we do go into some detail about issues that are unique to building applications that are designed for the cloud and prepared for broad-scale use. After all, one of the primary reasons for utilizing the cloud is to be prepared for, and to have an affordable economic model for, that wonderful "problem" of suddenly having too many users.

We'll describe the kinds of applications that fit well into the cloud model. And you'll learn about several design topics: building for internet scale (including the concept of sharding); building in on-demand capacity in your data center (cloudbursting); and storage that keeps expanding. First, let's examine a set of design patterns that fit well with the unique characteristics of the cloud.

5.1 High-scale application patterns that fit the cloud best

Let's begin with a discussion about broad types, or *patterns*, of high-scale applications and how they do or don't fit well into the model of cloud computing. The categories we'll consider are called transference, internet scale, burst compute, and elastic storage. These are the most common application patterns that motivate a move to the cloud to deal with high scale (lots of users, lots of compute, lots of data, or rapid swings of any of these). We'll look at these in order, first defining the category followed by a short discussion of the issues to watch out for.

5.1.1 Transference

Transference is when you take an existing on-premises application and move it to the cloud as is. This pattern is typically driven by economic factors (as you've read earlier in this book). It can be cheaper to use cloud resources than to run these applications in-house if you're not fully employing virtualization for higher utilization in your local data center. Commodity services, such as email, CRM, and other packaged applications, are candidates for this pattern.

Zillow.com—a website dedicated to providing consumers accurate expected home values on any U.S. residential address—is a small business that moved its application as is to the cloud because it couldn't afford the servers needed to process the large number of changes in home values across the entire country when the housing market bubble burst. It had a huge spike in compute work it needed to accomplish but didn't want to buy the necessary servers because they would be excess capacity in a few weeks.

When the transference pattern is the appropriate one to use, you need to watch out for customizations that work in your local data center but that the host/cloud doesn't support. For example, if the application depends on a custom device driver you built for Linux, you won't be able to transfer this application to a cloud: cloud providers won't allow you to re-create that device driver modification in their Linux implementation. This aside, you'll find no other design issues with this pattern, and it won't get further coverage in this chapter.

5.1.2 Internet scale

The *internet scale* design pattern involves creating an application for the cloud that has the ability to handle huge numbers of users, such as YouTube, Flickr, or Facebook, without requiring the corresponding substantial capital investment from day one. This is a common pattern for prototyping new applications because it allows a significantly lower entrance cost (no servers are being purchased). It also lets you start very small yet expand when needed.

When Facebook started, it was run off a single server and serviced only Harvard University students. Facebook built its own data center on its way to supporting 400 million users. If the cloud had existed, the company would have avoided a few growing pains caused by data center and application limitations along the way. Twitter also started as one guy on one server; and because it resonated with people, it grew at an unprecedented pace. It faced many outages because of scaling problems. If you're a small company with big visions of building a service that people want, you need to think hard about starting in the cloud with a strong, scalable design.

Finally, designing for and starting in a cloud is applicable as a risk-mitigation measure for applications with unpredictable growth. One of the most challenging design issues for this application pattern, when the application does have to scale, revolves around the database structure: without care, it quickly becomes the database that prevents scale. You'll see how to address this issue in detail later in this chapter.

5.1.3 Burst compute

Applications that fit the *burst compute* pattern have the ability to handle additional compute capability on an as-needed basis without idle, over-provisioned resources. Applications ideal for this pattern have large swings in capacity requirements, particularly if the spikes are somewhat rare.

A good example is the site Eventseer.net. It routinely bursts out to Amazon's cloud to statically generate changed pages on its 600,000-page site because it doesn't have the capacity internally to do this fast enough.

The burst compute pattern is driven by the economic factors of the cloud. The cost of additional hardware capacity required to support this pattern internally is prohibitive. Real bursts of load can be handled cost effectively in the pay-only-for-what-you-use cloud model. You'll read about *cloudbursting* as a nice solution for the burst compute application pattern later in the chapter.

5.1.4 Elastic storage

In the *elastic storage* application pattern, applications have the ability to grow exponentially from a storage perspective. Although local storage is relatively cheap, its management is fairly expensive. As a result, using a cloud platform can be a cheaper alternative to local storage management. But using this pattern requires careful thought and planning for accessing the data. For instance, if you're using the cloud purely to store data, but processing it locally, performance may be unacceptable; that would make this pattern not applicable.

5.1.5 Summarizing the application patterns

Table 5.1 summarizes the five major cloud application patterns. Note that the sense of the word *design* we're using in this chapter is *the act of working out the form of something.* And the word *architecture* is *the structure and organization of a computer's hardware or system software.*

Table 5.1 Summary of the five major cloud-scaling application patterns, their major issues, and the section in which they're discussed

Pattern	Description	Major issues	Section
Transference	Existing on-premises application moved to the cloud as is for economic benefits	Application customizations may not transfer or work.	N/A
Internet scale	New web-facing applications with unpredictable growth	Database design can throttle growth; consider sharding.	5.2
Burst compute	Applications with large swings of capacity requirements, particularly if spikes are rare	Load-balancing requires a strategy; database access from data center to cloud is the issue.	5.3
Elastic storage	Application storage that has the ability to grow exponentially	Local processing of cloud accessed data may preclude this pattern.	5.4

Let's suppose you're thinking about adapting or building from scratch an application that will run in whole or in part on the cloud, and it will deal with the implied scale of the huge population of the internet as well. What form should it take? What are the issues you must address to have it successfully take that form? What is the hardware configuration (potentially virtual hardware) required? What is the structure, and what are the components to be included in the software solution you create? Your answers lie in the design and architecture of the application. Let's now tackle the design and architecture issues for the internet scale application pattern.

5.2   Designing and architecting for internet scale: sharding

When you think *internet scale*—by which we mean exposure to the enormous population of entities (human and machine) that could potentially access your application—you may think of any number of the most popular services. Google is the obvious king of the realm, but Facebook, Flickr, Yahoo! and many others have faced these issues when scaling to hundreds of millions of users. eBay may surprise you by how big it's become and how much it's had to engineer in enormous scale (see figure 5.1).

Each of these services was throttled at some point by the way it used the database where information about its users was being accessed. For many internet companies, these problems were so severe that they required major reengineering, sometimes many times over. That's a good lesson to learn early as you're thinking about how to design internet scale applications.

5.2.1 *Application issues that prevent scaling*

Many best-in-the-industry applications had to completely reengineer their successful services as they grew and became more popular. Some weren't able to do so in time. Their experiences highlight two of the most impactful issues that prevent applications from achieving internet scale: too large a working set, and frequent and/or large database updates.

WORKING SETS TOO LARGE

If the amount of memory required to keep your frequently accessed data loaded in memory exceeds what you can (economically) fit in a commodity machine's main memory, your application has too large a working set. Five years ago, this was

- Over 89 million active users worldwide
- 190 million items for sale in 50,000 categories
- Over 8 billion URL requests per day
- Hundreds of new features per quarter
- Roughly 10% of items are listed or ended every day
- In 39 countries and 10 languages
- 24 x 7 x 365 service required
- 70 billion read / write operations per day
- 50TB of new, incremental data per day processed
- 50PB of data analyzed per day

Figure 5.1 Statistics that show why sites such as eBay can't survive with a centralized database. That database must be partitioned into multiple databases. Partitioning (or *sharding*) is a critical strategy for scaling.

4 GB; today it's 128 GB or even 256 GB. Note that this need not be the same size (or even near) the size of your entire database, assuming good database schema and indexing.

TOO MANY WRITES

If either the I/O system or a slave working on its behalf can't keep up with the number of writes—recording the data—being sent to the server, there are too many writes for the system to scale any further. The I/O system is throttling the application. Although you can improve the I/O system with a RAID approach (perhaps by 5X or even 10X), the slave-delay problem is hard to solve and only delays when the throttle point is hit anyway.

SOLUTION: PARTITION THE DATA

What is the solution? Partition the data. Easy as that may sound, it's extremely hard to do. But you can do it by splitting the data between multiple machines, and have a way to make sure you always access data from the right place.

For example, consider this simple scheme. Imagine you want to store data about customers, each of whom has a last name field. One partitioning scheme is to create 26 identical databases and assign each one a letter of the alphabet. Then, whenever you want to look up data about John Smith, you first connect to the S database, and then you fetch the data you want. The single-database solution, where all last names are stored, would have 26X more capacity added to it because each of the 26 databases contains all last names of a single letter of the alphabet. This process of partitioning a database is called *sharding*, and we'll delve into it in much more detail next.

5.2.2 *Sharding defined: a parallel database architecture for massive scaling*

The term *sharding* was coined by Google engineers and popularized through their publication of the BigTable architecture. But the concept of *shared-nothing* database partitioning on which sharding is based has been around for a decade or more. There have been many implementations over this period, particularly high-profile, in-house-built solutions by internet leaders such as eBay, Amazon, Digg, Flickr, Skype, YouTube, Facebook, Friendster, and even Wikipedia.

> **SHARDING** A decomposition of a database into multiple smaller units (called *shards*) that can handle requests individually. It's related to a scalability concept called *shared-nothing* that removes dependencies between portions of the application such that they can run completely independently and in parallel for much higher throughput.

There was a time when you scaled databases by buying bigger, faster, and more expensive machines. Whereas this arrangement is great for big iron and database vendor profit margins, it doesn't work so well for the providers of popular web-facing services that need to scale past what they can afford to spend on giant database servers (and no single database server is big enough for the likes of Google, Flickr, or eBay). This is where sharding comes in. It's a revolutionary new database architecture that, when implemented at Flickr, enabled that service to handle more than one billion transactions per day, responding to requests in less than a few seconds; and that scaled linearly at low cost. It does sound revolutionary, doesn't it? Let's look at it more closely.

SHARDING IN A NUTSHELL

In the simplest model for partitioning, as diagrammed in figure 5.2, you can store the data for User 1 on one server and the data for User 2 on another. It's a federated model. In a system such as Flickr, you can store groups of 500,000 users together in each partition (shard). In the simple two-shard design in figure 5.2, the criteria for shard selection is odd- versus even-numbered user identification values.

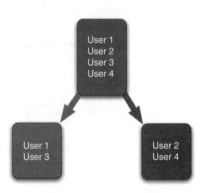

The more you examine sharding, the more advantages you'll discover:

Figure 5.2 Basic database sharding partitions the database based on who will access that part of the service. In this example, the criteria are that odd-numbered users go in one partition and even-numbered go in the other.

- *High availability*—If one box goes down, the others still operate. In the simple model, when some users stop getting service, the rest of the service is unaffected. Normally, there's some replication; even if a box with a shard goes down, its users can still be serviced on the replicated server.
- *Faster queries*—Smaller amounts of data in each user group mean faster querying. Services with a lot of experience with their particular usage pattern and database structure learn how to best partition their database onto shards to keep queries fast enough to keep users satisfied.

■ *More write bandwidth*—With no master database serializing writes, you can write to many shards in parallel. This increases your write throughput. Writing is *the* major bottleneck for many websites.

The bottom line is that sharding allows your application to do more work. It provides a parallel back-end, which means your application can do more things simultaneously. It can handle higher user loads, particularly when writing data, because there are parallel paths through your system on something that normally throttles performance: database writes. You can load-balance web servers that access shards over different network paths. These paths are processed by separate CPUs that use separate caches of RAM and separate disk I/O paths. The result is that few bottlenecks limit your application's performance. Now, let's look at a real example to substantiate this further.

WHY SHARD (OR PARTITION) YOUR DATABASE?

Let's take Facebook as an example. In early 2004, mostly Harvard students used the site as an online yearbook. A single beefy server handled the entire storage requirements and query load on the database. Fast-forward to 2008, when Facebook application-related page views were about 14 billion per month (more than 5,000 page views per second, each of which required multiple back-end queries to satisfy). In addition to query load, with its attendant IOPs, CPU, and memory cost, there's also storage capacity to consider.

Today, Facebook stores 40 billion physical files to represent about 10 billion photos, which is over a petabyte of storage. Even though the photo files aren't likely in a relational database, their metadata, such as identifiers and locations, still requires a few terabytes of storage to represent the photos in the database. You can be sure that originally Facebook didn't have terabytes of storage available to store photo metadata. And it correctly wasn't originally designed that way, because you can't know the exact usage patterns that will drive the best sharding strategy until you observe user behaviors as they interact with your application.

At some point during the development of Facebook, the company reached the physical capacity of its database server and probably suffered a lot of user dissatisfaction while it worked to rearchitect. The moot question was whether to scale vertically by buying a more expensive, beefier server with more RAM, CPU horsepower, disk I/O, and storage capacity; or to spread data across multiple relatively cheap database servers.

As we discussed earlier, if your service has rapidly changing data (lots of writes) or is sporadically queried by many users in a way that causes your working set not to fit in memory (lots of reads, leading to lots of page faults and disk seeks), then your primary bottleneck will likely be I/O. This is typically the case with social media sites, such as Facebook, LinkedIn, Blogger, MySpace, and even Flickr. In such cases, it's either prohibitively expensive or physically impossible to purchase a single server to handle the load on the site. Sharding the database, although challenging to design and implement correctly, provides the best performance and highest cost savings relative to the increased complexity of the system.

5.2.3   *How sharding changes an application*

In a well-designed application, the primary change sharding adds to your core application code is that instead of code that opens a single database and then does a query, such as this:

```
string connectionString =
    ConfigurationSettings.AppSettings["ConnectionInfo"];
OdbcConnection conn = new OdbcConnection(connectionString);
conn.Open();

OdbcCommand cmd = new OdbcCommand("SELECT Name, Address FROM Customers
                               WHERE CustomerID= ?", conn);
OdbcParameter param = cmd.Parameters.Add("@CustomerID", OdbcType.Int);
param.Value = customerId;
OdbcDataReader reader = cmd.ExecuteReader();
```

The actual connection information about the database to which it should connect depends on the data you're trying to store or access. You add a method `GetDatabase-For()` that opens one of many databases based on a `customerID` parameter. Now, you have the following:

```
string connectionString = GetDatabaseFor(customerId);
OdbcConnection conn = new OdbcConnection(connectionString);
conn.Open();

OdbcCommand cmd = new OdbcCommand("SELECT Name, Address FROM Customers
                               WHERE CustomerID= ?", conn);
OdbcParameter param = cmd.Parameters.Add("@CustomerID", OdbcType.Int);
param.Value = customerId;
OdbcDataReader reader = cmd.ExecuteReader();
```

We assume here that the `GetDatabaseFor()` method knows how to map a customer ID to a physical database location. For the most part, everything else should remain the same, unless the application uses sharding as a way to parallelize queries and not just access. The seemingly minor change of adding the `GetDatabaseFor()` method provides an application with a database architecture quite different from a traditional one.

5.2.4   *Sharding in contrast with traditional database architectures*

To understand how different and how powerful sharding is, let's contrast a sharded database with a traditional one in this section.

DATA ARE DENORMALIZED

Traditionally, we normalize data. *Normalizing* means you pull the data apart and relate data elements in a new record to the tables used to store the range of possible standard values. For example, if a user has a relationship status that has a fixed set of possible values (single, married, and so on), normalized data retains only an index into the relationship status table. Data are splayed out into tables without anomalies and then joined again when you need to use them. This makes databases smaller and easier for humans to understand but decidedly non-scalable.

But in sharding, the data are denormalized—you store together data that are used together. Every user record in this example retains the relationship status with the record and not an index into a single relationship status table. Now, if you need to move the data, it's all intact and doesn't have to refer to a table in a database that's shared by many and acts as a single point of congestion.

This doesn't mean you don't also segregate data by type. You can keep a user's profile data separate from their comments, blogs, email, media, and so on, but the user profile data is stored and retrieved as a whole. Although we don't know the top-secret internal workings of Facebook, the company must be employing something similar based on observed behavior and performance. This is a very fast approach. You get a blob of data and store a blob of data. You don't need any joins and can write data with one disk write.

DATA ARE PARALLELIZED ACROSS MANY PHYSICAL INSTANCES

Historically, database servers are scaled up (see figure 5.3). You buy bigger machines for more power. But it's not difficult to reach the limit of the server, the database, or both.

With sharding, the data are parallelized, and you scale by expanding horizontally. You can get more work done because it can be done in parallel. And as figure 5.4 implies, there's no limit to how many databases you can put to work.

DATA ARE KEPT SMALL

The larger a set of data a server handles, the harder it is to cache intelligently, because you have such a wide diversity of data being accessed. You need huge amounts of RAM that may not even be enough to cache the data when you need it. By isolating data into smaller shards, the data you're accessing is more likely to stay in cache. Smaller sets of data are also easier to back up, restore, and manage.

Starter system:
Small server + small database

Expanded system:
Large server + large database

Figure 5.3   The traditional approach to scaling a database. Bigger servers drive bigger databases. But the system is throttled by how fast the server and the disk subsystem can handle writes, and it quickly reaches its limits when dealing with internet scale.

Internet scaled system:
Many commodity servers + many parallel databases

Figure 5.4 The sharding approach to database scaling uses more modest servers (usually based on cheap commodity hardware) with modest databases, where each server and its associated database takes on a portion of the database load. A good partitioning scheme balances the load and allows continued expansion as the application continues to scale.

DATA ARE MORE HIGHLY AVAILABLE

Because shards are independent, a failure in one doesn't cause a failure in another. And if you make each shard operate at 50 percent capacity, it's much easier to upgrade a shard in place. Keeping multiple data copies within a shard also helps with redundancy, making the data more parallelized so more work can be done on the data.

You can also set up a shard to have master-slave (where the master database is the authoritative source and the slave databases are synchronized to it) or dual master (where each server functions as both a master and a slave to the other server) replication to avoid a single point of failure within the shard. If one server goes down, the other can take over.

DATA AREN'T REPLICATED

Replicating data from a master server to slave servers is a traditional approach to scaling. Data are written to a master server and then replicated to one or more slave servers. At that point, read operations can be handled by the slaves, but all writes happen on the master.

Obviously, the master becomes the write bottleneck and a single point of failure. And as load increases, the cost of replication increases. Replication costs in CPU, network bandwidth, and disk I/O. The slaves fall behind and have stale data.

Now that you've learned about the sharding concept and its attributes, let's explore the various common approaches to partitioning databases into shards.

5.2.5 Sharding in practice: the most common database partitioning schemes

Continuing to peel the onion, we'll discuss the most common types of sharding. The way the database is partitioned needs to match the characteristics of the application and its usage patterns. Do you separate out features, each to its own database? Should you divide segments of users to each have a separate database? Or is it best to use an even more sophisticated scheme, because your system may need to be repartitioned over and over as it grows? You have to make these choices early. To make an informed decision, you need to understand how your application is used.

VERTICAL PARTITIONING

A simple way to segment your application database is to move tables related to specific features to their own server. For example, placing user profile information on one database server, putting friend lists on another, and using a third for user-generated content, such as photos and blogs, may make sense.

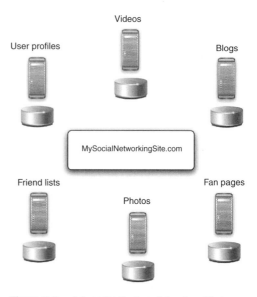

Figure 5.5 shows a hypothetical social networking site that employs vertical database partitioning (the real social networks guard their inner architectures like state secrets). The key benefit of this approach is that it's straightforward to implement and has low impact on the application as a whole. The drawback here is, if the site experiences additional growth, it may be necessary to further shard a feature-specific database across multiple servers (for example, handling metadata queries for 10 billion photos by 400 million users may be more than a single server can handle; but not many services will see Facebook's growth profile).

Figure 5.5   **A hypothetical social networking site that employed vertical (feature-based) partitioning when it implemented sharding to help it scale its application to ever-larger numbers of users**

RANGE-BASED PARTITIONING

When the entire data set for a single feature or table needs to be further subdivided across multiple servers, it's important to ensure that the data is split up in a predictable manner. One approach to ensuring this predictability is to split the data based on value ranges that occur within each entity. For example, you can split sales transactions by what year they were created or assign users to servers based on the first digit of their zip code.

The main problem with this approach is that if the value whose range is used for partitioning isn't chosen carefully, then the sharding scheme leads to unbalanced servers. In the previous example, splitting up transactions by date means that the server with the current year gets a disproportionate amount of read and write traffic. Similarly, partitioning users based on their zip code assumes that your user base is evenly distributed across the different zip codes. But this fails to account for situations where an application is popular in a particular region and the fact that human populations vary across zip codes.

KEY- OR HASH-BASED PARTITIONING

Key- or hash-based partitioning is often a synonym for user-based partitioning for Web 2.0 sites. With this approach, each entity has a value that can be used as input into a hash function whose output is used to determine which database server to use. For example, suppose you have 10 database servers, and your user IDs are numeric values that are incremented by 1 each time a new user is added. The hash function can perform a *modulo* operation on the user ID with the number 10 and then pick a database server based on the remainder value. This approach should ensure a uniform allocation of data to each server.

The key problem with this approach is that it effectively fixes the number of database servers, because adding new servers means changing the hash function—which, without downtime, is similar to being asked to change the tires on a moving car. This example illustrates the critical importance of thinking ahead when making sharding design decisions.

> ### Tips for avoiding unbalanced sharding
>
> Avoid bad hashing algorithms. You don't want to shard based on the first character of a username because our culture has many more *M* than *Z* names.
>
> Avoid the problem of users suddenly becoming unequal. The day Sarah Palin was announced as the vice presidential pick, one user became much more active than any other in any type of social networking service.

DIRECTORY-BASED PARTITIONING

A loosely coupled approach to this problem is to create a lookup service that knows your current partitioning scheme and abstracts it away from the database access code. This means the `GetDatabaseFor()` method hits a web service or a database that stores/returns the mapping between each entity key and the database server it resides on. This loosely coupled approach means you can perform tasks such as adding servers to the database pool or change your partitioning scheme without having to impact your application.

Remember the previous example, where there are 10 servers and the hash function is a modulo—the remainder after division of one number by another—operation? In spite of modulo being simple, it has a uniform distribution. Let's say you want to add five database servers to the pool without incurring downtime. You can keep the existing hash function, add these servers to the pool, and then run a script that copies data from the 10 existing servers to the 5 new servers based on a new hash function implemented by performing the modulo operation on user IDs using the new server count of 15. After the data is copied over (this is tricky because users are always updating their data), the lookup service can change to using the new hash function without any of the calling applications being any wiser that their database pool grew 50 percent and that the database they went to for John Doe's pictures 5 minutes ago is different from the one they're accessing now. Similar to any solution that creates a highly efficient layer of abstraction (or indirection), this is highly scalable. And after you write scripts to be able to migrate users to/from shards, you can tweak and rebalance to make sure all your hardware is utilized efficiently. The downside of this approach is that it's complicated.

In the next section, we'll explore the challenges and problems with sharding. You need to understand that although it's extremely powerful, sharding shouldn't be used too early or too often.

5.2.6 *Sharding challenges and problems*

Sharding isn't perfect. It has a few problems, not the least of which is that fact that it's very complicated.

When a database has been sharded, new constraints are placed on the operations that can be performed on the database. These constraints primarily center around the fact that operations across multiple tables or multiple rows in the same table no longer will run on the same server. The following sections describe some of the constraints and additional complexities introduced by sharding.

REBALANCING DATA

What happens when a shard outgrows your storage and needs to be split? Let's say a user has a particularly large friends list that blows your storage capacity for the shard. You need to move the user to a different shard. This can be a major problem. Moving data from shard to shard may require a service shutdown if this isn't designed extremely carefully.

Rebalancing must be built in from the start. Google's shards automatically rebalance. For this to work, data references must go through some sort of naming service so they can be relocated. In addition, references must be *invalidateable* so the underlying data can be moved while you're using it. You can see a simple example of this in figure 5.6.

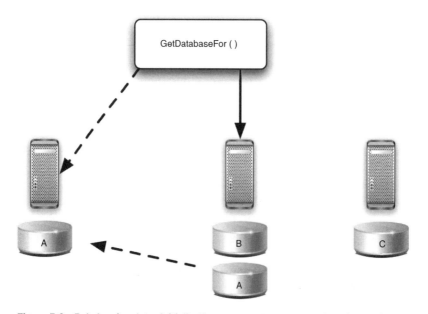

Figure 5.6   Rebalancing data. Initially, the `GetDatabaseFor()` function pushed requests for partition A to the center server. But that server's database shard has gotten too large and needs to be rebalanced. All or a portion of database A is moved to the server on the left. After that data is successfully moved, the function `GetDatabaseFor()` is modified so that future requests for shard A are directed to the leftmost server.

Using a scheme such as directory-based partitioning makes rebalancing more feasible at the cost of increasing the complexity of the system and creating a new single point of failure (the lookup service/database).

JOINING DATA FROM MULTIPLE SHARDS

To create a complex friends page, a user profile page, or a thread discussion page, you must pull together lots of different data from many sources. With sharding, you can't just issue a query and get back all the data. You have to make individual requests to your data sources, get all the responses, and build the page. Fortunately, because of caching and fast networks, this process is fast enough that your page-load times can be excellent. In the social-networking examples we've been using, human response time is a pretty forgiving upper bound.

REFERENTIAL INTEGRITY

It's extremely difficult to enforce data integrity constraints such as foreign keys in a sharded database. Most relational database management systems don't support foreign keys across databases on different database servers.

Sharded applications that require referential integrity must often enforce it in application code and run regular SQL jobs to clean up dangling references. Consequently, dealing with data-inconsistency issues due to denormalization and lack of referential integrity can become a significant development cost to the service.

LITTLE SUPPORT

Finally, the biggest problem with sharding may be the lack of experience and expertise you'll find to help you. You'll get ample help with traditional RDBMS tools. Thousands of books, experts, tool chains, and discussion forums can help you resolve your problem when something goes wrong or you're wondering how to implement a new feature. But the Eclipse IDE won't have a shard view any time soon, and you won't find any automated backup and restore programs for your shard.

With sharding, you're on your own, although the future looks promising. LiveJournal makes its tool chain available. Hibernate has a library under development. MySQL has added support for partitioning. But in the short term, sharding is something you must implement yourself.

5.2.7 Sharding in real life: how Flickr's sharding works

Let's look at how Flickr implemented sharding, to understand the concept more deeply. We've drawn this discussion from materials produced by Flickr's CTO Cal Henderson as well as the website High Scalability at http://highscalability.com, which is an excellent resource for sharding in practice and other topics relating to scaling to enormous levels. Let's begin by examining the overall profile of the Flickr service (see figure 5.7). Clearly, this service has a large number of registered users and a lot of data.

FLICKR'S DATABASE PARTITIONING SCHEME

Flickr's equivalent to the `GetDatabaseFor()` method assigns a random number for new accounts and uses this number as an index into the correct shard for this new user:

```
ShardToUse = RandomNumber mod NumberofShards
```

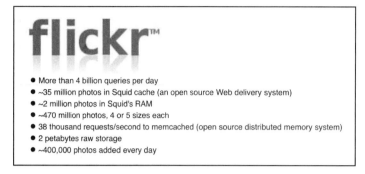

- More than 4 billion queries per day
- ~35 million photos in Squid cache (an open source Web delivery system)
- ~2 million photos in Squid's RAM
- ~470 million photos, 4 or 5 sizes each
- 38 thousand requests/second to memcached (open source distributed memory system)
- 2 petabytes raw storage
- ~400,000 photos added every day

Figure 5.7   The profile of the Flickr photo-sharing site, showcasing its large number of users and data

My data is stored on my shard, but the record of me performing an action on your comment is stored on your shard.

Shards contain a slice of the main database. The main database employs 100 percent replication in a dual-master architecture. Migration of certain users is done manually from time to time. A minor percentage of extreme power users destroy the nice balance between shards, and it's important to restore that balance by migrating these types of users off to a different area of the database. Even on a site as big and active as Flickr, migration can be done manually.

Each shard is designed to hold approximately 400,000+ users' data (apart from the photos themselves). Interestingly, a lot of data is stored twice. For example, a comment is part of the relation between the commenter and the commentee. Where is the comment stored? Both places. This is a good tradeoff between performance and disk use.

Certain operations, such as clicking a favorite, access several shards. First, the photo owner's account is pulled from cache to get the shard location for this user. Then, it pulls my information from cache to get my shard location. Next, a distributed transaction is started to answer a question like, "Who favorited my photo?"

FLICKR'S RELIABILITY STRATEGY

To get rid of replication lag, on every page load, the user is assigned to a bucket. If a host is down, Flickr goes to the next host in the list; if all hosts are down, it displays an error page. Flickr doesn't use persistent connections; it builds connections and tears them down. Every page load tests the connection. You can see the architecture that evolved to handle this level of demand in figure 5.8.

Each server in a shard is 50 percent loaded. Flickr can shut down half the servers in each shard. It's designed such that one server in the shard can take the full load if a server of that shard is down or in maintenance mode. To upgrade, all the company has to do is shut down half the shards, upgrade that half, and then repeat the process.

As you've seen, sharding is not only a powerful strategy for building high-scalability applications but also a common one. Google, Yahoo!, Flickr, Facebook, and many other sites that deal with huge user communities have found common ground that database

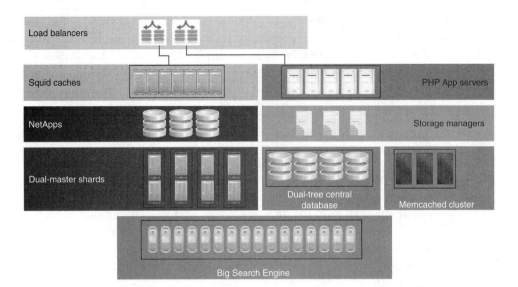

Figure 5.8 Flickr's architecture includes many levels. First is load balancing as incoming connection requests arrive. Squid caches are open-source web-delivery systems that operate as reverse proxies for HTML pages and images. The PHP App Servers connect to the shards and keep the data consistent. The storage managers do the actual mapping from an index to the correct shard. NetApps are for mass storage of photos. Their fundamental database architecture uses dual masters for each shard. This gives them resilience in the case of failure. The dual-tree structure is a custom set of changes to MySQL that allows scaling by incrementally adding masters without a ring architecture. The central database includes data, such as the users table, which includes primary user keys (a few different IDs) and a pointer to which shard a user's data can be found on. The Big Search Engine is a replication of the database Flickr wants to search.

partitioning in this way is a must to enable a good user experience. Next, let's look at how to design for scale that isn't necessarily based on a large user community—it may be compute-based—and that isn't consistent over time—demand ebbs and flows. For these scenarios, cloudbursting is proving to be the standard solution that's commonly employed.

5.3   *Designing for on-demand capacity: cloudbursting*

In the last section, we focused on the database issues that most inhibit scale. They can hopelessly throttle a cloud application that suddenly starts to see a dramatic spike in popularity and growth. Before you anticipate the kind of scale that warrants refactoring for sharding, you may have an application that runs in your data center that can or already does get to the point where it needs more capacity. You could buy more servers and keep them unused and on standby for when this situation occurs. Or you could keep only the capacity your application needs most of the time and, when it needs more, expand not within your own data center but out to the cloud. Think of it like having unexpected houseguests and not enough beds; you don't buy a bigger house with more bedrooms, you put up the overflow in a nearby hotel.

Another scenario where a data center application may need additional capacity is when a portion of your application involves highly sensitive data, and you want to process it only inside your data center. The rest of the application, which also presumably needs additional capacity you can't provide in the data center, runs in the cloud. You can handle both these capacity-related issues by careful design using a technique called *cloudbursting*.

5.3.1 Cloudbursting defined

What is cloudbursting? Let's define it more precisely. In earlier chapters, you read that the public cloud is a single application running on an elastic infrastructure that a third-party service provider buys and maintains. It's shared by many users simultaneously, all paid for on a pay-as-you-go basis. In chapter 4, we covered private clouds, where the third-party service provider attribute is dropped. Now, with cloudbursting, let's modify the single-application context as well and talk about applications that partially run in a local data center and partially in a public or private cloud.

> **CLOUDBURSTING** In 2009, the National Institute of Standards and Technology (NIST) published its formal definition of cloud computing, which included the concept of *cloudbursting* as cloud infrastructure that is a composition of two or more clouds (private, community, or public) that remain unique entities but are bound together by standardized or proprietary technology that enables data and application portability.

The *bursting* concept has been applied in IT before but normally to resource allocation and automated provisioning/deprovisioning of bandwidth. Today, in the cloud, it's being applied to resources such as application servers, application delivery systems, and other infrastructure required to provide on-demand computing environments that expand and contract as necessary without manual intervention.

5.3.2 The best of both worlds: internal data center plus cloud

Suppose an organization appreciates the benefits of cloud computing but would prefer to take a more careful and measured approach. It has the option of a hybrid approach

---

The (alternative) negative definition of a cloudburst

Here's a negative definition of the term *cloudburst*, by Nicholas Carr: "[It is] the failure of a cloud-computing environment due to the inability to handle a spike in demand." Carr was reporting on some issues that came out of poor performance from Intuit's cloud; he said, "The only way to do cloud computing efficiently is to share the cloud—to establish a broad, multitenant grid (or a number of them) that balances the loads of many different companies. Otherwise, it'll be one cloudburst after another, [alternating with] a whole lot of underutilized capital assets."

for moving to the cloud, where core business processes remain inside the firewall and periodic or overflow processing happens on the cloud. This best-of-both-worlds design pattern was the genesis of cloudbursting.

INTERNAL APPLICATION THAT ADAPTS DYNAMICALLY

Cloudbursting describes an evolving model that marries the traditional safe enterprise-computing model with cloud computing. The cloud shoulders the burden of some of an application's processing. For example, the cloud provides the basic application functionality, whereas more critical (revenue-generating) functions continue to be served from within the controlled enterprise data center.

BURSTS OUT TO THE CLOUD WHEN DEMAND SPIKES

How do you move from your local data center to the cloud? You need to add load-balancing (or some strategic control point that acts much the same). Such load-balancing provides a means to redirect requests to an external cloud in the event that corporate resources are depleted. When a request is received, the global load-balancer decides which data center (corporate or cloud) should handle the request based on its understanding of capacity. Because the data-center application suddenly comes out of the data center and immediately enters the cloud, this concept began being described as *bursting*.

5.3.3 Cloudbursting business case

The strongest business case for cloudbursting is both simple and compelling: seasonal or event-based peaks of traffic that push infrastructure over its capacity. But because they aren't consistent, they don't justify the cost of investing in additional hardware that would otherwise sit idle.

It's hard to provision an application correctly. To err on the side of safety, most data-center applications are overprovisioned, which has led to consistently low utilization of data-center compute resources. Often, data centers are either overprovisioned with servers that sit idle most of the time or have insufficient capacity planning that causes outages or (at a minimum) poor service for users. Buying exactly the right processing capacities from the start is impossible. Even with the best estimate, you'll either have excessive capacities or will miss some spikes.

Let's look at a cost comparison between data-center provisioning and elastic cloud provisioning.

AN EXAMPLE BUSINESS CASE

Take a hypothetical example: Reign.net provisions an application with a server costing $500. The server handles the target application it will be running at baseline user load. If Reign.net tries to provision for a huge two-day spike with 10 Amazon EC2 medium CPU virtual machines to handle spikes (the price is $0.20 per hour each), then the total cost of handling the projected spike is around $48. To adequately cover this spike locally would require an expense of $5,000 for 10 servers that would be idle most of the time.

Given this compelling business case, you may ask why you wouldn't move everything to the cloud. It's important to note several reasons:

- Cloud computing solutions are generally more expensive when it comes to long-term consumption (compared to existing offerings by hosting companies).

- Cloudbursting is a more complex solution to implement (from the delivery and maintenance standpoints).

- Today, using any cloud still comes with a certain vendor lock-in cost. When you have your entire infrastructure in a single cloud, it's not easy to move it to a different cloud (particularly because we don't have a well-established cloud computing market, or standards, or even portability yet).

To reduce the dependency on a single cloud provider, Reign.net can use several cloud-computing providers, picking whichever is better for the situation—but that further complicates the solution and makes it more expensive.

THE EVENTSEER CLOUDBURSTING BUSINESS CASE

Going back to a real-world example that we mentioned earlier, let's look at how Eventseer architected its solution to include cloudbursting. First, let's review the business problem the company was trying to solve. Eventseer is an academic event tracker that contains some 8,000 event listings. It has a database of 573,000 people, 4,000 research topics, and 3,000 organizations, each of which has its own page. This adds up to almost 600,000 worth of pages. All the pages are highly interconnected, so each added event tends to require a considerable number of page updates.

As traffic grew, Eventseer was becoming slower. Navigating the site involved noticeable delays. Traffic analysis showed the average server load to be consistently high. Some of the obvious solutions, such as reducing the number of database queries per page view or caching rendered pages, were helpful but not satisfactory.

The ultimate bottleneck was that each and every request was sent through the full dynamic page-rendering cycle. With increasing traffic, that overhead compounded. Spreading the load across additional servers only addressed the symptom, not the core problem. What pushed the site over the edge was search-engine traffic: being continuously pounded by multiple search engines crawling those 600,000 dynamically generated pages took its toll.

Eventseer.net decided to explore generating static pages every night to handle search-engine crawlers, first-time users, and other non-authenticated users for whom static pages are sufficient. This would speed up those users' experience dramatically and free up CPU cycles for the many fewer registered visitors who must have dynamically generated pages. Great solution, but it created a business problem because generating all 600,000 of these static pages every night took seven days on a single server. This led them to a cloudbursting architecture.

And architecture is the next topic we need to delve into. Assuming a compelling business case for your situation, how do the internal data center and the cloud communicate, and how does the application shift from one to the other? You'll find the answers in the next section.

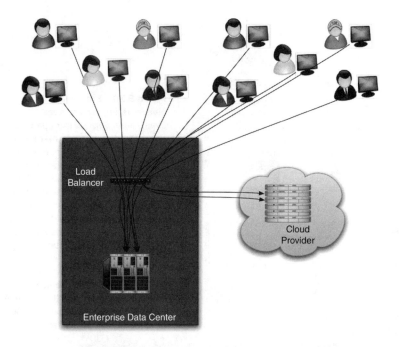

Figure 5.9   A highly simplified cloudbursting architecture showing that most users are directed by the load-balancer to the data center. After capacity is reached, additional users are directed to the cloud-resident portion of this application.

5.3.4 *Cloudbursting architecture*

A simple architecture diagram shows that cloudbursting, although backed by some compelling business-case numbers, isn't for the faint of heart. It's complicated. Figure 5.9 shows a highly simplified cloudbursting architecture.

Static page generation has no cross-page dependencies and can easily be split across several servers. Eventseer, from the earlier example, wanted to make sure the pages were done in a single night. The site divided the processing tasks into batches that each took roughly five hours to complete and split them across as many Amazon EC2 instances as needed (25 in this case). The cost was about $12.50.

You can see why IaaS works best for cloudbursting: an Amazon Machine Image (AMI) with the identical packages and software as your production server must be created. You only have to make sure the instances launched from that AMI are working with the freshest available data.

For Eventseer, the full database is regularly synced with Amazon Simple Storage Service (S3)—see figure 5.10. After launching the EC2 instances, each instance is instantiated with the latest data from S3. When the processing job is finished, the results are sent to the production server, the EC2 instances terminate themselves, and Eventseer stops paying for them.

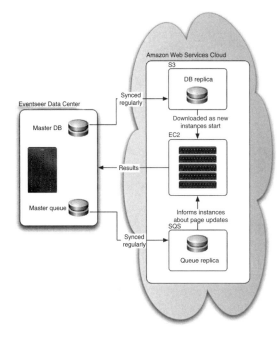

Figure 5.10   Eventseer's cloudbursting architecture. Eventseer's data center operates the production servers that serve all pages to site visitors, the master database, and the master queue of pages that need updating. The database is synced regularly over to Amazon's S3 so a replica of the current database is resident in the cloud when needed. Twice a day, an array of AMIs are spun up in EC2, and each is provided a copy of the database replica. Work to perform comes from the queue, which is updated periodically. Final static pages are sent back to the production data center at Eventseer.

Keeping the static files up to date is the most difficult part of Eventseer's dynamic-to-static conversion. Whenever an event is added, hundreds of pages may have to be updated. It would be too time-consuming and unnecessary to do these updates on the fly because it's not crucial that all pages be immediately updated. Delegating this task to regularly executed cloud-based servers is therefore workable.

To keep track of pending changes, Eventseer sets up a queuing system using Amazon's Simple Queue Service (SQS). Each page-update request is first added to a local queue that's regularly kept in synch with a remote queue on Amazon. The motivation for having two separate queues is for those times when Amazon is unavailable.

Twice a day, the required number of EC2 instances are automatically launched on Amazon. The most current version of the database is fetched from S3 and installed on each instance. Then, page-update requests are fetched one at a time from SQS until the queue is empty. Finally, all the generated static files are sent to the production server and installed at their correct location. When the EC2 instances are no longer needed, they shut themselves down.

This solution, when compared with the cost of purchasing dedicated server capacity, proved inexpensive for Eventseer.

5.3.5   *A recipe for implementing cloudbursting*

Let's get more specific and prescriptive now and walk through what your design has to include to cloudburst. Let's assume that at the top level, this application has an input task queue for work that it needs to do and an output queue for the results of the work it performs.

You begin by adding a Manager component to your system (it can be a separate process or a loop in a background thread). It continuously watches for the number of incoming requests (user sessions, perhaps) to be processed. Should it become obvious that your processing capacities aren't enough to keep up with the demand, it will issue requests to the cloud-computing API to deploy new virtual machines (Amazon EC2 already has such a REST-based API available; Windows Azure and others will follow suit).

Each virtual machine usually comes preconfigured with a worker role. This preconfiguration can be done by

- Deploying an application or scripts to the cloud (if this cloud service is a PaaS provider, such as Google App Engine or Windows Azure)
- Uploading a preconfigured VM image (if the cloud is an IaaS provider, such as Amazon EC2)

When this worker boots up in the cloud, it only needs the addresses of the task and result queues to start processing jobs. These parameters are usually passed as arguments along with the deployment calls.

To let the cloud workers access these queues in a secure way, you need to expose them via some encrypted service API, implemented in a flavor of communication framework of your choice (such as Amazon SQS).

When the Manager detects that you no longer need the same processing power from the cloud, it shuts down these workers, again providing you the cloud benefit of only paying for what you use.

A cloudbursting appliance

Nothing yet exists that meets the general need for cloudbursting, but it soon will. The idea would be to have a virtualized server environment that runs in your data center that builds virtual machine instances compatible with the cloud provider of choice. When the local environment is taxed to its limits, the next virtual machine instances are created by the same appliance up on the cloud, and the appliance handles all data-center-to-cloud communication transparently. Local users never know the application had to expand out to the cloud.

Note that the IBM cloudbursting appliance isn't this. It's useful only for building private clouds and wasn't appropriately named.

5.3.6 Cloudbursting: calling out for standards

Provisioning instances in Amazon EC2 is relatively easy; moving live workloads across a wide area network isn't. In most modern dynamic applications, the idea of having a *hot cloud standby* or a prebuilt virtual machine waiting in the wings would solve a lot of problems. But in reality, a number of complexities need to be overcome. These complexities range from network optimization to secure data transfer and replication to load-balancing across geographically diverse hosting environments, to name a few.

Case study: USA.gov

USA.gov, one of the busiest U.S. government websites, has achieved significant cost savings by embracing cloud computing. The U.S. General Services Administration (GSA) has migrated all the core resources of the USA.gov web portal to Terremark's IaaS platform, The Enterprise Cloud.

By cloudbursting to The Enterprise Cloud, USA.gov can maintain a small persistent footprint and deploy on-demand scaling as traffic fluctuates. GSA said this migration to the cloud has brought about a number of benefits and savings, such as avoiding idle server costs while still accommodating huge traffic spikes, acting on users' requests in real time, and applying security constraints on this platform. With infrastructure flexibility at the foundation, GSA has found both cost savings and capability improvement with its new cloud platform.

5.3.7 *The data-access problem with cloudbursting*

Cloudbursting promises to maximize agility while minimizing cost, but there's the nagging question of what exactly to do about the data such distributed applications require or generate. The original data-center-resident version of this application probably never envisioned that it might expand to the cloud; but when it does, where does it get its input data, and where should it store its output data? (In the Eventseer case study, the company addressed this head-on by having all interactions with the cloud extension of the data center in batch mode—see case 4 in the following subsections.)

Let's look at several strategies for dealing with cloudburst data. The following are five scenarios as described by Joe Weinman of AT&T Business Solutions. One of them may fit both your application's requirements and your enterprise's overall business model.

CASE 1: INDEPENDENT CLUSTERS

In the first scenario, minimal communication and data-sharing requirements exist between the application instances running in the enterprise and cloud data centers. Global load-balancers direct requests to either location, but the application instances running in the cloud don't need to communicate (much) with the ones in the enterprise data center. Because these load-balancers are probably already in place, you have no significant marginal cost of infrastructure to enable cloudbursting—only a requirement to keep contextual information, such as resource allocation, current. Applications that involve data coming to and from users that doesn't need to be saved between sessions—such as generating downloadable videos from uploaded photos—may not require much of a connection between the enterprise and the cloud.

Although this architecture provides excellent economics, it doesn't cover all situations. You may have data in the enterprise data center that needs to be accessed by the cloud-resident application, or new data may be acquired or produced as the cloud-based instances run. This must then be consolidated with what's in the enterprise data center. You'll see how to handle such scenarios next.

CASE 2: REMOTE ACCESS TO CONSOLIDATED DATA

The easiest approach to access and update enterprise data may be for application instances running in the cloud to access a single-instance data store. The viability of this approach depends on the pattern and intensity of reads and writes from the cloud data center to the enterprise. It also depends on the bandwidth, latency, and protocol support of the data-networking or storage-networking approach used to connect the cloud application to the enterprise-based data. This can be block-oriented, network-attached, content-addressed, or a database server.

CASE 3: ON-DEMAND DATA PLACEMENT

Placing cloud data centers on a global network backbone can enhance performance and latency. But if I/O intensity and/or network latency are too high for remote access, then any needed data that isn't already in the cloud must be placed there at the beginning of the cloudburst. Also, any changes must be consolidated in the enterprise store at the end of the cloudburst. The question is, "How much data needs to get where, and how quickly?"

You may require a large data set, either because all the data is needed for computation (such as with seismic or protein-folding analysis) or because the pattern of reads is unpredictable and as such needs to be present just in case. Then, even with fast file-transfer techniques, you have three options:

- Withstand delays when beginning cloudbursting (from trying to pass a lot of data through a small pipe or by using physical disk delivery).
- Pre-position a large-bandwidth pipe to quickly migrate the data, impacting cost.
- Move to more of an on-demand, pay-per-use approach for network capacity.

CASE 4: PRE-POSITIONED DATA PLACEMENT

Pre-positioning the data in the cloud to support application/server cloudbursting can be effective from a performance perspective. But it adds cost, because you must deploy a full secondary storage environment and a metro or wide-area network. This impacts the breakeven point for cloudbursting.

CASE 5: BUSINESS CONTINUITY/DISASTER RECOVERY PLUS CLOUDBURSTING

If the cloud location doubles as the data-mirroring or replication site for business continuity/disaster recovery, then support for cloudbursting can come with little additional cost, such as new operational procedures. But this may imply a requirement for bidirectional primary/secondary volumes. For example, data written at the enterprise site is replicated to the cloud, whereas data written in the cloud is replicated to the enterprise. And the primary/secondary volume designation must be fungible, or some sort of distributed data management and possibly distributed record-locking strategy must be implemented. Technology to do this is still evolving.

Understanding storage options is key for two reasons. First, the business case for cloudbursting may change. Saving a little on virtual server hours looks less attractive if you require expensive wide-area storage networking. On the other hand, an optimal architecture can kill multiple birds with one stone—agility, business continuity, and cost-minimization—while meeting transaction throughput and latency requirements through distributed, on-net processing. Second, different scenarios require different network interconnects between the enterprise and the cloud. The internet alone may be fine if clusters are independent; but for many scenarios, you may require much higher-speed mechanisms. We'll focus on the various options for large and expanding quantities of cloud storage in the next section.

5.4   Designing for exponentially expanding storage

In these days of Web 2.0, with picture and video sharing all the rage and some social networks growing bigger than 400 million registered users, it's not hard to understand why we need to talk about exponentially expanding storage. It's the rare application that needs the kind of storage that YouTube, Flickr, and Facebook require (see table 5.2). But even more modest applications are finding it desirable to include video- or photo-upload capability. Many more applications need to be designed for expanding storage than used to be the case. Not surprisingly, the cloud is excellent for providing expanding storage capacity. Let's address how applications take advantage of this capability.

Table 5.2   Some very large data hoarders

YouTube	1 billion video views per day (11,574 views per second)
Facebook	15 billion photos (and 60 billion image files with replication for different sizes)
	220 million new photos added every week
	1.5 PB of storage for photos; growing at 25 TB per week
Flickr	2 PB of storage to serve 2 billion photos from 4 billion queries per day
	400,000 photos added per day
PlentyOfFish	30+ million hits per day leading to 1.1 billion page views
	1 TB/day serving 171 million images
	6 TB storage array for millions of images uploaded per day

5.4.1   Cloud storage defined

Cloud storage is storage accessed over a network (internal or external) via web services APIs. Cloud storage access APIs are typically RESTful in nature. Representational state transfer (REST) is a style of software architecture for distributed hypermedia systems, such as the World Wide Web itself. RESTful means conforming to the REST model of an architecture consisting of clients and servers, where clients initiate requests to servers and servers process requests and return appropriate responses.

Similar to thinking of compute as elastic thanks to server virtualization, you can look at cloud storage as an abstracted layer of storage as opposed to the storage device directly. As you can imagine, this simplifies integration and development, and facilitates the introduction of many desirable features and options we'll discuss here.

5.4.2   *Amazon S3*

Amazon's S3 was the first and is the most successful cloud storage service. With the release of S3 in March 2006, for the first time, a large pool of storage was available for use where it was accessed via web services APIs on a nonpersistent network connection. You had immediate availability of very large quantities of storage, which operated on a pay-for-what-you use model. The most important attributes of cloud storage are that it must be scalable, reliable, fast, inexpensive, and simple.

Amazon was able to benefit from a decade of work on its own storage system that had all these requirements before exposing it to the outside world through a simple API. This is why S3 worked so well from the start and took off as a highly successful service.

5.4.3   *Example cloud storage API (using S3)*

It's useful to examine the API of the largest and most successful cloud storage service, because just as the API to Amazon's EC2 is being copied and may become a de facto standard, so too may the S3 API become an industry standard.

The basic units of storage S3 deals with are *objects* and *buckets*. Objects are the entities used to write, read, and delete collections of data. Objects can be from 1 to 5 GB in size. You can have an unlimited number of objects in S3. Objects are stored in buckets. You can specify whether the bucket is located in the United States or Europe. (Other locales will be available in the future. This becomes important when you're dealing with a specific country or region's regulations, such as a locale's privacy rules.) Access to a bucket is secure and can only proceed through a unique developer-assigned key. Within a bucket, each object can be made private, public, or with access rights granted to specific users. See table 5.3.

Table 5.3   Overview of the Amazon S3 API

API call	API description
GET *Service*	The GET operation returns a list of all the buckets owned by the authenticated sender of the request.
PUT *Bucket*	The PUT request operation with a bucket URI creates a new bucket. This is where you can specify a location constraint that affects where your data physically resides (such as U.S. or Europe).
PUT requestPayment	The PUT request operation with a requestPayment URI configures an existing bucket to be Requester Pays or not. With Requester Pays buckets, the requester, instead of the bucket owner, pays the cost of the request and the data download from the bucket. This is important when you want to share data but not incur charges associated with others accessing the data. You may, for example, use Requester Pays buckets when making available large data sets, such as various kinds of directories, reference data, and so forth.
GET *Bucket*	A GET request operation using a bucket URI lists information about the objects in the bucket if the requestor has READ access to the bucket.

Table 5.3 Overview of the Amazon S3 API *(continued)*

API call	API description
GET requestPayment	A GET request operation on a requestPayment resource returns the request payment configuration of a bucket: either Payer or Requester.
GET *Bucket Location*	A GET location request operation using a bucket URI lists the location constraint of the bucket. This can be very important when verifying that you're complying with certain E.U. regulations pertaining to data on E.U. citizens.
DELETE *Bucket*	The DELETE request operation deletes the bucket named in the URI. All objects in the bucket must be deleted before the bucket itself can be deleted. Only the bucket owner can do this.
PUT *Object*	The PUT request operation adds an object to a bucket. The response indicates that the object has been successfully stored.
COPY *Object*	The COPY operation creates a copy of an object already stored in Amazon S3.
GET *Object*	Objects are fetched using the GET operation. This operation returns objects directly from Amazon S3 using a client/server delivery mechanism.
HEAD *Object*	The HEAD operation is used to retrieve information about a specific object or object size, without fetching the object itself. This is useful if you're only interested in the object metadata.
DELETE *Object*	The DELETE request operation removes the specified object from Amazon S3. Once deleted, there is no method to restore or undelete an object.
POST *Object*	The POST request operation adds an object to a bucket using HTML forms. This is an alternate form of PUT that enables browser-based uploads.

Now, let's look at some sample code using a few of these APIs, to see how simple they are to use. First, the S3 API call to GET the service requires authentication with a valid access key user_ID. Here's the request:

```
GET / HTTP/1.1
Host: s3.amazonaws.com
Date: date
Authorization: signature
```

And here's the response:

```
HTTP/1.1 200 OK
x-amz-id-2: id
x-amz-request-id: request_id
Date: date
Content-Type: type
Content-Length: length
```

```
Connection: close
Server: AmazonS3

<?xml version="1.0" encoding="UTF-8"?>
<ListAllMyBucketsResult xmlns="http://doc.s3.amazonaws.com/2006-03-01">
  <Owner>
    <ID>user_id</ID>
    <DisplayName>display_name</DisplayName>
  </Owner>
  <Buckets>
    <Bucket>
      <Name>bucket_name</Name>
      <CreationDate>date</CreationDate>
    </Bucket>
    ...
  </Buckets>
</ListAllMyBucketsResult>
```

Next, the S3 API call PUT `Bucket` creates a new bucket identified by `request_id`. Here's the request:

```
PUT / HTTP/1.1

Host: destinationBucket.s3.amazonaws.com
Content-Length: 0
Date: date
Authorization: signature
```

And here's the response:

```
HTTP/1.1 200 OK
x-amz-id-2: id
x-amz-request-id: request_id
Date: date
Content-Length: 0
Connection: close
Server: AmazonS3
```

The S3 API call for reading an object uses GET `Object` with the `byte_range` of the object:

```
GET /destinationObject HTTP/1.1
Host: destinationBucket.s3.amazonaws.com
Date: date
Authorization: signature
Range:bytes=byte_range
```

The response is as follows:

```
HTTP/1.1 200 OK
x-amz-id-2: id
x-amz-request-id: request_id

Date: date
Last-Modified: Sun, 1 Jan 2006 12:00:00 GMT

ETag: "etag"
Content-Length: length
Content-Type: type
```

```
Connection: close
Server: AmazonS3
file_content
```

These code fragments demonstrate that each of the calls is simple and conforms to the standard HTTP GET and PUT structure. Each also has a Simple Object Access Protocol (SOAP) formulation as well as these RESTful versions.

5.4.4   Costs

Detailed cost information is available from each cloud storage vendor, but Amazon is setting the ceiling, and that ceiling is already low. Roughly, storage of a modest size (under 50 TB) runs $0.15/GB/month with an additional $0.10/GB data transfer in and $0.17/GB data transfer out. Amazon ties its services together by making transfers between S2 and EC2 free. All costs are higher for buckets located in Europe.

As low as these numbers look, be careful, because large-volume long-term storage can turn out to be very expensive. For example, to store 1 PB (remember, that's a quadrillion bytes or 1,000 TB or 1 million GB) on the cheapest commodity raw drives costs about $81,000. On EMC's NS-960, this would cost $2,860,000; and on Amazon S3 for three years, it would cost $2,806,000. That's not a typo! Granted, a petabyte is a lot of data; but as you saw at the beginning of this section on storage, the big video- and photo-sharing sites routinely get up to the petabyte levels.

S3 is about raw storage with no structure and no structured way for it to interact with applications running in the cloud. One type of storage structure that has been built on top of S3 is the ability to mount a file system so that applications think they're dealing with a file system as if they had formatted disk drives attached to each server.

5.4.5   Mountable file systems in the cloud

If the model of unstructured buckets containing objects of an arbitrary number of bytes used by S3 and other cloud storage services isn't the right model for an application, you have another model for elastic storage that looks like a file system or database to an application running in EC2—services, such as Elastic Block Store (EBS). When an instance in EC2 shuts down normally, its data is lost instantly. The only way to maintain its data after shutdown is through EBS. As you might imagine, EBS is additional functionality built on top of S3.

EBS volumes can be from 1 GB to 1 TB in size. After a volume is created, it can be attached to an Amazon EC2 instance. When it's attached, it appears as a mounted device similar to any hard drive or other block device. At that point, the instance can interact with the volume as it would with a local drive, formatting it with a file system or installing applications on it directly.

You can attach a volume to only one instance at a time, but many volumes can be attached to a single instance. This means you can attach multiple volumes and stripe your data across them for increased I/O and throughput performance. This is particularly helpful for database-style applications that frequently encounter many random reads and writes across the data set. If an instance fails or is detached from an Amazon EBS volume, you can attach the volume to another instance.

5.4.6 Addressing the challenging issue of latency

The delay from request for a chunk of data to its ultimate delivery—*latency*—is a big problem when you're transferring data across a wide area network or the internet. Local disk subsystems these days typically deliver data with latency of five milliseconds or less. What about the internet? Pinging 15 of the most popular sites as listed by Alexa once a second for a period of one minute produced the following results:

- *Average latency*—72 ms
- *Maximum latency*—142 ms
- *Minimum latency*—25 ms

An average latency almost 14½ times what even a disk read would be is a high price to pay to shift something to the cloud, and for some applications this is a show stopper.

The number-one strategy to combat latency is to move the data as close to users as possible. This is what content-delivery networks such as Akamai have built huge businesses on. The same concept of content delivery can be employed by cloud applications to take the data out to the network edge so the content is as close as possible to consumers of that data. Again, the cloud provider that has the longest lead over all the others in the market is Amazon. It has a mature enough service to have already developed a content-delivery capability called CloudFront to help solve the latency issue.

Content delivered to the edge can largely solve the latency problem for distribution of files to end users: the output side of the equation. But what about the input side? For example, what if you run your application in your data center but want to use the cloud strictly for storage? You probably need to carefully examine your application's data-usage patterns with latency for both the input and output sides clearly in mind. Output destined for end users should be pushed out to the cloud and from there out to the network edge using content delivery.

When you're planning for the input side of the data your application needs, make sure any data streaming in from cloud storage to your application is also as physically close to your data center servers as possible. This is because every router and switch between the portion of your application doing compute and where the data resides adds to the latency. Choose a cloud storage provider that guarantees you geographic control over your storage and has a facility close to yours.

Now you know why design and architecture issues need to be carefully considered when you're moving or building an application for the cloud and expect it to scale in terms of steadily growing user base, rapidly growing and shrinking user community, high-demand compute loads, or exponentially growing storage requirements.

5.5   *Summary*

In this chapter, we began to answer the question, "How do you move to the cloud?" We looked at design and architecture issues germane to both refactored applications being moved to the cloud and to new applications purpose-built to run in the cloud. The big design topics covered included using sharding to scale very large applications that have databases (because databases frequently become the barrier to scaling), using cloudbursting to keep an application resident in the local data center with overflow capacity provide by the cloud, and using cloud storage services to scale data-storage capacity quickly and easily.

In the next chapter, we'll focus on reliability issues that arise in the cloud when hundreds or even thousands of servers are employed by an application.

Achieving high reliability at cloud scale

This chapter covers
- SOA as a precursor to the cloud
- How loose coupling improves reliability
- Distributed high-performance cloud reliability, including MapReduce

The cloud is great for dealing with scale because the public Infrastructure as a Service (IaaS) as well as Platform as a Service (PaaS) clouds are large collections of thousands of virtualized servers with tools that allow you to expand and contract the number of instances of your application according to demand. But what happens when you try to have literally thousands of commodity (cheap) computers all working in parallel? Well, some of them will fail as they reach the mean-time-to-failure point. You learned about designing and architecting for scalability in chapter 5. But in the event that you create a popular application (there'll be another Google and Facebook, have no fear), you need to be prepared to deal with those hardware failures. You need to design and architect those applications for reliability. Reliability is important for any application, no matter where it resides, if it's going to be put into production and in any way become mission critical. But the cloud presents interesting challenges as well as opportunities with respect to application reliability.

131

In the first section, you'll read about distributed systems, loose coupling, and how those principles led to Service Oriented Architectures (SOAs), the precursor to the cloud. Distributed systems have been around for decades, but we'll focus on the aspects of this architectural principle most relevant to the cloud. In the second section in this chapter, you'll read about a powerful paradigm called MapReduce that's being used extensively in the cloud to make highly reliable and highly scalable systems that can perform rapid tasks on massive amounts of data.

Let's start learning how to design and architect for application reliability in the cloud by going back to the advent of SOA and how they're a direct ancestor of cloud computing.

6.1   *SOA as a precursor to the cloud*

Distributed, loosely coupled systems, which formed the basis for SOA, are by now widely used by virtually every organization with an active web presence. They formed the direct precursor to cloud computing. This architecture also presents one of the best approaches to reliable (or at least fault-tolerant) systems. Let's begin this section by examining distributed systems and loose coupling before delving into SOA more deeply and seeing how it has informed reliable cloud computing approaches.

6.1.1   *Distributed systems*

The most important point about distributed systems, and why they can be more reliable than nondistributed systems, is that when properly implemented, they have no single point of failure. Distributed web architectures typically fall into one of several basic categories:

- *Client-server architectures are two-tier.*   Smart client code contacts the server for data and then formats and displays it to the user. Input at the client is committed back to the server when it represents a permanent change. The server is frequently little more than a database.

- *Three-tier architectures add a business-logic middle tier.*   Three-tier systems (see figure 6.1) move the client intelligence (also called *business logic*) to a middle tier so that stateless clients can be used. This simplifies application deployment. Most web applications are three-tier.

- *N-tier architectures usually refer to web applications that utilize more services.*   N-tier (see figure 6.2) typically refers to web applications that further forward their requests to other enterprise services. This type

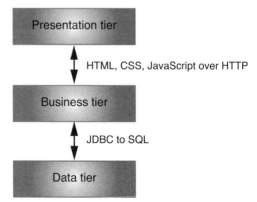

Figure 6.1   A three-tier architecture: Presentation layer + Business layer + Database layer

of application is the one most responsible for the success of application servers.

- *Tightly coupled (clustered) architectures are a form of parallel processing.* This refers typically to a cluster of machines that work closely together, running a shared process in parallel. The task is subdivided in parts made individually by each one and then put back together to make the final result.

- *Peer-to-peer is clientless and has no single point of failure that can cause total failure.* This type of architecture has no special machine or machines that provide a service or manage the network resources. Instead, all responsibilities are uniformly divided among all machines, known as *peers*. Peers can serve both as clients and servers.

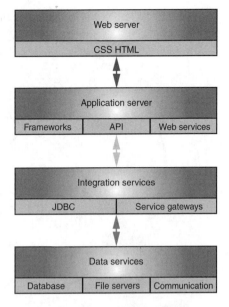

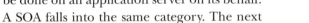

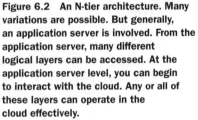

Figure 6.2 An N-tier architecture. Many variations are possible. But generally, an application server is involved. From the application server, many different logical layers can be accessed. At the application server level, you can begin to interact with the cloud. Any or all of these layers can operate in the cloud effectively.

This book focuses on the multitier architectures (three-tier and N-tier) because they apply best to the web and to the cloud. This is because the browser is the definition of a thin client *presentation* layer where the work has to be done on an application server on its behalf. A SOA falls into the same category. The next section will drill down into the SOA style of distributed application.

6.1.2 Loose coupling

In computer science, *coupling* refers to the degree of direct knowledge that one component has of another. It's the degree to which components depend on one another. What does this have to do with reliability or the cloud? Loose coupling affects reliability because each component that operates somewhat independently from all other objects can be built, tested, and replaced separately from all other objects. It's easier to build the other components such that they can handle when this component fails, either by failing gracefully themselves or by accessing another instance of this component running somewhere else. Earlier, you learned about humans interacting with websites through a browser, and one machine at one site interacting with another machine at another site. Loose coupling is the only application architecture that can provide reliable web applications, because one site never knows when another may be out, slow, or have made an unannounced change in its interface.

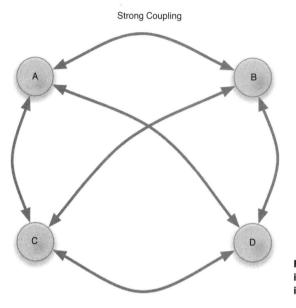

Strong Coupling

Figure 6.3   Strong coupling. Changes in A impact B, C, and D. Changes in B impact A, C, and D.

As some have pointed out, the ultimate way to make two components loosely coupled is to not connect them at all; short of that, make sure the communications between components don't depend on internals of the component and only access an abstract interface layer.

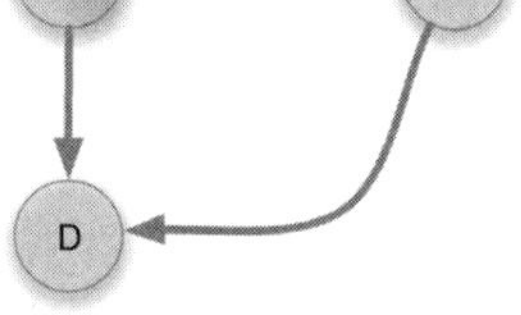

At the class level, *strong coupling* occurs when a dependent class contains a pointer directly to a concrete class that provides the required behavior. This is shown abstractly in figure 6.3. Loose coupling occurs when the dependent class contains a pointer only to an interface, which can then be implemented by one or many concrete classes. Loose coupling provides extensibility to designs (see figure 6.4). You can later add a new concrete class that implements the same interface without ever having to modify and recompile the dependent class. Strong coupling doesn't allow this.

Tight coupling leads to a situation where a change in one module forces a ripple effect of changes in other modules. Further, assembly of modules requires more effort and time due to the increased intermodule dependencies. One module may be harder to reuse because dependent modules must be included with it. Loosely coupled systems benefit from the negation of each of these characteristics.

Loose Coupling

Figure 6.4   Loose coupling. Modifications in A's behavior don't impact B, C, or D. Modifications in B's behavior *may* affect A but nothing else.

Tight versus loose coupling is an important concept for application reliability, SOAs, and ultimately reliable cloud applications. Table 6.1 lists a series of important characteristics of applications that can be measured against an application tightly

Table 6.1 Critical application attributes in tightly vs. loosely coupled architectures

	Tightly coupled	Loosely coupled
Technology mix	Homogeneous	Heterogeneous
Data typing	Dependent	Independent
Interface model	API	Service
Interaction style	RPC	Document
Synchronization	Synchronous	Asynchronous
Granularity	Object	Message
Syntactic definition	By convention	Self-describing
Semantic adaptation	By recoding	Via transformation
Bindings	Fixed and early	Delayed
Software objective	Reusability	Broad applicability
Consequences	Anticipated	Unintended

versus loosely coupled. This table is based on ideas originally expressed by Doug Kaye on his blog called Loosely Coupled (www.looselycoupled.com/blog/).

You can use a list of techniques to help create and maintain loose coupling in your application components. To achieve the desired loose coupling, use the following:

- Vendor- and platform-independent messages
- Stateless messaging where possible and appropriate
- Coarse-grained, self-describing, and self-contained messages
- Constrained, well-defined, extensible, and versionable interfaces
- Human-readable strings (URIs) for service and instance addresses
- Humans controlling clients where possible and appropriate
- Asynchronous exchange patterns where possible and appropriate

Web applications followed many of the attributes of loose coupling. When we moved toward machine-to-machine communication over the web, we retained the loose coupling and created the concept of SOA. Here, a remote *service* publishes its interface (via a WSDL), and a consuming service has to abide by that interface to consume the service. SOA was an important evolutionary step to get to the cloud. Let's look much more closely at how SOA works.

6.1.3 SOA

Computing has several different definitions of SOA. SOA is an attempt to provide a set of principles or governing concepts used during the phases of systems development and integration. It attempts to package functionality as interoperable services in the context of the various business domains that use it. Several departments in a company or different organizations may integrate or use such services—software modules provided as a service—even if their respective client systems are substantially different.

SOA is an attempt to develop yet another means for software module integration toward a distributed application. Rather than defining an API, SOA defines the interface in terms of protocols and functionality. An endpoint is the entry point for such an SOA implementation.

> **SOA** A flexible set of design principles used during the phases of systems development and integration. A deployed SOA-based architecture provides a loosely coupled suite of services that can be used in multiple business domains. SOA separates functions into distinct units, or *services*, which developers make accessible over a network (usually the internet) in order to allow users to combine and reuse them in the production of applications. These services, and their corresponding consumers, communicate with each other by passing data in a well-defined, shared format (usually XML), or by coordinating an activity between two or more services.

SOA is about breaking an architecture down to its functional primitives, understanding its information and behaviors, and building it up again using service interfaces abstracted into a configuration layer to create business solutions. SOA naturally fits the definition of loose coupling because it treats services as black boxes of functionality with a simple internet standards-based interface between these service components.

6.1.4 *SOA and loose coupling*

SOA in its simplest form was aimed at allowing one computer to access a capability across the internet on another computer that previously might have been accessed by a human through a browser. For example, an early web service allowed a site selling domain names to also start selling digital certificates, where the authentication of the certificate buyer was performed at a third-party site. (Previously, you would have gone to that third-party site and, using the browser, followed the authentication process, thus breaking the *stickiness* of the original vendor—which lost a buyer in the middle of a transaction.)

SOA enabled a form of aggregation where a web application could be constructed out of services, some of which were yours and some of which were delivered by others. In this way, SOA aims to allow users to string together fairly large chunks of functionality to form ad hoc applications built almost entirely from existing software services. The larger the chunks, the fewer the interface points required to implement any given set of functionality. But large chunks of functionality may not prove sufficiently granular for easy reuse. Each interface brings with it some amount of processing overhead. You must consider performance in choosing the granularity of services. The great promise of SOA suggests that the marginal cost of creating the nth application is low, because all the software required already exists to satisfy the requirements of other applications. Ideally, you require only orchestration to produce a new application.

For this to work well, no interactions must exist between the chunks specified or within the chunks themselves. Instead, you have to specify the interaction of services (all of them unassociated peers) in a relatively ad hoc way with the intent driven by newly emergent requirements. This is why services must be much larger units of functionality than traditional functions or classes, lest the sheer complexity of thousands of such granular objects overwhelm the application designer. Programmers develop the services themselves using traditional languages such as Java, C, and C++.

SOA services feature loose coupling, in contrast to the functions that a linker binds together to form an executable to a dynamically linked library, or to an assembly. SOA services also run in safe wrappers (such as Java or .NET) and in other programming languages that manage memory allocation and reclamation, allow ad hoc and late binding, and provide some degree of indeterminate data typing.

6.1.5 SOA and web services

Web services can implement a SOA. Web services make functional building blocks accessible over standard internet protocols (such as HTTP) independent of platforms and programming languages. These services can represent either new applications or wrappers around existing legacy systems to make them network-enabled.

Each SOA building block can play one or both of two roles: service provider or service consumer.

SERVICE PROVIDER

A *service provider* creates a web service and possibly publishes its interface and access information to a service registry. Each provider must decide which services to expose, how to make trade-offs between security and easy availability, and how to price the services or (if no charges apply) exploit them for other value. The provider also has to decide what category the service should be listed in for a given broker service and what sort of trading partner agreements are required to use the service. It registers what services are available within it and lists all the potential service recipients.

The implementer of the broker then decides the scope of the broker. You can find public brokers through the internet, whereas private brokers are only accessible to a limited audience—for example, users of a company intranet. Furthermore, you must decide on the amount of offered information. Some brokers specialize in many listings. Others offer high levels of trust in the listed services. Some cover a broad landscape of services, and others focus within an industry. Some brokers catalog other brokers. Depending on the business model, brokers can attempt to maximize look-up requests, number of listings, or accuracy of the listings.

The Universal Description Discovery and Integration (UDDI) specification defines a way to publish and discover information about web services. Other service broker technologies include (for example) Electronic Business using eXtensible Markup Language (ebXML).

SERVICE CONSUMER

The *service consumer* or web service client locates entries in the broker registry using various find operations and then binds to the service provider in order to invoke one of its web services. Whichever service the service consumers need, they have to take it into the brokers, bind it with respective service, and then use it. They can access multiple services if the service provides multiple services.

Note that Amazon's cloud services are called Amazon *Web Services,* and Amazon is a web service provider in the way described here.

6.1.6   *SOA and cloud computing*

SOA and cloud computing can be paired to gain the benefits both of service deployments and of the scale and economics of the cloud. With cloud computing, enterprises can access services hosted on third-party servers over the internet. With SOA, enterprises use integrated application services in a more lightweight fashion than traditional application platforms.

Because cloud computing is a way of creating a system in which some or all of its IT resources exist within a third-party cloud computing resource, such as Amazon EC2 or Force.com, cloud computing can involve part or all of an architecture. The core difference is that the system is extended to resources that you don't own or host locally.

Putting this more simplistically, SOA is all about the process of defining an IT solution or architecture, whereas cloud computing is an architectural alternative. We can say that SOA can't be replaced by cloud computing. Most cloud computing solutions are defined through SOA. They don't compete—they're complementary notions.

Adopting SOA can prepare an enterprise for cloud computing by showing what challenges the organization faces internally in supporting service components— challenges that using cloud services will exacerbate. The service orientation in SOA and the cloud make for similarities, such as both concepts requiring a governance layer and a strong understanding of processes.

Both the cloud and SOA determine what some of the major reusable components are and what the right technologies to run large-scale components over open networks are. An organization that has moved toward SOA in a modular fashion is in a better position to move modules to the cloud.

Further, the cloud serves as a good way to deploy services in an SOA environment. SOA and the cloud support each other but aren't based on the same ideas. Cloud computing is a deployment architecture, not an architectural approach for how to architect your enterprise IT, whereas SOA is.

Components that reside on different computers (some or all of which are in the cloud) and must communicate over the network—potentially over the public internet— require communication between those components (or processes). It's important that your understanding of interprocess communication is current. The next section delves into a typical type of interprocess communication used in the cloud.

6.1.7   *Cloud-based interprocess communication*

Amazon Simple Queue Service (SQS) is a way of sending messages between applications (components in a distributed application) via web services over the internet. The intent of SQS is to provide a highly scalable and hosted message queue.

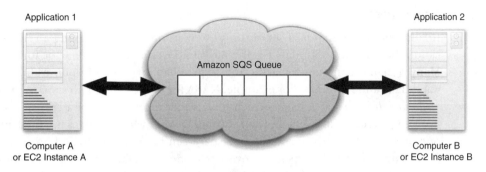

Figure 6.5   The simple structure of Amazon's SQS interprocess communication web service

SQS works in a complementary fashion with EC2. (See figure 6.5.) It's a highly reliable, scalable message queuing service that enables asynchronous message-based communication between distributed components of an application. Those components are typically EC2 instances. You can send any number of messages to an Amazon SQS queue at any time from any component. The messages can be retrieved from the same component or a different one right away or at a later time. No message is ever lost in the interim; each message is persistently stored in highly available, highly reliable queues. Multiple processes can read, write from, and write to an Amazon SQS queue at the same time without interfering with each other.

Now that you've delved into loose coupling, its incarnation in distributed applications, and the way in which those distributed application components may communicate across the internet, let's look at a framework called MapReduce that handles much of this infrastructure for you and yet allows scaling to a massive level, all the while giving you a simple way to maintain high reliability.

6.2   *Distributed high-performance cloud reliability*

In all engineering disciplines, *reliability* is the ability of a system to perform its required functions under stated conditions for a specified period of time. In software, for application reliability, this becomes the ability of a software application and all the components it depends on (operating system, hypervisor, servers, disks, network connections, power supplies, and so on) to execute without faults or halts all the way to completion. But *completion* is defined by the application designer. Even with perfectly written software and no detected bugs in all underlying software systems, applications that begin to use thousands of servers will run into the mean-time-to-failure in some piece of hardware, and some number of those instances will fail. Therefore, the application depending on those instances will also fail.

The cloud, with its tendency to use commodity hardware and virtualization, and with the potential for enormous scale, presents many additional challenges to designing reliable applications.

6.2.1 *Redundancy*

In addition to the standard set of things to consider when designing a reliable application, building in redundancy is the most important additional factor for the cloud. Many design techniques for achieving high reliability depend upon redundant software, data, and hardware. For example, NASA for decades has built systems called *triple modular redundancy with spares*, which means that three copies of a critical system are live and producing answers that run through a voter who produces the final answer. If one or more of the live systems fails, a spare can be powered up and brought online. Such redundancy helps ensure recovery from detected failure conditions. These techniques are expensive and complex but can be less so in the cloud because some of the hard stuff is provided by the cloud vendors.

For redundant software components, this may consist of double- or triple-redundant software components (portions of your application) running in parallel with common validation checks. One idea is to have the components developed by different teams based on the same specifications. This approach costs more, but extreme reliability may require it. Because each component is designed to perform the same function, the failures of concurrent identical components are easily discovered and corrected during quality-assurance testing. You should be cautious, because it's possible for separate developer teams to make the same error in reading the specification. Such common-cause errors are infrequent but do happen.

Although redundant software components provide the quality-assurance process with a clever way to validate service accuracy, certain applications may want to deploy component redundancy into the production environment. Such runtime component redundancy may be useful for situations where the runtime environment is hazardous and can't be strictly controlled (such as the space shuttle). In such hazardous conditions, multiple parallel application processes can provide validity checks on each other and let the majority rule. Although it's true that redundant software components cause extra resource consumption, the tradeoff between reliability and the cost of extra hardware may be worth it.

Another redundancy-based design technique is the use of services such as clustering (linking many computers together to act as a single faster computer), load-balancing (workloads kept balanced between multiple computers), data replication (making multiple identical copies of data to be processed independently and in parallel), and protecting complex operations with transactions to ensure process integrity. There is a lot less complexity when you use a cloud provider because it has in-built infrastructure that does this for you.

Redundant hardware is one of the most popular strategies for providing reliable systems. This includes redundant arrays of independent disks (RAID) for data storage, redundant network interfaces, and redundant power supplies. With this kind of hardware infrastructure, individual component failures can occur without affecting the overall reliability of the application. It's important to use standardized commodity hardware to allow easy installation and replacement.

6.2.2 *MapReduce*

MapReduce is a software framework invented by Google to solve the massive search problem it has across all content on the web, which, by the end of 2008, exceeded one trillion unique URLs. MapReduce is loosely coupled distributed computing on a massive scale, working on large data sets operated on by clusters of commodity (cheap) computers.

Why commodity computers? Because the numbers got so large that Google had no choice but to give up on hardware reliability and switch things over to have reliability provided by the software. The law of large numbers took over; and with hundreds of thousands of servers, even when each individual server has excellent reliability statistics, there will still be multiple failures per day as one machine or another reaches its mean-time-to-failure. The only way to build a reliable system on top of that is to have the software prepared to deal with those failures.

The name *MapReduce* has its roots in functional programming, inspired by the `map` and `reduce` functions first called out in the programming language Lisp.[1] In Lisp, a `map` takes as input a function and a sequence of values. It then applies the function to each value in the sequence. A `reduce` combines all the elements of a sequence using a binary operation. For example, it may use + to add all the elements in a sequence.

In addition to addressing reliability, this is parallel programming potentially on a massive scale, achieving huge performance gains. This is as important as reliability because given problems with data sets as large as the web, not doing the job with massive parallelism may mean the job won't get done.

THE PROBLEM MAPREDUCE SOLVES

MapReduce achieves reliability by parceling out operations on the data set to each node in a network. Each node reports back periodically with results and status updates. Obviously, a failed node remains silent. That node's master notes the dead worker node and sends its work out again. You can see the roles of master and worker illustrated in figure 6.6.

The master does the following:

1 Initializes the array and splits it into tasks according to the number of available workers
2 Sends each worker its subarray task
3 Receives the result from each worker

The worker does the following:

1 Receives the subarray task from the master
2 Performs processing on the subarray task
3 Returns the result to the master

---

[1] Harold Abelson, Gerald Jay Sussman, and Julie Sussman, *Structure and Interpretation of Computer Programs,* 2nd edition (MIT Press, 1996).

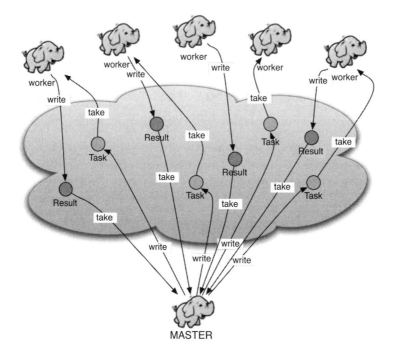

Figure 6.6   The roles of master and worker are depicted using the little elephant logo of the open source Hadoop implementation of MapReduce. The master divides the problem into tasks and assigns them to workers. Each worker performs its task and writes back a result that the master gathers into an overall result.

THE MAP STEP

Map, written by a user of the MapReduce library, takes an input pair and produces a set of intermediate key/value pairs. The MapReduce library groups together all intermediate values associated with the same intermediate key I (an arbitrary user-defined handle to organize intermediate results) and passes them to the reduce function.

A master node takes the input, chops it up into smaller subproblems, and distributes those subproblems to worker nodes.

Worker nodes may repeat the process as many levels as needed until they get the desired problem size. A worker node receiving appropriately sized problem processes the work and passes the result back to its parent node. Figure 6.7 shows the map function in the context of the entire MapReduce model.

Now, let's look at the reduce part.

THE REDUCE STEP

The reduce function, also written by the user, accepts an intermediate key I and a set of values for that key. It merges together these values to form a possibly smaller set of values. The master node takes the answers to all subproblems it spawned and combines them appropriately to produce an answer—the answer to the problem it was handed in the first place.

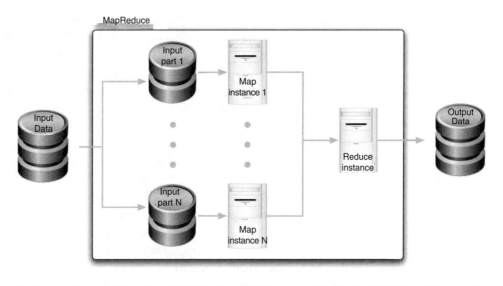

Figure 6.7   The `map` and `reduce` functions in a MapReduce model. The input data is partitioned into subparts, each of which is handed to a `map` function. It passes the output of all the `map` functions to a `reduce` function that prepares the final output.

Consider the problem of counting the number of occurrences of each word in a large collection of documents. The following shows the MapReduce code for such a problem:

```
void map(String name, String document):
  for each word w in document:
    EmitIntermediate(w, 1);

 void reduce(String word, Iterator partialCounts):
  int result = 0;
  for each pc in partialCounts:
    result += ParseInt(pc);
  Emit(result);
```

On the first line, `name` is the document name and `document` is the document contents. Then, for the `reduce` function, `word` is a word, and `partialCounts` is a list of aggregated partial counts.

The `map` function emits each word plus an associated count of occurrences (1, in this example). The `reduce` function sums together all the counts emitted for a particular word.

HOW MAPREDUCE WORKS

MapReduce implementations are sophisticated frameworks for reliable parallel processing in a highly distributed fashion. They specifically allow distributed processing of the `map` and `reduce` functions. Provided all `map` functions are independent of each other, all `maps` can be done in parallel. The key is any dependencies in the data set. There may in practice be limitations caused by the data source and/or number of CPUs near that data. The set of reducers operating on the same key produced by the map operations can perform the reduction phase in parallel as well.

At first glace, MapReduce may appear inefficient compared to more streamlined sequential algorithms. But remember, you can apply MapReduce to gigantic data sets much larger than any commodity server can handle. For example, a large server farm can use MapReduce to sort a petabyte (1 million GB) of data in only a few hours. More important, this massive parallelism allows smooth recovery from failures of servers or storage devices during processing, because you can reschedule map and reduce work as long as that step's data is still available.

Figure 6.8 shows a fairly detailed step-by-step examination of how MapReduce works. The MapReduce library in the user program first shards the input files into M pieces of typically 16 MB to 64 MB per piece. It then starts up many copies of the program on a cluster of machines. MapReduce then operates in the following way:

❶ One of the copies of the program is special: the master. The rest are workers assigned work by the master. M map tasks and R reduce tasks need to be assigned. The master picks idle workers and assigns each one a map task or a reduce task.

❷ A worker assigned a map task reads the contents of the corresponding input shard. It parses key/value pairs out of the input data and passes each pair to the user-defined map function. The intermediate key/value pairs produced by the map function are buffered in memory.

❸ Periodically, the buffered pairs are written to local disk, partitioned into R regions by the partitioning function. The locations of these buffered pairs on the local disk are passed back to the master responsible for forwarding these locations to the reduce workers.

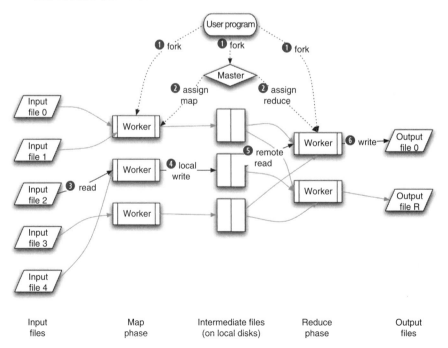

Figure 6.8   How MapReduce operates (see reference numbers in the above diagram)

④ When a reduce worker is notified by the master about these locations, it uses remote procedure calls to read the buffered data from the local disks of the `map` workers. When a `reduce` worker has read all intermediate data, it sorts it by the intermediate keys such that all occurrences of the same key are grouped together. If the amount of intermediate data is too large to fit in memory, an external sort is used.

⑤ The `reduce` worker iterates over the sorted intermediate data and, for each unique intermediate key encountered, passes the key and the corresponding set of intermediate values to the user's `reduce` function. The output of the `reduce` function is appended to a final output file for this `reduce` partition.

⑥ When all `map` tasks and `reduce` tasks have been completed, the master wakes up the user program. At this point, the MapReduce call in the user program returns back to the user code.

After successful completion, you can get the output of the MapReduce execution in the *R* output files.

RELIABILITY IN THE EVERYDAY CLOUD

According to published interviews with Google IT managers, in each cluster's first year, it's typical that 1,000 individual machine failures will occur; thousands of hard drive failures will occur; one power distribution unit will fail, bringing down 500 to 1,000 machines for about 6 hours; 20 racks will fail, each time causing 40 to 80 machines to vanish from the network; 5 racks will go wonky, with half their network packets missing in action; and the cluster will have to be rewired once, affecting 5 percent of the machines at any given moment over a 2-day span. Also, the cluster has about a 50 percent chance of overheating, taking down most of the servers in less than 5 minutes and taking 1 to 2 days to recover.

With this kind of scale, reliability has to be built into the software, not the hardware. As you've read, for this reason and to minimize hardware costs, Google opts to go with bare-bones commodity hardware and not high-end, supposedly bullet-proof machines.

You can better appreciate MapReduce by looking briefly at the handful of examples in table 6.2. It's been effectively employed by the largest web companies on the planet, such as Google and Yahoo!.

Table 6.2 Examples where MapReduce is used in high-scale production applications

Application	How MapReduce is employed
Distributed grep	The `map` function emits a line if it matches a given pattern. The `reduce` function is an identity function that copies the supplied intermediate data to the output.
Reverse web-link graph	The `map` function outputs `<target, source>` pairs for each link to a target URL found in a page named `source`. The `reduce` function concatenates the list of all source URLs associated with a given target URL and emits the pair `<target, list(source)>`.

Table 6.2   Examples where MapReduce is used in high-scale production applications (*continued*)

Application	How MapReduce is employed
Term-vector per host	A *term vector* summarizes the most important words that occur in a document or a set of documents as a list of `<word, frequency>` pairs. The map function emits a `<hostname, term vector>` pair for each input document (where the hostname is extracted from the URL of the document). It passes the `reduce` function all per-document term vectors for a given host. It adds together these term vectors, throwing away infrequent terms, and then emits a final `<hostname, term vector>` pair.
Inverted index	The map function parses each document and emits a sequence of `<word, document ID>` pairs. The `reduce` function accepts all pairs for a given word, sorts the corresponding document IDs, and emits a `<word, list(document ID)>` pair. The set of all output pairs forms a simple inverted index. It's easy to augment this computation to keep track of word positions.

6.2.3 Hadoop: the open source MapReduce

Fortunately, MapReduce hasn't stayed locked inside the proprietary domain of Google. Hadoop has been created as an Apache open source project to provide the rest of the world with the benefits of MapReduce. One of its major subprojects is its implementation of MapReduce, which is heavily used by many groups:

- *Amazon*—A9 product search, and also Elastic MapReduce as part of Amazon Web Services (tied to Elastic Compute Cloud)
- *Adobe*—Social services
- *Baidu*—Leading Chinese language search engine
- *Facebook*—4,800 CPU cluster used to store copies of internal log and dimension data sources
- *Hulu*—Log storage and analysis
- *IBM*—Blue Cloud, which is based on Hadoop
- *NetSeer*—1,000 EC2 instances running Hadoop for crawling, processing, servers, and log analysis
- *New York Times*—Large-scale image conversions run on EC2
- *Rackspace*—30-node cluster that parses and indexes logs from the email hosting system
- *Yahoo!*—Over 100,000 CPUs on more than 25,000 servers running Hadoop

A high-quality open source community has grown up around Hadoop. With the caliber of its various production deployments, it will remain robust and healthy going forward. The Manning book *Hadoop in Action* by Chuck Lam delves deeply into MapReduce as implemented in the open-source community, with lots of practical programming examples.

6.3 *Summary*

Designing and architecting for handling the potentially massive scale of users accessing your cloud-based application is important. Equally vital is preparing for keeping such an application and the massive number of servers (or instances) it may require up and running, with no failures affecting its users. In this chapter, we've done a quick review of the relevant reliability concepts when thinking about cloud applications, leading up to a detailed discussion of MapReduce, one of the most successful frameworks for reliability even on Google's massive scale. You now have the knowledge and tools necessary to plan for handling large numbers of users as well as handle the failures that will naturally occur given a large numbers of servers, providing for those users in a smooth and tractable way.

The next chapter builds on chapters 5 and 6 by getting into the practical issues of how to build, test, deploy, and operate an application in the cloud.

Testing, deployment, and operations in the cloud

Contributed by Patrick Lightbody[†]

This chapter covers

- How the typical software deployment model is improved by the cloud
- Using the cloud to improve development, testing, and operations
- Using parallelization for testing in all forms

The process of testing software is, and likely always will be, inherently a *spiky* activity. Companies aren't *always* testing. Even in software groups that employ the most rigorous agile methodologies, it's unlikely that automated tests are running 24x7—if only because the humans who trigger those tests by making software changes aren't working around the clock. For this reason, testing is quickly becoming one of the killer apps for cloud computing.

[†] Patrick is the founder of BrowserMob, a cloud-based website monitoring and load testing service provider. He is also the founder of OpenQA and a core contributor to Selenium, a popular open-source browser-testing framework. You can learn more about Patrick and his company at http://browsermob. com or by emailing him at patrick@browsermob.com.

In this chapter, we'll explore deployment models that are optimized for the cloud, and how clouds can have a drastic impact on how teams manage operations and testing. We'll also look at the various elements of testing that can be accelerated using the cloud.

To help you fully appreciate the sea change that cloud computing brings to testing and operations, we'll also spend some time looking at how people approach testing without the cloud. This includes how companies traditionally buy hardware for new projects, who is responsible for provisioning the software and hardware, and the typical breakdown between automated and manual testing.

In examining these different aspects of testing, we'll discuss not only how traditional Infrastructure as a Service (IaaS) vendors such as Amazon can accelerate automated testing, but also how new Software as a Service (SaaS) and Platform as a Service (PaaS) vendors (many of whom are built on Amazon EC2) are offering new services and cloud-based APIs that can accelerate manual and semi-automated testing. Let's get started by investigating some of the typical deployment models for software.

7.1 Typical software deployments

Before we can discuss how the cloud impacts testing, we need to be clear what the traditional deployment model looks like. For this exercise, let's use a fairly standard web-based application built on top of the Linux, Apache, MySQL, PHP (LAMP) stack. We'll rely on four well-known deployment environments you probably already use for most IT projects:

- *Production*—The place where your users/customers access the application and store their data.
- *Staging*—A clean environment meant to clone the production environment as closely as possible and be used as a final sanity check before deployment. You may do performance testing here in addition to final system testing.
- *Testing*—Typically smaller than staging and production, meant to contain test data and in-progress software that can be periodically checked for errors and regressions. Often utilized for functional testing and some performance testing.
- *Development*—Often a developer's desktop or laptop, this is where most of the code is written and initial testing and debugging takes place.

Prior to cloud computing, you could purchase these environments as physical machines or lease them from managed hosting providers, such as Rackspace. In an ideal world, the production, staging, and testing environments would be identical in terms of hardware and software configuration. But in the real world, budget constraints often result in staging and testing being considerably smaller than the production environment they aim to emulate.

7.1.1 Traditional deployment architecture

Consider a public-facing web application required to support at least 10,000 users browsing the site. Up until this point in the project, the web application has only been deployed on the developers' desktop computers. It's now time to purchase the hardware for these various environments.

The architect, working with performance engineers, estimates that the bottleneck will most probably be the web servers and that each web server can sustain up to 2,500 users browsing the site. Therefore, they should purchase four web servers, a load-balancer, two database servers (one master and one slave), and a networked file server. You can see the production environment in figure 7.1.

For green field projects, this hardware may be used first for testing, then for staging, and finally for production. During each phase of development and testing, the servers are wiped clean and reconfigured, ensuring that the environments don't carry over any junk data from previous testing. This only works for version 1 of this product. After the project is released and work begins on version 2 and beyond, you need separate staging and/or testing environments, because what is in production must not be perturbed. Completely separate and distinct environments must be used to test new versions of the software about to be moved to production.

7.1.2 *Defining staging and testing environments*

At this point, what the staging and testing environments (if any) look like is dictated by a variety of factors, including budget, the software architecture, and risk factors, such as how confident the team is that the master/slave configuration is necessary and sufficient.

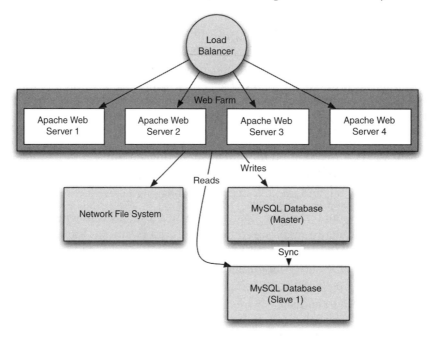

Figure 7.1   A typical production environment, which includes four web servers, a load-balancer, two database servers, and a networked file server, which hosts files shared to all four web servers

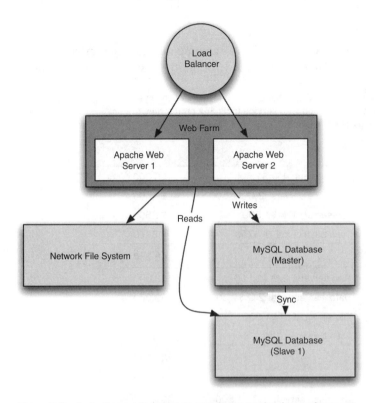

Figure 7.2   A staging environment to match the production environment in figure 7.1

Suppose the engineering and operations teams have decided that they need both load-balancing and MySQL master/slave replication in the staging environment to be confident in any configuration changes they push to production. They also want staging to be as similar as possible (within budget) to production. They decide on the deployment illustrated in figure 7.2.

As you can see, the basic architecture is kept intact: it includes load-balancing and MySQL data replication. The team has chosen to have fewer web servers, still believing that the web server is the main bottleneck and that adding double the web servers should double the number of users they can handle.

For the testing environment, the team has decided that neither the load-balancing nor MySQL replication is critical for the functional testing the QA team will do. As such, they opt for a simple two-server configuration, illustrated in figure 7.3.

Note that there is a risk that bugs related to functionality may be caused by either web server load-balancing or MySQL data replication. The team has determined that the cost savings in hardware is worth that risk.

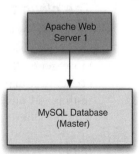

Figure 7.3   A simple testing environment with a single web server and single database

7.1.3   Budget calculations

You may ask, what is the final cost? Let's assume that each server costs $1,500 and the load-balancers cost $750 each. Each environment's cost is outlined in table 7.1.

Table 7.1   The capital expenditure budget calculations for the systems needed to support a production web service including production, staging, and testing versions of the service

Production		$11,250
	Web servers: 4 @ $1,500	$6,000
	Database servers: 2 @ $1,500	$3,000
	File server: 1 @ $1,500	$1,500
	Load balancer: 1 @ $750	$750
Staging		**$8,250**
	Web servers: 2 @ $1,500	$3,000
	Database servers: 2 @ $1,500	$3,000
	File server: 1 @ $1,500	$1,500
	Load balancer: 1 @ $750	$750
Testing		**$3,000**
	Web server: 1 @ $1,500	$1,500
	Database server: 1 @ $1,500	$1,500
Total		**$22,500**

The total of all systems is $22,500. And yet half of it is for staging and testing environments that are almost certain to spend long periods of time sitting idle. Even the production hardware isn't likely to be 100 percent utilized all the time. Let's explore how the cloud can not only cut down these costs but even make testing faster and operations better prepared to scale.

7.2   The cloud to the rescue

If you've ever worked in a development or operations team, the architecture and purchasing decisions we walked through in section 7.1 are likely familiar. The cloud—or, more generally, virtualization—is changing how people go through the previous exercise. Although it certainly saves money, it's also making businesses more efficient at testing and more prepared to scale with customer demand. Let's look at some of the ways the cloud can help your company.

7.2.1   Improving production operations with the cloud

The most commonly cited reason for moving to cloud computing is its ability to achieve *internet scale*. For example, if your hypothetical web application suddenly needed to scale to 100,000 users (10X growth) because the site was mentioned on *Oprah*, the traditional deployment model we went through earlier wouldn't work. There's no way to acquire another 36 web servers and some number of database servers on demand.

Although this scalability argument is one of the best for moving deployments and operations to public or private clouds, there are many good reasons to consider the cloud even if your applications will never get surges of traffic such as this.

ELASTIC BANDWIDTH

Whether you're building your own data center or renting space from an Internet Service Provider (ISP), you have to pay for bandwidth. Bandwidth is almost always metered, usually by a combination of total bytes transferred per month and peak throughput in terms of megabits per second. If you have your own data center, your data throughput may be limited by the size and type of network connection coming into your data center, possibly limiting the speed at which you can deliver content to your users.

Either way, it's often impossible or at least costly to quickly surge up to extreme levels of network throughput. Yet in a cloud model, you get the benefit of pooling resources to have much larger network throughput than you'll typically ever need but can tap into on occasion.

For example, I've seen my own pool of machines on the Amazon EC2 network, capable of collectively transferring more than 3 GBps. That's the equivalent of downloading a full, uncompressed CD in less than 2 seconds, or a complete Blu-ray movie in about a minute.

Even if the number of machines you need can stay completely constant, the cloud's massive network infrastructure is a benefit that's often overlooked. Most network operations teams can easily spend hundreds of thousands of dollars getting only a fraction of the performance that large public and private clouds can provide immediately.

ELASTIC DISK STORAGE

A local, redundant, high-speed storage area network (SAN) is often a massive infrastructure investment. And when you eventually outgrow your original storage space, increasing the size can be extremely difficult. But in the cloud, your data may be practically unlimited in terms of scalability.

For example, for any data stored in Amazon S3, it's unlikely you'll ever need to think about disk space. Amazon's pricing page talks about 5 PB (5,000,000 GB) as one of its pricing tiers—and you can go well beyond that if needed. For that, your architecture must work with S3's basic capabilities and remote nature. See chapter 5 for more on architecting for the cloud.

A local SAN will always offer much faster performance than fetching objects in a remote file store, such as Amazon S3. Consider that it may cost $250,000 or more just for the initial hardware for a 100 TB SAN, plus hundreds of thousands more in personnel and electricity costs. You can store that same 100 TB in Amazon S3 for less than $15,000/month.

Whereas those cost savings are reason enough for people to re-architect their applications to work with the cloud, there's another factor to consider. If you ever outgrow the maximum capacity of your SAN (that is, the SAN controller's CPUs or RAM are fully utilized), the cost of building a new, larger SAN and migrating the data over can be a massive or even crippling expenditure.

RESPONDING TO BAD HARDWARE

Similar to the growing pains of expanding SANs, another area that network operations often spends a lot of time on is responding to emergencies when hardware fails. Practically everything in a server will eventually fail: disks, CPUs, RAM, fans, and so on. How quickly you can respond can greatly affect customer satisfaction.

In the non-cloud world, if a server suffers a crash from hardware failure, it's taken out of rotation, and replacement parts are installed as quickly as possible. This can take hours, days, or even weeks, depending on where the servers are located and whether you can readily find replacement parts.

In the cloud world, hardware still goes bad. Although it's just as rare as with physical hardware, we've seen hundreds of Amazon EC2 instances fail all at the same time, likely due to hardware problems. The difference is how we responded to the issue. Because our software was designed for the cloud, all we had to do was click a few buttons: those machines were replaced with new ones in a different availability region where there were no hardware issues.

AUTOMATING DEPLOYMENT

Being able to respond to failing servers or instantly provision new ones for scale greatly depends on the software architecture and whether it allows for truly automated deployment. Although there are many benefits of public and private clouds, you can't take advantage of them if you rely heavily on manual processes.

If your team needs to manually bring up a server, install Apache, copy over your PHP web application, configure the application to point to the MySQL database, and then finally add the new IP address to the load-balancer for production rotation, you probably aren't ready for cloud scale (or, heaven forbid, a mention on *Oprah*).

But if you can answer "yes" to some or all of the following questions, you may be cloud-ready:

- Do you have automated scripts for setting up the operating system and installing all necessary software?
- Do you package your software in such a way that all the configuration files are bundled with the binary artifacts, ready for one-click deployment?
- Do you run your software stack inside of virtual machines that can be cloned?
- Are common maintenance tasks (such as vacuuming the database, announcing maintenance windows, and backing up data) happening automatically or easily automated with a single click?
- Is your software designed to scale horizontally by adding new web servers or other machines?

By putting some time into automation efforts that allow you to answer "yes" to these questions, you not only prepare yourself to be able to address hardware issues and dynamically scale using the elasticity of the cloud, but also put yourself in position to accelerate your development and testing.

7.2.2 Accelerating development and testing

Whereas we've been highlighting the merits of the cloud for production operations, the rest of this chapter will focus on how the cloud changes the software when testing is done. Before diving into specific types of testing, let's explore the two primary reasons you should consider cloud-based testing: cost savings and test acceleration.

COST SAVINGS

Remember that half of the $22,500 of hardware purchase in the earlier hypothetical testing environment was for testing and staging, both used for a variety of QA and testing. But that hardware is unlikely to be used 100 percent of the time. Let's assume that both environments are needed only 50 percent of the time during normal business hours. That comes out to approximately 1,000 hours per year of required usage.

Table 7.2 compares physical hardware utilized 100 percent of the time (24 hours × 365 days) to that of equivalent cloud-based deployments.

Table 7.2 Comparing staging and testing cloud fees to production hardware costs

	Production	Staging	Testing	Staging (Alt)	Testing (Alt)
Servers	7	5	2	7	7
Annual hours	8,760	1,000	1,000	250	1,000
Cores/server	8	8	8	8	8
Hardware cost	$11,250	-	-	-	-
Annual cloud cost	-	$4,025	$1,600	$1,406	$5,625

The costs are estimated at approximately 10 cents per CPU per hour, plus a 2.5 cents-per-hour fee for a load-balancer. These prices reflect the public prices of Amazon's EC2 service at the time of publication of this book.

As you can see, when the hardware is used only 1,000 hours per year, the combined cost of staging and testing is $5,625 per year—much less than the hardware costs of both smaller environments.

But also consider the alternative deployment layouts represented in the last two columns of table 7.2. In this situation, you're re-creating a full production environment with all seven servers in both environments for not much more. In doing so, you can also use the staging environment less often, because the testing environment is now much larger and can be used for performance testing.

Note that to take advantage of these savings you have to be able to quickly deploy and tear down the environments. That's where the investments put in by the operations staff and developers can help out. Often, you can reuse the tools and processes used for cloud-based disaster recovery and scalability to save thousands of dollars each year.

SPEEDING UP TEST AUTOMATION AND MANUAL TESTING

Although the savings in hardware costs are nice, the largest expense for most businesses is usually employee salaries. As such, anything that can make testers more productive is often worth the effort. That's why as agile software methodologies have taken hold over the past decade, a major focus on automated testing has been central to the agile movement.

Whether it's for load testing, functional testing, or unit testing, the cloud and various cloud-based tools (commercial and open source) are helping with test automation. Even for manual testing, various cloud-based services are making individual testers more productive.

Before we go deeper into how the cloud is speeding up test automation and manual testing, let's take a moment to quickly review the various kinds of testing most QA teams do:

- *Unit testing*—Involves using tools such as JUnit or NUnit to build and run automated tests that exercise the internal algorithms of your software.
- *Functional testing*—End-to-end testing of the entire application, from the end user's perspective. Also known as *acceptance testing*.
- *Visual testing*—Verifies the user interface on a variety of different platforms. Between mobile devices, several versions of Windows, and at least five major browsers, this is particularly important for most web applications.
- *Load testing and performance testing*—Measures the performance of an application from when it's barely being used all the way up to heavy utilization. Also used to determine the failure point of an application.
- *Usability testing*—Collects subjective feedback on how real users react to the application's interface and functionality.
- *Ad hoc and manual testing*—A broad bucket of various types of manual testing efforts that can't or shouldn't be automated.
- *Penetration testing*—Evaluates the security of a computer system or network by simulating an attack from a malicious source.

Each of these types of testing can benefit from the cloud. Some, such as load testing and functional testing, benefit through the use of new testing tools designed for the cloud. Others, such as manual testing, benefit when the application under test (AUT) can be deployed quickly to the cloud.

For example, suppose two testers need to have exclusive access to the testing environment at the same time—one plans to run a large load test, and the other needs to run the entire suite of automated tests. Without the cloud, one would have to wait for the other to finish. With the cloud, the environment can be cloned, and both testers can get on with their job without interruption. Let's explore ways the cloud allows for tasks to run in parallel, allowing developers and testers to operate more efficiently.

7.3 The power of parallelization

Whether it's optimizing the speed at which testers can operate or increasing the performance of a production application, the common theme of cloud computing here is parallelization. By now, you probably know that in the world of computing performance, parallelization is king. Thanks to the work done by companies such as Intel and AMD, which now ship almost exclusively multicore chips, most consumers enjoy the same benefits scientists have had for years with supercomputers. Everything from photo manipulation to super-realistic 3D video games to software-compilation tasks has been dramatically improved through the use of parallel computing techniques.

And yet when it comes to software development and testing, we're still remarkably single-threaded in the way we operate. Whether it's automated unit tests, which almost always run in sequence, or the agile-less inefficiencies that organizations unknowingly employ, such as forcing their test team to wait idle for the next release candidate to be pushed to the testing environment, the software industry has been surprisingly slow to use parallelization to improve its own internal processes.

Perhaps it's because we're so maniacally dedicated to making our users have better experiences that we selflessly put off improving our own processes. Clearly the software industry understands and can take advantage of parallel computing. Ask any PlayStation or XBox game developer who routinely takes advantage of the multiple cores in those platforms.

In a way, that's what's happening. But usually, the motivation is more about cost savings and corner cutting than about being customer focused. Convincing management that you should spend more time building new features is always easier than arguing for time to speed up your unit tests. Consider figure 7.4, which shows how you can augment limited internal resources (personnel and hardware alike) with cloud-based resources, all for the purpose of testing against your test environment.

CPUs have been gaining more cores in recent years; many desktop-class systems now routinely ship with eight processor cores. There's an opportunity in the cloud to make a generational leap in the number of resources you can utilize in parallel. You no longer have to look within your own organization to try to achieve a 5X or 10X increase in throughput; rather, you can look to the cloud and achieve a 100X or greater throughput increase.

This isn't limited to raw CPU resources, either, although that's a huge area that benefits testing. You'll find new growth in cloud-based services that employ real people to do specialized tasks on demand, paying as you go, following many of the same principles of cloud computing. Let's explore the various types of testing and see how they can be improved by using cloud-based resources in parallel.

7.3.1 Unit testing

Almost every software project has some number of unit tests. The quantity varies greatly from team to team and project to project, but tools such as JUnit (and their xUnit equivalents in other programming languages) have become ubiquitous in software development projects.

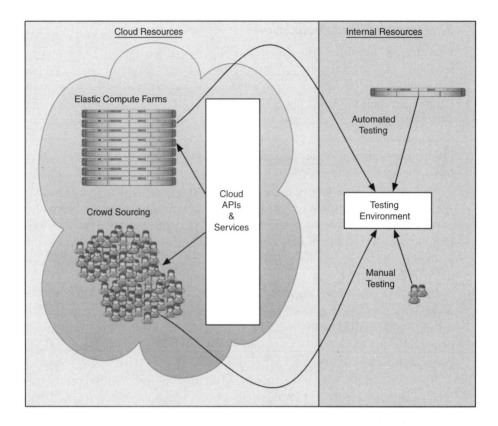

Figure 7.4 How cloud resources can augment internal resources (personnel and hardware) for testing. Instead of a small staff being responsible for all manual testing, a crowd-sourcing scenario is backed up by a potentially vast number of virtual servers in an elastic compute farm.

Most unit tests require little in terms of complex setup and teardown logic. They're often designed to test algorithms and blocks of code that are fairly static. Because there is little to set up, they often run quickly and demand few resources. As such, many projects can run hundreds of unit tests in a few minutes.

Unless you're using the parallelization features of your unit-testing framework (many of which were only added in the last year or two), you're likely running all those tests in sequence. By turning on parallelization in your unit tests, you can use up all those idle CPU cores and potentially speed up your unit test execution by 5X or 10X.

BEYOND PARALLEL CORES: PARALLEL MACHINES

If your team is writing unit tests, there's a good chance they're also using continuous integration (CI). In small teams with only a few projects, CI servers usually aren't busy—only a few builds may run every day.

But larger teams and complex projects often quickly overuse CI servers. For example, one open-source project I contribute to has more than 40 different builds/ projects configured in our CI server, with build times ranging from 30 seconds to over

---

About continuous integration

Software packages such as Hudson (open source) and Atlassian Bamboo (commercial) automatically detect source-code changes and run build and test scripts to check if anything broke. The result is constant feedback about the quality of the software project. For CI to work well, it also needs to be installed on remote servers, because it's no use if it's on a developer's laptop that may be turned off for the day.

For more information, see http://hudson-ci.org/ and www.atlassian.com/software/bamboo/. For an in-depth discussion of CI, you may also want to read *Continuous Integration in .NET* (Marcin Kawalerowicz and Craig Berntson, Manning).

---

15 minutes. Because multiple developers usually work on many projects at the same time, our CI system often has to put some tasks in a queue, waiting for resources to become available.

The solution to an overloaded CI system is to add more *build agents.* You can install a build agent on additional servers, and it's remotely controlled by the CI server to build and test code on those remote machines. For example, if your CI system is constantly in a state of backlog with 10 jobs in its queue, you can decrease the queue wait time by purchasing 10 servers and deploying build agents on each server.

The problem with this approach is that you have to buy 10 servers. Although hardware isn't too expensive these days, it's still wasteful when you think about the fact that those 10 servers will likely be busy only during normal business hours. For weekends and the remaining 16 hours of the workday, they will sit idle.

CI servers such as Hudson and Bamboo embrace the cloud in a big way. For example, Hudson can detect when your internal build farm is too busy and automatically spawn new machines in the cloud. When the activity dies down, it knows to turn them back off. Now, instead of waiting 20 minutes for your 1-minute build to get to the front of the queue to run, it can start immediately.

7.3.2 *Functional testing*

Compared to unit tests, functional tests are much heavier weight. They rely on the entire software application stack to be running, including database, web server, and web browser. As such, they take considerably longer to run. A typical unit test may take 1 to 2 seconds to run, whereas a functional test may take 1 to 2 minutes.

You've seen how you can make a unit test suite take 1 minute instead of 5 minutes by using multiple CPU cores. You've also seen how the turnaround time on a CI build for that same unit test suite can be taken from 21 minutes (20 minutes in the queue + 1 minute to build and test) to 1 minute by dynamically scaling up more build agents in the cloud.

But you have to take a different approach when the test suite itself takes hours. Spinning up more build agents can keep the CI queue empty, but it doesn't reduce the time it takes for the test results to be reported back. That's because you're still running with one build agent for each individual test run.

Often, these test runs take so long that the developers and QA team decide to run them only at night or only a few times during the project. The downside is that you end up catching errors later. Let's explore ways you can reduce the time it takes for a functional test suite to complete.

USING SELENIUM FOR FUNCTIONAL TEST AUTOMATION

For this exercise, let's examine the popular open-source project Selenium, which has gained wide traction among developers and testers as a simple, low-cost way to write automated functional tests for web applications. Figure 7.5 shows Selenium IDE, which can record user interactions and create scripts based on them.

A traditional Selenium test suite first automatically sets up the web application by deploying the code to a web server, such as Apache, and also sets up a clean database. Figure 7.6 illustrates how each Selenium test then runs in sequence against the local test environment.

The problem is that each Selenium test needs to start a fresh browser and walk through the web application. This not only takes a lot of time (1 minute+), but

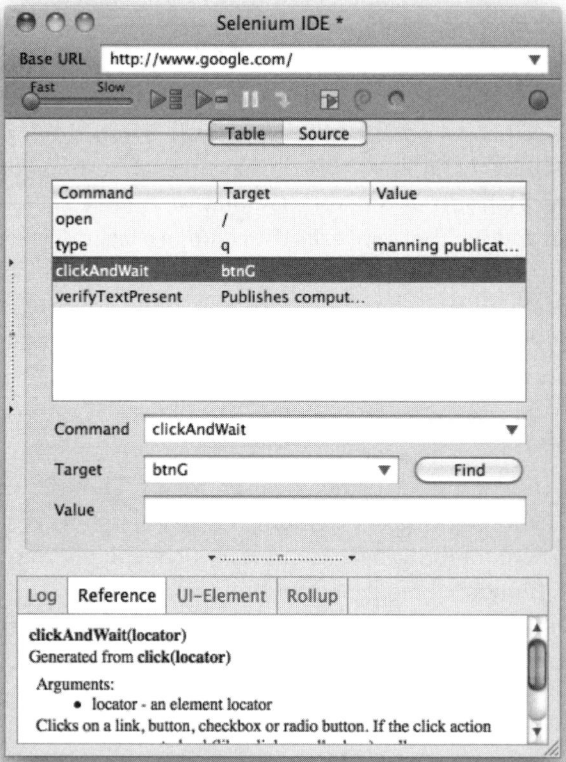

Figure 7.5   Selenium IDE after recording a Google search

About Selenium

Selenium is a popular open-source, cross–operating system, cross–programming language, cross-browser automation framework. Using Selenium, you can drive Internet Explorer, Firefox, Google Chrome, Safari, and Opera on Windows, OS X, and Linux, and write your tests in Java, C#, PHP, Python, Ruby, and Perl. Selenium is a suite of tools and libraries, including a recorder (Selenium IDE), APIs for most modern programming languages, and a distributed browser farm build for Amazon EC2 (Selenium Grid). You can learn more at http://seleniumhq.org.

it's also resource heavy (modern web browsers can easily use up a full CPU core and hundreds of MB of RAM.) Unlike with unit tests, you can't run dozens of Selenium tests in parallel on the same machine. If you want to try to tighten the feedback loop for these important automated functional tests, you have to do something else.

A SECOND LAYER OF PARALLELIZATION IN THE CLOUD

The solution is to go beyond parallel build agents in the cloud and to introduce a second layer of machine parallelization, also in the cloud. Instead of running one Firefox browser at a time on your build agent, you run dozens in parallel on a *browser farm* that you're hosting in the cloud. With a pool of, say, 20 browsers ready to execute tests in parallel for each build agent, you can take what was a 3-hour build down to less than 10 minutes.

The good news is that building a browser farm is neither hard nor expensive. The open-source project Selenium Grid uses Amazon EC2 and makes it easy to talk to one central dispatch (the Grid server), which then handles allocating a browser in the farm exclusively for your testing. Also, several commercial Selenium Grid-like solutions are available on the market today. Figure 7.7 illustrates how the Selenium tests now can run in parallel.

By dramatically decreasing the time it takes to run your functional tests, you move from running them once a night to running them continuously in your CI infrastructure. This means you can learn about critical user-facing issues within minutes of code changes, rather than hours or days. This newfound convenience creates a positive feedback loop, in which developers and testers alike write more tests, further benefiting the team and the project and underscoring the value of automation.

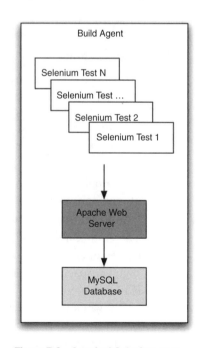

Figure 7.6 A typical Selenium test suite running on a CI build agent that includes an Apache web server and a MySQL database

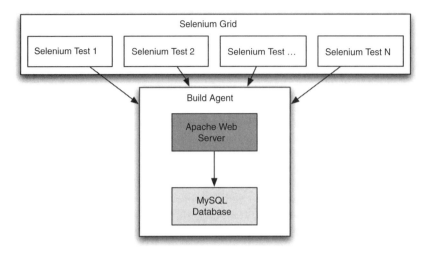

Figure 7.7 Selenium tests running in parallel against a single test environment on a CI build agent

Similar to CI build agents, these cloud-based machines don't need to be on all the time. Your QA team can start and stop them based on demand and cost requirements. It's easy for the team to do the cost/benefit analysis of employing a browser farm and a build-agent farm, allowing them to dynamically change resource allocation based on business needs.

7.3.3 Load testing

Probably the best example of testing in the cloud is load testing. *Load testing* is the act of simulating hundreds, thousands, or even millions of users hitting your site. By doing this, you can find out if your website can handle the expected load that you may get on Cyber Monday or after airing a Super Bowl commercial.

The cloud is great for load testing because whereas all QA tasks tend to be spiky in nature, nothing is spikier than load testing. You may go weeks without running a load test; and then, as you get close to a release, you may suddenly need dozens or hundreds of machines to generate enough load to meet your testing goals.

TRADITIONAL LOAD TESTING

The common approach to load testing prior to the cloud involved running commercial or open-source software on your own hardware. Performance testers used tools such as Apache JMeter and Mercury LoadRunner to create a test script that issued HTTP requests similar to the traffic a real user caused by browsing the site.

But when it comes time to run a load test, testers need to find enough hardware to generate the required load. Because load testing doesn't happen all the time, it's hard for businesses to justify the purchase of dedicated hardware for this task. As a general rule of thumb, a single web server can handle approximately 250 concurrent users, whereas a single midsized server can generate approximately 1,000 concurrent users for load. That means you need one load generator for every four web servers.

Because this physical hardware is difficult to procure, testers tend to try to push more simulated users on each load generator. The risk of doing this is that if you overload the load generator, your results can be skewed or incorrect because the observer (the load generator) suffers from its own performance problems.

THE ECONOMICS OF CLOUD-BASED LOAD TESTING

Because hardware is often a scarce resource, testers try to make the most out of what they can get access to, increasing the number of simulated users on each load generator. But in the cloud, virtual machines are a commodity. That's why load testing in the cloud is such an appealing concept.

Several companies have recently rolled out new load-testing services specifically built for the cloud. Some, such as LoadStorm (http://loadstorm.com), focus on the cost savings of cloud-based operations and pass those savings on to the end user. Others, such as SOASTA CloudTest (http://soasta.com), use the massive scale of the cloud to generate tests for some of the largest websites, such as Intuit's TurboTax website and MySpace.

If you have a large website and want to test what happens when 50,000 visitors hit it at the same time, you have to find 50 load generators. Getting hold of 50 physical servers can be extremely difficult and costly in many organizations, but you can do so in the cloud for less than $5 per hour.

Because it's so cost effective to generate load from the cloud, you don't have to be nearly as aggressive in trying to maximize your load generators. See table 7.3 for hourly prices of various load-generation configurations.

Table 7.3 Various cloud load-testing configurations, ranging from aggressive to conservative

	Aggressive	Moderate	Conservative
Concurrent users	1,000	1,000	1,000
Users/generator	1,000	250	50
Generators required	1	4	20
Hourly cost	< $0.10	< $0.40	< $2.00

As you can see, even when you're extremely conservative and generate only 50 concurrent users per generator, the cost is trivial. You may want to consider a moderate or conservative configuration because if you're too aggressive and get bad test results, then at a minimum you'll waste the time of your testers and developers as they analyze and try to make sense of fundamentally flawed data. Or worse, you may miscalculate your server capacity, putting yourself at risk of an unexpected crash. When viewed from that perspective, an extra $2 per hour is a no-brainer.

BROWSER-BASED, CLOUD-BASED LOAD TESTING

A new development in the world of load testing takes this concept one step further. One of the most time-consuming parts of load testing is the process of creating and maintaining test scripts that simulate your end users. Traditional load testing—even cloud-based load testing—is still based on the concept of simulating 50, 250, or even 1,000 users from a single computer.

To accomplish this, load-testing tools don't run a browser. Instead, they play back only the HTTP traffic that a browser would issue if a real user were to visit a site. The following listing shows a typical load-test script that simulates a user visiting Google and searching for "manning publications".

Listing 7.1   Typical load-test script simulating a user visiting Google

```
var c = openHttpClient();
c.setBaseUrl('http://google.com/');
c.get('/');
c.get('/logos/olympics10-bg.jpg', 200);
c.get('/logos/olympics10-sskating-hp.png', 200);
c.get('/extern_chrome/c26c79a56c95bda8.js', 200);
c.get('/generate_204', 204);
c.get('/images/nav_logo7.png', 200);

var search = "manning+publications";
var partial = '';
for (var i = 0; i < search.length; i++) {
    partial += search[i];
    c.get('/complete/search?hl=en&client=hp&q=' + partial);
}

c.get('/csi?v=3&s=webhp&action=&e=23868,23933&...', 204);
c.get('/search?hl=en&source=hp&q=manning+publications&...', 200);
c.get('/csi?v=3&s=web&action=&ei=AWuJS4bmLs7VlAev85DPAQ...', 204);
c.get('/verify/EAAAAH3CAnvqlBhsQW-xnu2kZmE.gif');
```

The challenge with this approach is that the script must be written to simulate advanced Ajax functionality. Scripts such as this can take days or weeks to create and maintain. Today, even the simplest sites, such as www.google.com, contain Ajax functionality. In this case, as users type each key in their search query, a background Ajax request is made to provide search suggestions (see figure 7.8).

A Google engineer wrote the autocomplete functionality with JavaScript to work inside a web browser. But because traditional load-testing tools don't run a browser, it's up to the script writer to simulate the autocomplete behavior. Note the `for` loop in listing 7.1, which incrementally sends requests to Google's servers, first with *m*, then *ma*, *man*, *mann*, and so on.

But there has been some movement toward using web browsers to generate load, including a company I founded in 2009 called BrowserMob (http://browsermob.com). The basic idea behind this approach is that although you can't run 50 users per CPU core as you can with traditional load testing, the cost is still small.

For example, suppose you run only one browser per CPU core in the cloud (a conservative approach). The same 1,000-user test that cost $2 in the old conservative model now costs $100. Although a 50X jump in cost is quite a lot, relatively speaking, consider the following code, which is an equivalent script using a real web browser:

Figure 7.8 Demonstration of Google's Ajax-based autocomplete functionality

```
selenium.open("http://google.com/");
selenium.typeKeys("q", "manning publications");
selenium.click("btnG");
selenium.waitForTextPresent("books for professionals")
```

As you can imagine, this script is much simpler to write and maintain. Because it also uses Selenium, testers can even reuse automated functional tests. Money spent on writing scripts can now be allocated toward running completely realistic tests. This is the ultimate promise of the cloud—not merely saving money on infrastructure, but making employees more productive, too.

7.3.4 Visual testing

Another area that takes a lot of time is cross-browser visual testing. We're in the middle of Browser Wars 2.0, and Microsoft, Google, Mozilla, and Apple show no sign of relenting. In chapter 9, we'll discuss where the browsers are going. Although the new choices are great for consumers and have pushed the HTML standards to new heights of functionality, QA teams are left with more work than ever to ensure that the user interface looks and works well on every platform.

The most common approach to this problem is for QA teams to retain dozens of physical or virtual machines, each with a different operating system and selection of browsers. The problem is maintenance: hundreds of combinations of operating systems, browsers, screen sizes, and versions/releases can influence how a web page functions and looks. Similar issues exist when you're trying to test whether emails sent out by marketing programs or automatically from your software look good on the dozens of desktop- and web-based email clients.

Fortunately, some commercial services address this issue. Three such companies are Litmus (http://litmusapp.com), BrowserCam (http://browsercam.com), and Adobe BrowserLab (http://browserlab.adobe.com). Figure 7.9 shows Litmus displaying results of how an email looks in 12+ different email clients, including web-based clients such as Gmail and Yahoo! Mail.

By using these services, you offload the maintenance of these different environments to a company dedicated to that task. In addition, because these companies share their resources among all their customers, you end up paying a lot less than if you tried to virtualize and host each test environment in the cloud by yourself. In a February 2010 case study with Amazon,[1] Litmus reported that at times they're running more than 400 computers in the Amazon EC2 network!

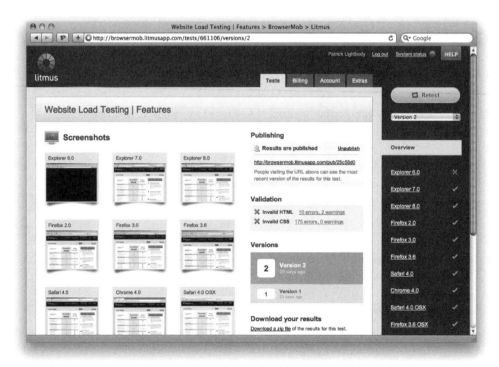

Figure 7.9   Litmus provides cross-browser testing services entirely hosted in the Amazon cloud.

---

[1] http://aws.amazon.com/solutions/case-studies/litmus/

7.3.5 *Manual testing*

Until now, we've only discussed how the elasticity and parallelization of technical in-frastructure can improve the ways you build software. But you shouldn't focus only on nonorganic resources when building software. People are finite resources as well, and crowd-sourcing networks backed by cloud APIs are a powerful way to augment your QA process.

Every software project has some sort of QA phase. Unfortunately, prior to the QA handoff, testers tend to be underutilized. Even worse, after the handoff, they become over-utilized, resulting in increased stress and potential for missing critical bugs. Although automated tests can help even out the workload, the reality is that manual testing will never go away. After all, where do those automated tests originate? From a QA engineer running a first manual test.

As such, it's important to think about ways you can take advantage of new services that let you get access to *elastic people*. No, not the Mr. Fantastic kind of elasticity, but rather the kind of people who can be counted on for short, burstable periods of time. Thanks to the reach of the internet and some innovative new services, you can tap into people power with relative ease.

Amazon provides a service called Mechanical Turk (https://www.mturk.com/), shown in Figure 7.10. Amazon calls it "artificial artificial intelligence."

The service has tens of thousands of human "workers" (also known as *Turkers*) who are ready to do arbitrary tasks, written in plain English, for small bounties. For example,

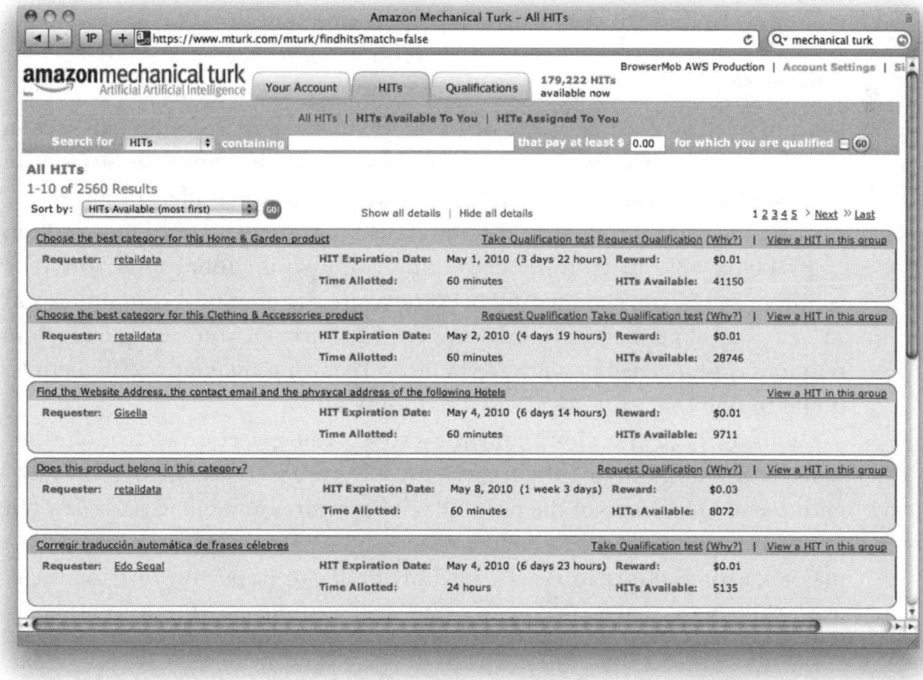

Figure 7.10   The view a "worker" sees when logging in to Amazon Mechanical Turk

suppose you've received reports that your site isn't accessible from home computers in Japan. A Turker located in Japan may be able to help confirm that for 5 or 10 cents.

Keep in mind that these Turkers aren't QA professionals. They aren't trained in the world of software testing, and their technical skill level may range greatly from Turker to Turker. But if your QA team needs help, such as checking hundreds of pages on your website for visual defects on all the major web browsers, it may be a cost-effective, elastic solution. Even better, your core QA team gets freed up to focus on more intellectual tasks, such as automation engineering or better understanding core product requirements.

Mechanical Turk isn't the only crowd-sourcing option out there. If you need access to a more professional staff of manual QA testers, look toward services such as uTest. They can get you access to thousands of people with QA backgrounds to help with manual functional testing efforts. With uTest (http://utest.com), you can recruit dozens or even hundreds of QA professionals to help you with the final testing of a project without having to pay full salaries for those testers.

Another interesting use of crowd sourcing is for usability testing. In a world where good design and bad design are often determined in subjective ways, services such as Mechanical Turk and UserTesting (http://usertesting.com) let you ask dozens of random people to record their experiences using your software.

This new way to use the power of people lets you, for brief periods, increase your QA team from 2 people to 20, similar to how you can use the power of elastic machines to scale up your browser farm or build agents. Those who use these new techniques effectively find that it opens up new opportunities in how they build their software.

7.4   *Summary*

Continuous integration was a major shift in the way we build software and receive near-instant feedback on basic quality metrics such as compilation status and unit-test success rates. But the new ability to elastically deploy parallel resources (machines or people) means you can move beyond basic tasks, such as compiling and unit testing.

By being able to continuously run in-depth functional tests and receive results within minutes, you can quantitatively measure the quality of your entire software stack in near real time. Similarly, by using crowd sourcing, you can quickly determine the readiness of a particular software build by receiving qualitative/subjective results and doing testing that isn't possible with automation.

By using both the cloud and the crowd, you get close to a model of *continuous deployment*. In this model, the time between changes to the software by developers and end-to-end QA shrinks to the point that it isn't unreasonable to push new releases every day while maintaining complete confidence in the quality of the release. Although it may take some effort to reach this holy grail, we hope you're encouraged to begin exploring these new technologies and services and use them to make incremental improvements to the way your team builds and tests software.

Now, let's move on to the next chapter, where we'll discuss the practicalities of putting cloud applications into production.

Practical considerations

8

It's been one week since you launched the new corporate collaborative portal on the cloud to great fanfare. You're still basking in the accolades of your colleagues as you log in to the application to see the CTO's latest blog posting on the wonders of cloud computing, only to find out that your new site is unreachable. It must be a glitch, you think, trying again. Same result. Frantically, you try other sites within the intranet. You can reach the cafeteria menu application without any problem. Next, you try reaching other sites on the internet, such as yahoo.com—again, success. You try your portal once more. Still unavailable. You're starting to get that sinking feeling, as you imagine going from hero to goat in the short span of a week. But it's your lucky day. The gods of IT look down mercifully on you, and lo and behold, 10 minutes later the portal is back online. What happened, and how did the situation resolve itself?

Applications running in your corporate data center are typically monitored and managed using network management-systems software. How can you gain similar insight into the operation of an application running in the cloud?

Running applications in the cloud is different from running an application in your data center in the level of control you have over the resources that make up the application. You need a good level of visibility to understand how a cloud application is operating and to fix and find problems when they occur. The last three chapters looked at topics related to applications in the cloud. Specifically, in chapters 5 and 6, you read about the design and architecture related to scalability and reliability of cloud applications. You continued through to the development and testing of cloud applications in chapter 7. Now, armed with an understanding of how to design, build, test, and deploy applications for the cloud, let's shift our focus to the practicalities of putting cloud applications into production.

In this chapter, we'll look at the business considerations important in choosing a cloud provider by examining the key criteria for evaluating various vendor offerings. We'll also look more closely at the technical operational issues most important for cloud applications. Finally, you'll be able to measure how a cloud application is doing and how well the cloud vendor is living up to their end of the bargain.

8.1   Choosing a cloud vendor

Choosing a cloud vendor is a momentous decision. Let's explore the two most critical aspects of making that decision: the business considerations and the technical operational considerations.

8.1.1   Business considerations

When choosing a public cloud provider, you're often able to purchase services in an on-demand fashion. The advantage of this sort of arrangement is the ability to stop using it at any time. You can experiment with the services at little cost, and if the quality and reliability of the service leaves something to be desired, you can choose to go elsewhere. If you're running an application requiring significant investment that has high business criticality, or if you're considering an annual contract to lower costs, it probably makes sense to proceed cautiously. In this case, the selection and evaluation of a potential cloud provider bears some similarity to how you choose a traditionally outsourced service, such as web hosting or collocation.

The questions you should research and ask regarding the basic facts about a business providing cloud services should be along the lines of the questions you ask any outside vendor:

- Financial viability:
    o   How long has the vendor been around?
    o   Are they financially stable? Is it a public company or a well-financed privately held company?
    o   Is it profitable?
- Operational viability
    o   Does it have the requisite core assets, such as multiple data centers, and is it reasonably located?

- o Can it provide references of satisfied customers?
- o Does it have an operating history as a service provider?
- ■ Contractual viability
  - o Are its operations audited and in compliance with best practices for service-based operations (SAS 70 Type II)?
  - o What are its SLAs, and how are they enforced?

SAS 70 Type II Compliance

SAS 70 is an acronym for Statement of Auditing Standards, developed by the American Institute of Certified Public Accountants. Being SAS 70 Type II compliant means that a service organization has the appropriate infrastructure and controls in place to handle and process its customer's data in a satisfactory manner. SAS Type II certification is a costly process and represents a significant investment by a cloud provider. It involves a six-month data-collection process followed by a lengthy and comprehensive audit; it concludes with a detailed report produced by an independent accounting firm.

At a minimum, before entrusting a cloud provider with your business-critical applications, you should be comfortable that it is in a strong financial position and has a good operational track record and good operational assets, such as appropriate data-center facilities and network connectivity. When business issues have been satisfactorily addressed, the next step is to evaluate the technical considerations germane to cloud operations, which we'll talk about next.

8.1.2 Technical operational considerations

Many of the issues often cited as barriers to general cloud adoption end up being issues that you need to deal with when managing a deployed cloud application. In this section, we'll look at the main technical operational issues you'll encounter when you put your business in the cloud. Let's start with a discussion of availability and performance, which are traditionally the bread and butter of operational management. Next, we'll discuss elasticity and scale, operational security and compliance, and, finally, issues around interoperability and platform compatibility.

AVAILABILITY AND PERFORMANCE

Most people who work in the IT industry, or who are responsible for running IT operations, have an intuitive feel for what availability and performance mean. The simplest definitions are as follows:

- *Availability*—Whether an application performs its design function
- *Performance*—How fast or slow the application is

To proceed further, let's be more specific and provide precise definitions of these terms. Let's start with availability.

In the context of applications, whether delivered via the cloud or not, it's important to measure the availability as experienced by the intended user of the application—was the end user able to get what they came for? Most applications perform several business functions or services, and you can measure the availability of each. For any specific application, the starting point is to determine what the important business processes or services are and measure the availability associated with them. For example, consider an e-commerce site that sells books. A myriad of business services constitute such a site, but four are the primary ones important for generating revenue:

- *Search*—Find a book.
- *Browse*—Look at the description of a book.
- *Shopping cart*—Select a book for purchase.
- *Purchase*—Buy the book.

To measure the availability of the e-commerce site, you need to determine whether each of these business services works properly when you try to use it. You can attempt to measure these services independently and assign an availability measure to each. Alternatively, you could define a composite business service that looked at the total availability as being able to perform each of these business services. The product of the individual availability measures would be the result for each business service measured independently.

One way to define availability is as the number of successful uses of the application divided by the number of attempts to use the application:

$$Availability = \frac{(Total \text{ \# } of \text{ } successes)}{(Total \text{ \# } of \text{ } attempts)}$$

Although technically correct, this definition has some drawbacks. In practice, it's generally straightforward to measure the number of successes in using an application by looking, for example, at log files or other records of activity. The number of tries is less straightforward to measure. Whereas you can measure the number of errors that caused an availability issue when the application is more or less running properly, in the event that the system is down, you have no way of knowing how many users tried to use the application when it wasn't available.

The traditional way of defining availability looks at what percent of the time a given application or service is able to service users successfully over a given duration. We can sum up the definition of availability in the following equation:

$$Availability = \frac{(Total \text{ } time \text{ } the \text{ } service \text{ } is \text{ } usable)}{(Total \text{ } duration \text{ } of \text{ } measurement \text{ } period)}$$

The availability of a system is often measured in *9s*, which describes the percent value of availability. *Three 9s* refers to 99.9% availability, and *five 9s* refers to 99.999% availability—truly a high bar for reliability.

"To the 9s": measures of application availability

Service-level agreements (SLAs) on availability are often measured in 9s. This describes the target percent of unplanned availability to be achieved, typically on a monthly or annual basis. Each 9 corresponds to a 10-fold decrease in the amount of downtime. For an important application, such as email or a CRM system, three 9s might be a reasonable target, whereas critical services such as public utilities would tend to target five 9s. The following table describes the amount of acceptable downtime per year for the corresponding level of availability:

# of 9s	SLA target	Maximum downtime per year
2	99%	3 days, 15 hours, and 40 minutes
3	99.9%	8 hours and 46 minutes
4	99.99%	52 minutes and 36 seconds
5	99.999%	5 minutes and 16 seconds
6	99.9999%	31.56 seconds

You should measure performance, like availability, as experienced by the end user, for each specific business process important for an application. You can measure the performance for each individual transaction but track aggregates over a given time interval to understand the overall performance of the system. Typically, you measure the average of the performance at a specific percentile level—such as 95th or 99th percentile over a period of time—to develop a baseline expectation for the delivered performance.

The availability and performance of applications in a cloud environment are due to three primary factors. The first factor involves the performance and reliability of the underlying hardware and software offered by the cloud vendor. The robustness of the infrastructure depends on how redundant and well provisioned the cloud vendor's data centers are. As you saw in the previous chapters, cloud infrastructures are built with huge numbers of commodity servers and are designed with the expectation that the individual components in the system might fail. If a particular server running several instances in a cloud goes down, it doesn't impact the overall advertised availability of the cloud. But if the particular instance that goes down is the one supporting your application, the failure is indeed a problem for you. The best way to deal with this sort of occurrence is to plan for it. You can adopt two possible strategies:

- *Design with the possibility of failure in mind.*   This strategy is included in the inherent design of the application and uses techniques such as horizontal scalability and balancing between multiple instances.

- *Plan to fail fast but recover quickly.*   Make sure you have a good handle on detecting the occurrence of a failure and can react quickly to bring up an alternate instance to take over immediately.

The second factor relates specifically to the application's design and robustness as well as its quality. This is the realm of the application developer and is fundamentally no different from traditional application development except for the ability to design applications in the context of the resources available in a cloud environment. In the early days of computing, when memory and computing capacity were expensive, it was necessary to build applications that were stingy in their consumption of these precious resources. As CPU and RAM became less expensive, this requirement could be relaxed. In the same way, with the advent of the cloud, the ability to shard and horizontally scale with less regard to cost means you can trade off stringent quality control against the ability to dynamically distribute the load. But don't take this idea to imply the extreme, where the code is so unreliable that it crashes repeatedly. Rather, in a cloud environment you have an additional degree of flexibility and freedom as tradeoffs between code quality and dynamic scaling, to reach a desired level of robustness.

Another factor that comes into play is somewhat different from traditional application development. It relates to the fact that, by definition, the application's end users are necessarily connecting to the infrastructure via the public internet. The network connectivity between the cloud infrastructure and the client used to access the application affects the cloud application's performance and availability for end users. The availability of the application can suffer for a variety of reasons. The first involves the loss of connectivity between the cloud provider's data center and the internet—or, equivalently, the loss of connectivity between the client side and the internet. The best way you can deal with the former is to choose a cloud provider with data centers that have multiple connections to the internet backbone. In the event of an interruption to one, you'll still have connectivity. Similarly, if end users are accessing the application from within your corporate network, redundancy of connection with multiple different network access providers can improve application availability. In the case of applications accessed by those outside the corporate network, such as consumers of an e-commerce application, providing such redundancy isn't possible.

Don't forget, for a cloud-based application, availability is subject to the macro conditions of the internet at large. A recent error at Google related to DNS for its free Google Analytics offering caused general slowdowns and unavailability for several hours on the internet. For a cloud application serving an intranet audience, such an availability hit would be avoidable for a traditional deployment. For an internet-facing application, you probably would have a good case for getting a free pass on the performance and availability hits taken for an event such as this, because "everyone else in the world" is also down.

The last point to mention with regard to network effects relates to the geographic dependence of performance on cloud applications. In a study on cloud performance,

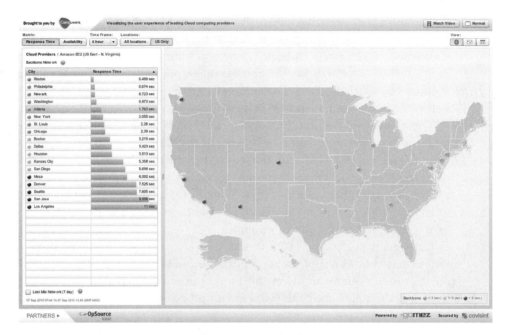

Figure 8.1   A comparison of the average time it takes to access the same web page for an application running in a sample cloud provider from 18 different cities across the U.S., as measured by Gomez

Gomez measured significant variations in the response time experienced by end users in different geographies. Figure 8.1 shows the performance of a simple web application deployed at a sample cloud provider, as experienced by end users from 18 different geographies. If the primary users of your application are in Virginia or the mid-Atlantic, for example, Amazon in VA may be an ideal choice. For an internet-facing application, you can expect a wide variation in the performance experienced by end users from their points of access around the world.

To improve the performance users experience, you could look to deploy the application in multiple cloud data centers. Another approach would be to use content delivery network (CDN) technologies such as those provided by Akamai and Limelight.

ELASTICITY AND SCALE

In the architecture and design of traditional applications, an important consideration relates to the scale at which it must run. When deploying the application, you provision the appropriate amount of hardware and system capacity to meet expected demand. In a cloud world, one of the primary assumptions is that an infinite resource pool is available. As long as the cloud application is appropriately designed using sharding and other appropriate horizontal-scaling techniques, you can reach a certain scale or capacity by bringing online more instances as the situation dictates. The problem then comes down to being able to bring resources online quickly enough for a given situation.

The term that describes the attribute of a cloud system to respond with rapidity or velocity in response to spikes in demand is *elasticity*. A typical application that may stretch the elasticity of a cloud is a media website that gets spiky load due to a news event, such as a natural disaster. You can drive peak loads to a website in less than a minute. The elasticity of a cloud can vary based on the underlying cloud technology as well as intrinsic boot times of OS images.

The elasticity of Amazon EC2 and a cloud built using the open-source Eucalyptus platform have been measured by looking at the time it took to launch one and then eight virtual images by the team that created Eucalyptus. In figure 8.2, you can see that on average, it took less than 20 seconds to launch 1 new instance on EC2 and less than 25 seconds for 8 new instances. For most applications, this level of elasticity is sufficient to scale up in times of peak demand, provided you're able to detect the need for the extra computing power quickly enough.

In addition to the time taken to start a base image, you also need to factor in the time required for the application to initialize and be ready for work. The general load on the cloud system can affect the time required to start new instances. It can be subject to variability due to the volume of traffic requests within the cloud for various administrative functions.

OPERATIONAL SECURITY AND COMPLIANCE

Security- and compliance-related issues tend to top the list in any survey on the primary inhibitors to widespread adoption of the cloud for business critical applications. The two main compliance standards often cited as potentially problematic for a cloud-style deployment include the Payment Card Industry Data Security Standards (PCI DSS) for e-commerce related businesses and the Health Insurance Portability and Accountability Act (HIPAA) that governs privacy within the healthcare industry. Both

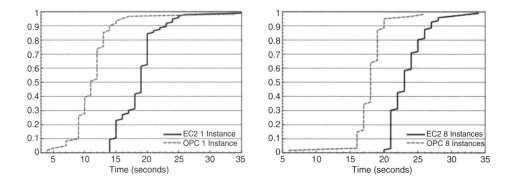

Figure 8.2 Elasticity of EC2 and a private cloud deployment based on Eucalyptus. The left graph shows the cumulative probability as a function of time for an instance to be available after the request has been made to start it. The right graph shows the cumulative probabilities of the time it takes before eight instances are available. Source: Daniel Nurmi et al, "Eucalyptus: A Technical Report on an Elastic Utility Computing Architecture Linking Your Programs to Useful Systems," UCSB Computer Science Technical Report Number 2008–10, August 2008.

are very detailed specifications on the proper way to handle data in a safe, secure, and auditable manner. A cloud provider, assuming it has deployed the appropriate base security architecture, maintains sufficient physical infrastructure, and has put in place the proper processes and procedures, can provide the necessary base for a generically secure infrastructure. SAS 70 Type II certification, as we discussed earlier, is a measure of whether a cloud provider has all of these necessary ingredients in place, and can be seen as a prerequisite for PCI DSS or HIPAA.

In addition, the cloud application must be deployed with the appropriate security standards, including correctly configured firewalls, appropriate encryption of sensitive data, appropriate practices for key management, and so on. None of these practices are much different than those required for an internally hosted compliant application. The primary difference, and regulatory hurdles that often can't be overcome, are strict requirements for such things as direct inspection of hardware infrastructure that may not be practical within the context of a cloud environment. (See chapter 4 for a more comprehensive discussion of cloud security considerations.)

INTEROPERABILITY AND PLATFORM COMPATIBILITY

Interoperability and platform *compatibility* refer to how easy or difficult it is to switch between different providers. These factors are often cited as primary blockers to cloud adoption. But it's probably arguable whether these are major practical issues worth worrying about. In the simplest public cloud adoption scenario, where you choose one provider, are happy with it, and stick to it, interoperability and compatibility never come into play. Also, when choosing something more complex than a basic IaaS provider (such as PaaS or SaaS), it's your choice. You make the implicit choice of trading richer functionality for portability.

Several potential levels of interoperability exist. The simplest forms involve provisioning and management interoperability. More complex forms may include the ability to copy instances from one cloud provider to another or even migrate between them dynamically in real time. You can argue that the only kinds of interoperability that really matter are command and control. Next most important are a common framework for monitoring. Interoperability of VMs and also the ability to move them dynamically sounds cool but is probably impractical in a public cloud-type deployment because it would take too much time to move stuff around. The good news is that the current state of interoperability isn't bad.

Let's consider a scenario where you need to switch from one provider to another. This case requires, at some level, provisioning compatibility, but not much more. For a one-time move, a little friction and some manual processes are probably acceptable. Let's look at another scenario in which you need multiple simultaneous providers. This is rare, but it can be driven by two potential business requirements. The first relates to applications that require more capacity for short bursts than is available from any given provider. Here, at a minimum, once again, you need provisioning. The second potential use case, which is even rarer today, is the ability to arbitrage the IaaS providers. Again, this can only work in an IaaS world because for services to be tradable, they (by definition) need to be easy to switch between, and that must happen at minimum cost. You can consider arbitrage between like services on several factors. Some of these may include cost or performance. The final case is a hybrid private-public cloud scenario. In these scenarios, you'll see a similar requirement regarding interoperability of provisioning. As of today, two primary standards are used for provisioning: Amazon-style APIs and VMware.

For a public cloud provider, interoperability is a two-edged sword. Interoperability with your competitors means it's easy for their customers to leave them and come to you. But the flip side is that it can work in reverse. In a world of perfect interoperability and functional equivalence between vendors, only two factors remain for a cloud vendor to compete on: the price of the offering and the quality and reliability of the service they provide. SLAs are documents that cloud providers publish, detailing their level of service. They also serve as contractual commitments to delivery of that service level. In the next section, we'll look in detail at the SLAs provided by several major cloud vendors.

8.2   Public cloud providers and SLAs

As you've seen, much of the apprehension associated with moving applications to the cloud is because of people's uneasiness at ceding control over something they've grown accustomed to managing on their own. SLAs are a tangible way for cloud providers to address these concerns.

An SLA lays out specific criteria or service levels that a provider is committing through a contractual obligation to provide. Generally written as quantifiable or measureable metrics, they describe the satisfactory operation of the service. These metrics must be met on a continual basis, and the inability to meet them constitutes an SLA violation. An SLA is a way for cloud vendors to "put their money where their mouth is" concerning any claims they may make on the quality of their offering. The customer is entitled to compensation, usually in the form of a credit, to make up for the vendor not being able to meet the SLA targets.

SLAs aren't new and are commonly offered by managed service providers for their data-center offerings. Cloud SLAs are structured similarly to those offered for traditional hosting services but may differ in the specific metrics incorporated into the SLA. Let's look at the SLAs published by three major cloud providers: Amazon EC2, Microsoft Azure, and the Rackspace Cloud. At the time of this writing, Google App Engine had no published SLA for its offering.

8.2.1   Amazon's AWS SLA

Amazon offers an SLA for EC2 compute and S3 storage services. The EC2 service level is calculated on an annual basis, whereas the S3 service level is calculated over a monthly interval. The EC2 SLA guarantees an uptime over the previous year of 99.95%. This equates to about 4 hours and 20 minutes of allowable unavailability over a 1-year period. In the simplest terms, Amazon's EC2 SLA guarantees two things:

- The ability to access instances
- The ability to start new instances

Amazon's *Region Unavailability* refers to the availability of its compute regions across multiple availability zones. Region Unavailability is defined as the customer being unable to either access or instantiate replacement instances in more than one availability zone in a region over a 5-minute interval. Each of these 5-minute intervals can be tallied over a rolling 1-year window; and if at any time the total calculated unavailability exceeds 4 hours and 20 minutes, there is a violation of the SLA. Amazon only guarantees access to the instances up to the edge of its own network and for factors reasonably under its control. It excludes instance failures not specifically due to Region Unavailability. In the event of an SLA breach, the customer of EC2 is entitled to a 10% credit for the monthly service charges for that month, excluding any one-time fees charged during that month.

Amazon S3 monthly service levels are determined on the basis of a quantity defined as the *Error Rate*, which is the ratio of service requests that result in an InternalError or ServiceUnavailable divided by the total number of requests made in a 5-minute interval. The Monthly Uptime Percentage is defined as 100% minus the average Error Rate over all of the 5-minute intervals in the month. The customer gets a service credit of 10% of the monthly bill if the Monthly Uptime Percentage is lower than 99.9% and a credit of 25% if it falls below 99%. The equivalent outage durations for the 99.9% and 99% Monthly Uptime Percentages are 40 minutes and 7 hours, respectively.

In order to get credit for service level violations for either EC2 or S3, a customer must send a claim to Amazon within 30 days of the event and provide a detailed summary of their case.

8.2.2 *Microsoft Azure SLA*

Microsoft Azure SLAs are published for Azure Compute, Storage, AppFabric Access Control, and SQL Server. The Azure Compute SLA is similar to that published by Amazon for EC2. Like EC2's, the Azure Compute SLA is set at a 99.95% level. The Azure Compute SLA has two components: governing the connectivity of internet roles and governing the uptime of all customer role instances. You calculate Connectivity Downtime as the aggregate of 5-minute intervals when two or more internet-facing roles in different update domains are unavailable. You use this number to calculate the Monthly Connectivity Uptime Percentage that defines the Compute SLA as follows:

$$\frac{\textit{Monthly connectivity}}{\textit{uptime percentage}} = \frac{(\textit{Maximum connectivity minutes} - \textit{Connectivity downtime})}{(\textit{Maximum connectivity minutes})}$$

You calculate the second component of the Compute SLA similarly for the uptime of all customer roles instances.

The Azure Compute SLA is somewhat more stringent than the EC2 SLA in that it calculates the 99.95% level every month, meaning that it can be initially tripped with 20 minutes of downtime, whereas in the EC2 case calculating over a yearly interval means no penalty until more than 4 hours and 20 minutes of downtime. Availability of less than 99.95% entitles the customer to a 10% service credit for compute services, and less than 99% means a 25% credit.

The Azure Storage SLA closely mirrors the Amazon S3 SLA. It defines an error rate in a manner similar to S3, with a minor difference: the aggregation interval for measurement by default is 1 hour for Azure compared to the 5-minute interval defined by S3. Both Azure Storage and S3 define SLAs on a monthly basis and have service credits of 10% and 25% due for misses of the SLA at the 99.9% and 99% levels, respectively.

The Azure AppFabric Access Control and SQL Server SLAs have no direct comparables with Amazon. Both are defined on a monthly basis, with service credits of 10% and 25% at the 99.9% and 99% levels. For AppFabric, the SLAs govern connectivity and processing uptime percentages to the Access Control Services. For SQL Server, they govern connectivity and basic read and write operations. Additionally, the SQL Server SLA allows exclusion for scheduled maintenance for up to 10 hours per annum that doesn't count against the SLA. To claim credit for an Azure SLA violation, the customer has to send a notification to Microsoft within 5 days of the incident of the intention to file, and the claim must be sent in before the end of the next monthly billing cycle.

8.2.3 Rackspace Cloud SLA

The three relevant Rackspace SLAs are called Cloud, Sites, and Files. These SLAs are structured differently from the SLAs from Amazon and Microsoft. Unlike the other providers' SLAs, the SLAs from Rackspace can entitle customers to credit up to the entire monthly fee. But as in the case of the other vendors, customers must notify Rackspace about the SLA violation to receive credit.

The Rackspace Cloud SLA governs the functioning of the infrastructure of the Rackspace cloud, including the HVAC in the data center, network connectivity, and the virtual server, including compute, storage, and the hypervisor. In the case of the data center's power and network connectivity, Rackspace guarantees 100% uptime and offers 5% credit for each hour of unavailability up to 100% of the total monthly bill. In the event of a virtual server failure, the Cloud SLA guarantees a 1-hour replacement time after the problem is discovered and a 3-hour migration time for a virtual server operating in a degraded mode. For each hour past the initial replacement or migration window, a 5% credit is due to the customer until the situation resolves.

The Rackspace Sites SLA governs the availability of websites, email, and databases, and offers a service credit of 1 day per 1 hour of downtime. This SLA governs the availability of authentication, storage, and content delivery network (CDN) services. The minimum acceptable availability for the file-access SLA is set at 99.9%. For availability levels lower than this, the credit due to the customer is calculated on a sliding scale (see table 8.2).

Table 8.2 Rackspace credit amounts for SLA violations on cloud files availability at different levels of total availability recorded during a year

Total cloud files available time	Credit amount
100.0%–99.9%	0%
99.98%–99.5%	10%
99.49%–99.0%	25%
98.99%–98.0%	40%
97.99%–97.5%	55%
97.49%–97.0%	70%
96.99%–96.5%	85%
< 96.5%	100%

Now that you better understand the SLAs of several major cloud providers, let's look at how to measure how well they're performing and whether the vendors are living up to the standards they've set for themselves.

8.3 Measuring cloud operations

Running an application in the cloud involves using resources and infrastructure that you don't have ultimate control over. It's critically important to have visibility so you can see what's going on, to identify and react to problems quickly. In the event that your cloud provider caused the outage, you need to have visibility to enforce committed SLAs and hold them accountable.

In this section, we'll look at the various ways of tracking the level of your cloud provider's performance. Let's start with resources provided by the cloud providers themselves and then look at third-party solutions to the problem.

8.3.1 Visibility, as provided by cloud vendors

At first glance, it may seem that the logical place to look for solutions to the visibility of cloud operations is with the cloud providers themselves, and this is true to a point. Transparency in their operations helps build credibility with customers; but ultimately, if performance and availability aren't good, it's not in their self-interest to publicize it. Furthermore, too much detail about their weaknesses could provide fodder to competitors looking for an advantage. As you saw in the construction of SLAs, the onus is on the customer to prove and document the SLA violation before the vendor will credit you for it. Cloud providers do publish data related to how well they're doing, but the specificity and details of the disclosures are uneven.

WEBSITE NOTIFICATION PAGE

The simplest form of visibility that cloud providers offer their customers is a web page that reports any abnormal operating conditions or outages that may affect a customer's application. These sites are typically updated when the operations staff detects a

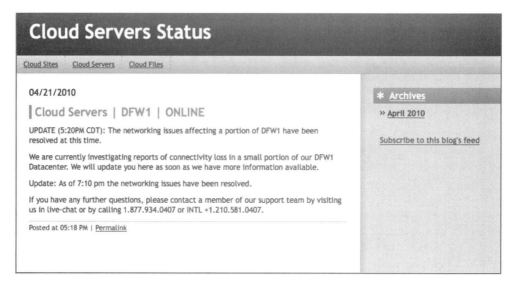

Figure 8.3   A screenshot of the Rackspace Cloud system status web page, displaying active and resolved incidents (http://status.rackspacecloud.com/cloudservers/)

problem and on an ongoing basis as it discovers information related to the issue's cause and resolution. You can see an example of this type of notification page in figure 8.3, which shows the Rackspace Cloud status page.

OPERATIONAL DASHBOARDS

The next, more detailed approach that cloud providers take to provide visibility into the health of their operations comes in the form of dashboards that are updated in real time. These dashboards show the performance of the cloud vendors' major service offerings on an aggregate basis. They display historical data, typically over the last month.

When operations are normal, they're marked by a green indicator. Abnormal states are depicted in yellow, often with annotations describing the general cause. Red, as you may imagine, indicates a critical failure of the service, such as a total outage. In figure 8.4, you can compare the operational dashboards of Amazon and Azure. You can see a remarkable similarity in the look and feel of the two screens with respect to their layout and the style with which they're rendered.

Some vendors also give a more granular breakdown of the performance of their major systems by publishing real-time statistics of the core operational parameters important for each specific system. These views provide a historical look-back capability over the last month to figure out any trends developing over time. In figure 8.5, you see that Google AppEngine Datastore service performance is described in terms of three parameters:

- *I/O throughput*—The average number of Mbps available for applications
- *I/O latency*—The time it takes for requests to be processed
- *Processing time*—The time it takes for a canonical request to be processed

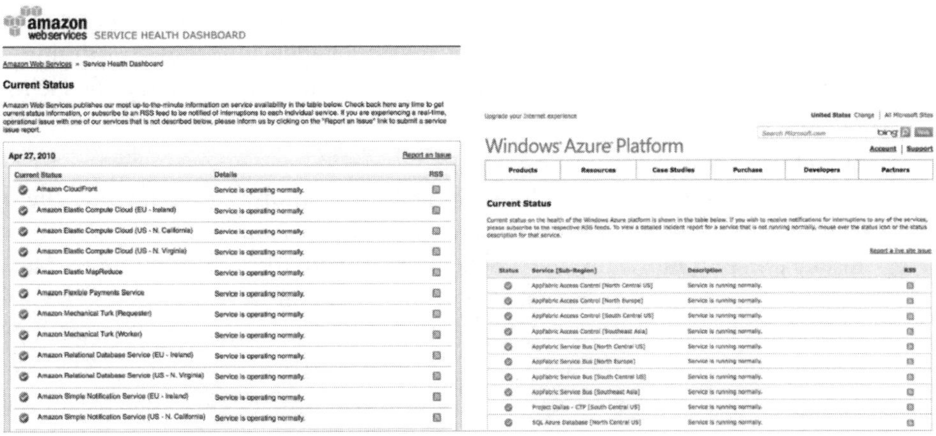

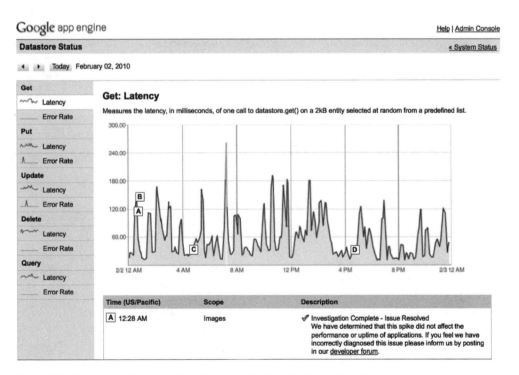

Figure 8.4 These two parallel screenshots show the real-time status dashboards for Amazon EC2 (http://status.aws.amazon.com/) and Windows Azure (www.microsoft.com/windowsazure/support/status/servicedashboard.aspx).

Figure 8.5 Datastore status from the Google AppEngine dashboard. Variations in performance as well as annotations describing incidents are shown in this display (http://code.google.com/status/appengine/detail/datastore/2010/02/02#ae-trust-detail-datastore-get-latency).

Whereas these statistics are good at an aggregate level and can tell you whether a global issue is taking place, you need more detailed information to understand the behavior of any specific application running on the cloud. You may be facing an issue isolated to a small portion of the infrastructure.

APIS AND VALUE-ADDED VISIBILITY SERVICES

Amazon CloudWatch is an additional feature to improve visibility into the operation of instances running on EC2. You can access it for an additional charge of $0.015 per instance hour. Once activated, you can access CloudWatch via the AWS Management Console (see figure 8.6) as well as via Web Services APIs.

Statistics are provided as aggregated metrics with a minimum aggregation period of 1 minute and are available for retrieval for the last 14 days. You can see data on running AMIs as well as load balancers. The following three metrics are available for AMIs:

- *CPU*—The average CPU utilization over the specified time interval, measured in percent
- *Network throughput*—The aggregate amount of inbound and outbound data to the AMI over the specified interval, measured in bytes
- *Disk usage*—The number and size in bytes of disk reads and disk writes over the specified time interval

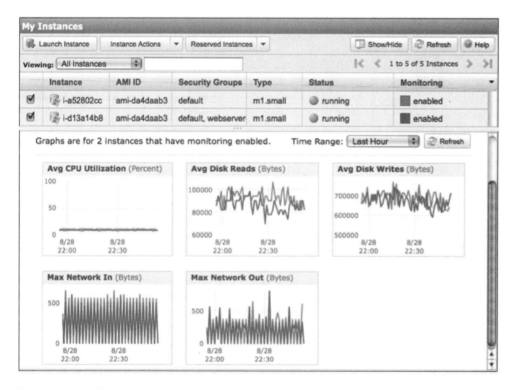

Figure 8.6   The CloudWatch feature of Amazon EC2 lets the cloud customer see metrics related to the performance of instances. Data is reported for CPU, network I/O, and disk utilization.

You can collect the statistics created for each running instance and baseline them over time. When you understand the system's normal steady-state behavior, you can apply thresholds to the data to create alerts when the system's behavior is outside its normal operating range, signaling a potential problem. The absence of data or the monitoring service itself also is an indication of a potential problem with the system.

8.3.2 *Visibility through third-party providers*

Solutions to provide visibility for cloud applications are in their early stages of development, but they can be placed in two main categories:

- *Solutions that attempt to instrument the virtual instances running the cloud application to provide more data than is made available through the monitoring services*—These can be existing network systems management solutions that have been embedded within AMIs: for example, offerings from providers such as IBM and HP.
- *Solutions that treat the cloud application as a black box*—These solutions create test transactions, sometimes called *synthetic transactions*, and measure the time it takes for the cloud application to respond. For cloud applications whose primary consumers are in the corporate environment, it's relatively simple to set up a process from within the corporate firewall that sends test transactions to the cloud application at periodic intervals. You can baseline the response time for processing the transactions. You can configure alerts either when response times fall out of an acceptable range, or when the system detects that the application isn't responding.

For a cloud application whose consumers are across the internet, several services can measure the system's performance and availability from multiple locations around the globe, such as AlertSite, Gomez, and Keynote. Some third-party vendors—such as Apparent Networks with its Cloud Performance Center (CPC) and Hyperic with CloudStatus—have put together publicly accessible dashboards that track the performance and availability of the various cloud vendors as seen from different geographical perspectives. They also provide advisory notices when they detect a serious outage of a cloud provider.

Figure 8.7 shows Apparent Networks' real-time cloud visibility dashboard. This dashboard allows you to compare the performance and availability of various leading cloud providers and also create composite metrics to stack-rank the providers according to parameters you consider the most important.

Independent third-party measurements of the operational reliability of the various cloud vendors are an important element of the cloud ecosystem. They provide needed visibility to cloud customers seeking to understand the relative merits of various providers and help to provide transparency into the nature and duration of outages when they do occur. Also, the competitive aspect of public benchmarks provide the cloud vendors an unvarnished view of their performance with respect to their peer group and can help them to understand what it takes to be the best.

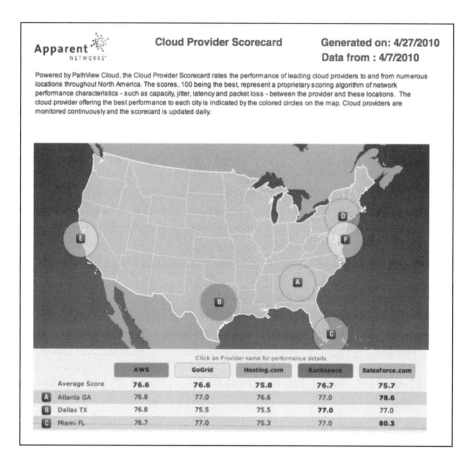

Figure 8.7   Apparent Networks provides a free service that monitors and compares the performance of various cloud providers as measured from geographical locations across the U.S. The interface includes a user-definable scorecard that can be configured with different weighting factors to rank the providers. The company also has an advisory service that documents outages of major cloud providers (www.apparentnetworks.com/CPC).

8.4   Summary

A cloud application is different from a conventionally deployed application in the level of control that's ceded to a third party. In a traditional deployment of an application with a colocation provider, you cede control over physical security, power, and network connectivity to a third party, but you retain control over the server hardware, operating systems, and application software. In a cloud deployment, you extend the ceding of control to include the server hardware and the operating system (through the virtualized environment). In comparison, this should be a good thing, because there's less to worry about as long as the provider's systems operate at a sufficient level of reliability.

The operating principle for these systems can be summed up using former President Reagan's approach to nuclear disarmament: "Trust, but verify." You'll need the necessary data to measure the cloud provider's compliance to the committed service levels. A practical strategy for maintaining good performance starts by assessing availability and performance as experienced by end users through continuous monitoring of the deployed application. When you detect a problem, instrumentation of the cloud applications is useful in determining whether the problem is of your own creation or is due to a problem with a cloud provider. Independent third-party assessments of cloud availability and performance can serve as a useful check before you draw conclusions.

Now that you've spent some time looking at the practical operational issues involved in managing an application deployed to the cloud, it's time to switch gears and get back to the bigger picture. In the final chapter of the book, let's leave the world of cloud computing as it exists today and fast-forward to see what the long-term future of IT looks like and how cloud computing will impact it.

Cloud 9:
the future of the cloud

The previous chapters as well as the introduction have covered a broad range of topics—defining who can best use this book, what the cloud is, and the what, when, and how of moving to the cloud. It's consistent with that progression to end with a set of predictions for the future of cloud computing. We'll do our best to paint both a medium- and long-term picture, keeping with the themes of the rest of this book to make them *useful*. We'll give you more information and perspective about what this means for you and your business, and prepare you to make informed decisions about how and when to begin utilizing some aspects of the cloud.

You'll also see how we think IT will look a generation from now—it will look like what people have for years been calling *utility computing*.

188

UTILITY COMPUTING   The packaging of computing resources, such as computation and storage, as a metered service similar to a traditional public utility (such as electricity, water, natural gas, or a telephone network). This system has the advantage of a low or no initial cost to acquire hardware; instead, you can rent computational resources. Customers with large computations or a sudden peak in demand can also avoid the delays that would result from physically acquiring and assembling a large number of computers. This term predates cloud computing; but as you can see, this is what cloud computing is becoming.

Making predictions, particularly long-range ones, is a risky business, as the short list of failed past predictions—at times both wrong and irrelevant—in figure 9.1 shows.

9.1 *The most significant transformation IT has ever undergone*

In the case of the cloud, we're confident that the future will involve a pervasive, game-changing reconstruction of IT from the ground up that'll take a full generation to occur. We'll break this section into two parts and look first at consumers and the cloud—including mobile computing—followed by the cloud in enterprises.

9.1.1 *The consumer internet and the cloud*

According to William Gibson (*The Economist*, December 4, 2003), "The future is already here—only, it's not evenly distributed." This quotation describes the present cloud position well. If you look at the consumer-facing internet, cloud usage is already pervasive. But for enterprise computing, widespread use of the cloud is still in the future.

1943	IBM's T. J. Watson predicted, "I think there is a world market for maybe five computers."
late 1970s	"The mainframe will always be the prevalent computing platform. The minicomputer is a toy."
early 1980s	"The PC will never be successful. People do not need their own personal computers."
mid-1980s	"The minicomputer will prevail. PC and networked computers are merely toys."
early 1990s	"The Internet has no real future as a computing platform. Too unreliable. Too hard to use. Could never support millions."
mid-1990s	"Electronic commerce is a joke. The Web is just a way to provide marketing information."
late 1990s	"There is no business model giving software away for free. The concept of collecting 'eyeballs' will never make money."

Figure 9.1   This list of predictions made about computing over the decades is now amusing.

Cloud Computing Activities by Different Age Cohorts

Internet users in each age group who do the following online activities (%)

	18-29	30-49	50-64	65+
Use webmail services such as Hotmail, Gmail, or Yahoo! mail	77%	58%	44%	27%
Store personal photos	50	34	26	19
Use online applications such as Google Documents or Adobe Photoshop Express	39	28	25	19
Store personal videos	14	6	5	2
Pay to store computer files online	9	4	5	3
Back up hard drive to an online site	7	5	5	4
Have done at least one activity	87%	71%	59%	46%
Have done at least two activities	59	39	31	21

Source: Pew Internet & American Life Project April-May 2008 Survey. N=1,553 Internet users. Margin of error is ±3%.

Figure 9.2   Cloud computing activities by different age cohorts from the Pew Internet & American Life Project of 2008. The survey shows that the younger age groups are using the cloud heavily and will continue to do so. The greatest usage is in the millennial group (87%), which does at least one activity (email, photos, online applications, video, storage, or backups) using the cloud.

The original generation of cloud computing infrastructure was built by companies such as Amazon and Google to solve their own problems in the internet-consumer space (referred to here as *internal clouds*). A 2008 survey conducted by the Pew Internet & American Life Project (see figure 9.2) found that in every age group other than 65 plus, the majority of users used the cloud infrastructure in at least one activity.

In the near future, probably within the next two to three years, we expect that the use of applications backed by the cloud will be ubiquitous, with practically all internet users using the cloud in some form or another. Three primary drivers are responsible for this shift to the cloud:

- Application standardization on the browser platform
- Miniaturization and standardization of device based computing
- The mobile revolution

Let's now discuss each of these three drivers in more detail in turn.

APPLICATION STANDARDIZATION ON THE BROWSER PLATFORM

Browsers first came out in 1991. The initial browser with significant adoption was Mosaic's Mozilla browser, which had rudimentary graphical capabilities. The browser sent a request to retrieve bits of static text and images, and the server on the other end of the network sent the requested data. From there, browsers and the web itself evolved to become more dynamic, through the introduction of client-side scripting capabilities such as JavaScript by Netscape in 1995 and Flash by Macromedia in 1996. You can see

Figure 9.3   Major browsers and their initial release dates: the original Mozilla browser, Netscape's Navigator, Microsoft's Internet Explorer, Opera Software ASA's browser, Apple's Safari, Mozilla's Firefox, and Google's Chrome.

in figure 9.3 Mozilla and the rest of the highly popular browsers in the order in which they were initially released.

In 1999, the Servlet Specification version 2.2 introduced the concept of the *web application* in the Java language. At that time, both JavaScript and XML had already been developed, but Ajax hadn't been announced, and the `XMLHttpRequest` object had only been recently introduced in Internet Explorer 5 as an ActiveX object.

In 2005, we heard the term *Ajax* (acronym for Asynchronous JavaScript and XML) for the first time. Applications such as Google Maps and Gmail started to make their client sides more interactive with Ajax. Web applications could retrieve data from the server asynchronously in the background without interfering with the display and behavior of the existing page. Today, browsers and servers interacting over the internet form a highly interactive, generally useful application delivery system for content, commerce, and collaboration.

JavaScript finally began the process of browsers enabling rich web-based applications. This step moved us away from the "submit-button web" applications of that generation (fill in edit boxes, and click a submit button) more toward the "green screen" applications of mainframe days (full-fledged applications running on a remote computer). A key point to note is that the increased capabilities have, for the most part, proceeded without major loss of interoperability. For application developers today, the web is the platform, period. All web-based applications work as they would in any standards-compliant browser. As the cloud has more to offer and as client devices get simpler, a rich browser becomes all you need to interact with all the applications you use. You can access everything via a browser (considered a *thin client*) and a set of network-enabled applications downloaded over the network. Because browsers are so rich in their capabilities and because applications today provide functionality via these browsers that used to be available only via *fat clients* (think of Microsoft Office versus Google Docs), there need not be a loss of capability or productivity.

With Chrome, Google is the first to acknowledge that the browser is evolving into an operating system. Google Chrome OS is an open-source, lightweight operating system that can run on a device with limited computing and storage capacity. As the operating system and the browser merge, the importance of the cloud increases as it serves as the de facto home for applications demanding large compute or storage.

Let's move on to the second trend—the evolution of client hardware devices—and how that relates to the future of cloud computing.

MINIATURIZATION AND STANDARDIZATION OF DEVICE-BASED COMPUTING

The idea of a *network computer* was floated as early as the mid-1990s. Sun was the first to come up with a network computer to follow through with the corporate tag line "the network is the computer." These machines, primarily deployed in an enterprise environment, weren't broadly adopted. Figure 9.4 shows a sampling of the attempts at less powerful computers that operate with little or no local storage.

Apple also came out with a concept aimed at the business or *prosumer* audience. Apple's eMate was a subcompact laptop—sort of a cross between the Newton PDA and a conventional laptop. Like the Newton, it wasn't a hit and faded from view and memory quickly.

Much more recently, we've seen the emergence of a new category of personal computers called *netbooks* (sometimes called mini notebooks or ultraportables). Netbooks are small, light, and inexpensive laptop computers suited for general computing and accessing web-based applications (the cloud) and often marketed as "companion devices," because they augment a user's other computer access.

Taking this a step further is the *tablet* concept. In general terms, a tablet PC refers to a slate-shaped mobile computer device, equipped with a touchscreen or stylus. This form factor offers a more mobile computer. The term *tablet PC* became popular through a product announced in 2001 by Microsoft. The concept was too new, and few were sold. In 2010, when Apple finally released the iPad, the concept of the mobile device being only a tablet PC finally stuck.

Figure 9.4   The evolution of network computers, clockwise from upper left: Sun's Network Computer, Apple's eMate, Microsoft's Tablet PC, Apple's iPad, and the current generation of netbook

Parallel to these developments, mobile phones were evolving from devices exclusively used for voice communications to those able to function as a PDA, send text messages, and interact with simplified web pages. These evolved into what is known as a *smart-phone*—a mobile phone offering advanced capabilities, often with PC-like functionality. Most important, a smartphone has a fully functional browser and can therefore act as a thin client for any application that runs in the cloud.

Smartphone adoption

In the U.S., 19% of consumers use a smartphone now; 49% plan to purchase one within two years (source: The Kelsey Group).

The smartphone market is growing at 30% per year and is now more than 180 million units per year, surpassing unit sales of PCs. Smartphones globally already make up 37% of handsets and continue to grow at 30% annually.

Apple transformed and energized this market with the iPhone's large touch screen, powerful networking, and huge number of applications; in a record short time, the iPhone snared 15% market share.

Over 2 billion iPhone applications have been downloaded. All run in the cloud. The iPad runs all iPhone applications and will only accelerate the use of mobile applications running in the cloud, as will Android phones, the smarter Blackberries, and new internet-browsing-capable phones coming out all the time.

In the future, you'll see tablets and smartphones displace the primacy of the PC as the primary personal computing device. These devices will run a combination of resident applications and cloud applications and will be backed by data storage in the cloud. This time, the idea is sticking because the concept of a cloud has finally caught up with the visionary client idea.

THE MOBILE REVOLUTION

Cloud computing is a disruptive force in the mobile world for two reasons: the number of users the technology has the power to reach—all the smartphones *plus* all the users of cloud applications on their PCs (Facebook alone represents 400 million consumers using the cloud from their computer or their smartphone); and the way applications are distributed today. Currently, mobile applications (including iPhone applications) are tied to a carrier. If you want an iPhone application, for example, you must first have a relationship with the mobile operator that carries the iPhone. If you want a Blackberry application, the same rule applies. But with mobile cloud-computing applications, as long as you have access to the web via a browser, you have access to the mobile application.

The future of mobile computing is simple to predict. In lots of different form factors, from netbooks to iPads, and on countless forms of smartphones that get increasingly smarter, you'll do most computing in an untethered (that is, wireless) fashion on lightweight computers accessing the cloud. And this will be true within the next cycle of cell phone contract renewal. (The cell phone industry has fostered a culture of highly accelerated consumer upgrades through their two-year contract renewal process aided by handset prices they subsidize.)

By the end of the first decade of this millennium, it became clear that consumers, not business users, were now driving smartphone adoption. It also indicated the start of the massive use of the cloud. (Hence, the major cloud providers went on a frantic building spree to create those $500 million data centers.) This simple change of putting consumers in the driver's seat cemented the acceptance of the cloud.

Consumers have no concerns about running their applications in the cloud (they use Google search, Gmail, Flickr, YouTube, and Facebook with no hesitation) and will continue to gravitate to applications that have the full features and responsiveness they like. As consumers take over the lead role in this massive shift in the way computing is done, their vast demographics will drive more enterprises to drop their reluctance and move to the cloud.

9.1.2 *The cloud in the enterprise*

Enterprise adoption of the cloud will proceed more slowly than the rapid rise for consumer-facing internet applications. This isn't surprising, because enterprise applications are less often entirely new as is most often the case for the consumer internet; they often rely on reusing existing functionality. Compuware, in working with its customers and market analysts, gathered data about where it sees the mix between mainframe, client-server, and various forms of cloud computing going over the next few years; see figure 9.5.

Looking longer term, we see the future of cloud computing in the enterprise proceeding through the following phases over the next 20 years:

- *Phase I*—Startups doing it hard and manually
- *Phase II*—Internal cloud migration

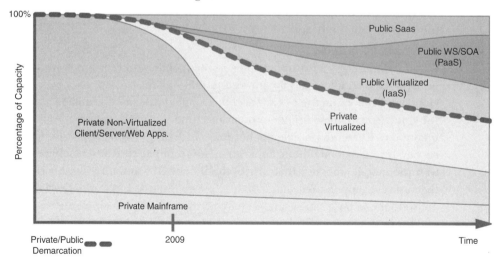

Figure 9.5   The projected mix of computing done via mainframe, client-server, and various types of clouds in enterprises over the next few years. Source: Compuware.

- *Phase III*—Ascendancy of the private cloud
- *Phase IV*—Transition to utility computing

In the subsequent sections, we'll go through these phases in sequence. You should view the phases as general characteristics of how the cloud will look over time, with the elements of each phase present throughout. Refer to figure 9.5 as you go through this discussion. Let's begin by looking at where we are today.

PHASE I: STARTUPS DOING IT HARD AND MANUALLY

We're today at an admittedly difficult stage: the beginning. This stage only works well for the smallest companies that have little-to-no existing IT infrastructure investment. They'll lease, buy, or build all applications. Many venture capitalists won't fund startups to purchase any IT equipment. For most startups this is no hardship, and it's natural for them to begin using the cloud for all their computing needs from day one. Amazon still leads the way in terms of customer share. Most of its estimated 500,000 customers are small companies.

This stage doesn't have enough standardization to avoid the lock-in that the cloud critics worry so much about. Not enough vendors and not enough competition make this an uneasy place to live. Big companies are worried about security and still believe (somewhat erroneously, as you've seen) that their data is more at risk in someone else's cloud than in their own data centers.

At this stage, SaaS is well established and growing; the next most successful cloud model is IaaS. In IaaS, as you've learned in this book, it takes pretty sophisticated programmers to lead the way, and everything has to be done manually the hard way. But there's light on the horizon as standards, frameworks, and tools make this increasingly less difficult. The bigger enterprises may remain hesitant and reluctant during this early phase.

PHASE II: THE INTERNAL CLOUD MIGRATION

Phase II, which should take place in the short term (the next five years), will be the shift to an *internal cloud* model. This is where an enterprise with existing IT infrastructure investment applies the concepts of cloud computing (on-demand resources, pay-as-you-go pricing, and the appearance of infinite scalability) to resources wholly owned by the enterprise consuming the service. They're building this out now as the adoption of virtualization leads companies down this path naturally.

Internal clouds are appealing to IT departments at many levels, although obviously they won't provide the economies of scale that public clouds will offer over time. But those standing outside the enterprise too quickly forget about the inability of most public clouds to support legacy applications without which the enterprise would cease to operate. In contrast, you can build internal clouds to handle old and new applications alike.

Perhaps the most pervasive argument is that internal clouds allow you to maintain control over security, service levels, and regulatory compliance in a way that public clouds aren't yet able to offer.

The move to internal clouds makes sense as a first step, and it should help to prepare enterprises for the real cloud. What will push them in that direction is the fact that choosing an internal-cloud approach doesn't provide the full benefits of public-cloud computing offerings. With much smaller scale, the economics aren't in an internal cloud's favor. Consequently, this phase of the evolution won't last long for any given company.

PHASE III: ASCENDANCY OF THE PRIVATE CLOUD

Private clouds, unlike internal clouds, will have a long-term role in the cloud ecosystem. And they'll play a dominant role in the medium term of 2 to 10 years from now.

As you saw in chapter 4, private clouds overcome the "rewrite everything" effect of "own nothing" cloud computing, rendering a much lower barrier to adoption for enterprises. Additionally, they provide the degree of trust that enterprises seek from internal clouds, including the ability to change the mix of cloud services consumed completely at their own discretion.

In general, those that opt for internal clouds will move to private clouds. And many will see private clouds initially as the best way to migrate. Once ensconced in a private cloud, there's a direct route to migrate all application workloads from wholly owned infrastructure to public clouds, where the economics of owning nothing come into play. The best part about this strategy—and the reason for the popularity of the private cloud computing model for years to come—is that it gives enterprises the perception that everything is running in their own data centers under their complete control.

PHASE IV: TRANSITION TO UTILITY COMPUTING

Utility computing has been a dream of many for several decades. But the infrastructure and maturity of both the cloud environment and enterprises hasn't been anywhere close to what is needed to make utility computing a reality. The basis of the dream goes back to the analogy of electric power in the early 1900s. Previously, many beer breweries had their own power generators. They needed lots of power, and power from an electric utility either wasn't available or was unreliable. Being an expert in electricity shouldn't be a prerequisite to brew beer. The beer brewers couldn't wait to dump their own generators and start using electricity provided by experts to whom they paid a monthly fee. Similarly, enterprises realized that they needed computers to run their businesses. But unlike the beer brewers buying electricity from a utility, enterprises couldn't opt not to run their own computer centers—until the day of ubiquitous cloud computing. Many today see the utility-computing model finally on the horizon as the solution.

It won't arrive quickly. It may take a generation (20 years) to fully transform computing. But these transformations happen both faster and slower than anticipated. In hindsight, things always seem to have happened faster than expected. But from the forward-looking perspective, living through these transformations makes them appear slower than desired. Big shifts similar to the one underway now have, in the past, taken a decade or so to fully wash in—for example, general adoption of client-server and personal computers. This one will take even longer because many of the current generation of corporate decision-makers will have to retire before their organizations can release their psychological commitment to keeping local physical control of data.

Figure 9.6, similar in concept to the Compuware diagram shown in figure 9.5, is our view of the next 20 years. It shows what percentage of overall computing capacity is allocated to what type of IT infrastructure, be it private cloud, internal cloud, public cloud, or the more traditional captive data center.

Now that you've seen the general pattern of the evolution and future of cloud computing, let's look at some specific predictions of what you can expect to happen.

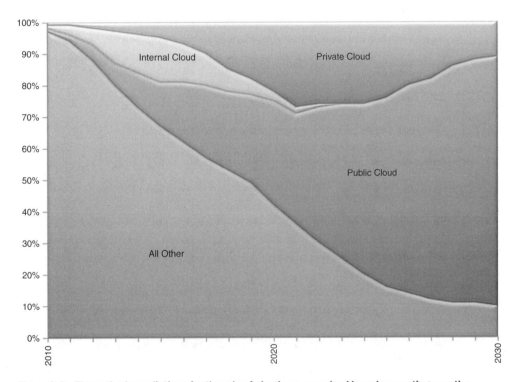

Figure 9.6 The author's predictions for the role of clouds vs. non-cloud-based computing over the next 20 years. Today, less than 3% of computing is done via clouds. Twenty years from now, public clouds will be the dominant approach for corporate IT services. Private clouds, which will initially grow to more than 35% of all IT, will shrink back to under 25%; internal clouds will all but disappear; and the remaining percentage of do-it-yourself IT (such as corporations with their own data centers) will be only 10%.

9.2   Ten predictions about how the cloud will evolve

In the first of two prediction sections, we'll focus on how the infrastructure evolves. In short form, the list of predictions about how the cloud will evolve is as follows:

- The cloud will be cheaper, more reliable, more secure, and easier to use.
- The cloud will become a real engine of growth for early adopter companies.
- Cloud providers' costs will be less than 25% of what corporate data centers cost.
- Cloud mega-data centers will contain 500,000 servers costing $1B by 2020.
- The best cloud provider operator's ratio of administrators to servers will go from 1:1,000 servers to 1:10,000 servers by 2020.
- Open source will dominate the future of the cloud.
- Pragmatic standards come from market leaders; Amazon's API will lead the way.
- An ultimate ISO cloud standard will emerge.
- Government will lead enterprises in cloud adoption.
- SaaS will grow and stay current by using the basic web standards that will themselves continue to advance.

Let's begin with our first prediction.

9.2.1   Cheaper, more reliable, more secure, and easier to use

The cloud will be cheaper, more reliable, more secure, and easier to use. Relentless economies of scale are driving down cloud providers' costs as cloud providers build bigger data centers, get volume discounts from commodity hardware providers, demand better rates from power companies, and continue to use as much open-source software as possible. Fierce competition keeps prices low. As de facto standards emerge and with the promise of more widely adopted international standards to come, less and less lock-in will be possible; that will further drive competition until cloud services are a pure commodity based almost entirely on price.

Meanwhile, competition and strident demand from customers will force cloud providers to promise stronger SLAs to which they'll have to adhere. Most providers will have multiple locations each with excess capacity to compensate hardware or network failures by moving workloads to different banks of servers or entirely different facilities if the failure is broad in scope.

The effort expended to make clouds more secure and compartmentalized for data integrity and for privacy will pay dividends in the long term. Ultimately, as we have noted, even the public clouds will provide better data security and protection than the vast majority of either government or enterprise data centers. Because data in transit and data stored in cloud storage facilities will remain encrypted in all types of clouds, data security in non-cloud data centers will improve as they adopt best practices initially demonstrated by the public and private clouds.

Ease of use will continue to improve, as all competitive software systems tend to do, as users provide feedback and vote through their dollars for the best service providers. Amazon is winning today, and that'll push many cloud providers to use the Amazon API more broadly; but usability will still come under heavy scrutiny and will improve as more customers use the systems and report issues.

The end result means that the cloud will be cheaper, more reliable, more secure, and easier to use than corporate data centers.

9.2.2 *Engine of growth for early adopters*

The cloud will become a real engine of growth for early adopter companies. Five hundred thousand companies are already using Amazon's AWS. As discussed in chapter 2, most startups no longer buy servers; instead, they use the cloud for everything they formerly would have expended significant capital equipment dollars for. This leaves precious dollars for other things that can help companies get to market faster and out-market and out-sell competitors that aren't using the cloud.

As is always the case, the real engine for growth in any market is innovation. The reason the cloud strongly supports innovation—and therefore drives growth—is that it changes a company's willingness to experiment. Because it's so cheap to provision new virtual instances and build a product to test a new idea, companies want to try it. Paying only for what you use means failures are quickly turned off and de-provisioned and are immediately no further drain on the company's resources. But experiments that are a big success take off, get broader exposure, and, because they're running in the cloud, can expand to keep up with demand. Companies try things they couldn't try before. This becomes a vehicle for growth for companies that are early adopters of the cloud.

The cloud will be such an important engine of growth for early adopters that those companies will get to market faster, will compete better, and will win compared to laggards that don't use the cloud.

9.2.3 *Much lower costs than corporate data centers*

Cloud providers' costs will be less than 25% of what corporate data centers cost. Already, the cloud providers' data center costs are much lower than what corporate data centers spend because the mega centers get huge economies of scale, receive significant tax breaks, and continue to drive down costs each year.

These mega data centers may quickly become an "if you can't beat them, join them" proposition. Intel now says that by 2012 mega data centers will account for 25% of its server chip sales. Dell created a specialized division to address the needs of customers buying more than 2,000 servers at a time and now declares that division as the fourth- or fifth-largest server vendor in the world. This also means the big server consumers can profoundly influence Intel (or Dell) design decisions and can negotiate huge volume discounts that no one else can get.

The big cloud data centers are using more scale-based approaches to wring out even more cost. For instance, they're beginning to eliminate redundancy in each facility (such as generators and batteries) by building sophisticated software that can move workloads to other facilities when failures occur.

The gap between corporate data savings and cloud provider data center savings will continue to widen, and by 2020, cloud provider costs will be less than 25% of what corporate data centers cost.

9.2.4 *500,000 servers costing $1 billion by 2020*

Cloud mega data centers will contain 500,000 servers costing $1 billion by 2020. A small list of enormous cloud providers, including Amazon, Apple, Google, Microsoft, Oracle, IBM, and even Facebook, are in a class by themselves when it comes to the size of their data centers. Examples of centers this expensive include Microsoft's Chicago facility, which is 700,000 square feet and cost $500 million; and the company's San Antonio facility, which is 11 acres and cost $550 million. Apple also has one in North Carolina (chosen because of the tax breaks); it's over 500,000 square feet and is shown in a rare photo in figure 9.7. Google has 40 data centers around the globe, all roughly this size.

All of these cloud providers are building data centers that have in the range of 50,000–100,000 servers; on the low end, when amortized over three years, such a center costs about $53 million per year. That constitutes about 45% of the total cost of the data center. Another 25% goes to power distribution and cooling ($18 million/year); 15% is for electric utility costs ($9 million/year, of which 59% is for IT equipment, 33% for cooling, and 8% for power losses); and 15% is for network costs. These data centers consume as much power as aluminum smelters, silicon

Figure 9.7   A rare photo of Apple's new 500,000 sq. ft. North Carolina cloud data center site

manufacturers, and automobile factories. All the data centers in the world combined use more power then Holland.

9.2.5 Ratio of administrators to servers: 1:10,000 by 2020

The best cloud provider operator's ratio of administrators to servers will go from 1:1,000 to 1:10,000 servers by 2020. Note that the breakdown of costs in the previous section didn't list labor. This is because mega data centers have so much scale that the cost of labor becomes miniscule, particularly because they've invested heavily in software to automate the operation. A typical corporate data center operates at a ratio of about 1 staff member to every 100 servers, whereas the best cloud providers operate instead at a ratio of 1:1,000 servers. These facilities draw the best IT professionals because they're so advanced and specialized that it's a good career move. Also, the cloud providers pay employees better for their skills than corporate data centers do.

The cloud data centers run so efficiently because they've had to build high levels of automation into their operations to offer a basic cloud offering. One way they can achieve high levels of automation is by standardizing their platforms. You can request only a handful of different platforms from Amazon. But a typical corporate data center has a huge number of applications (frequently in the thousands) with literally hundreds of different possible configurations of hardware and software. Exacerbating this complexity is the fact that forecasts for usage patterns and scale requirements are usually uncertain. This pushes a tendency to overprovision so as not to get caught short of capacity on important applications.

The end result of this constant drive for more automation, hiring the best people, and creating larger data centers, will get the cloud providers to a ration of 1 administrator for every 10,000 servers in the next decade.

9.2.6 Open source dominance

The cloud of the future will be dominated by open source. Linux is the operating system of choice in the cloud. Frequently, you see cloud providers running RedHat Linux. Xen is the hypervisor of choice. In the hypervisor world, the most common alternatives to Xen are Microsoft and VMware, neither of which is cheap. Amazon's hundreds of thousands of servers supporting EC2 run the Xen hypervisor as do cloud providers 3Tera and Rackspace. Such heavy-duty usage will keep the open-source community building the basic infrastructure for the cloud busy and vibrant.

Open source is a powerful force because acquisition and licensing costs of open-source software is 80% lower than comparable proprietary offerings. You've already seen how cost sensitive (due to their scale) the cloud providers are. Naturally, open source has been driving the cloud evolution and will continue to do so. But it works both ways—the rapid advancements of the cloud fuel the open-source movement as well. The cloud is perfect for open-source developers to use for development, testing, and storage at low cost for the sometimes shoestring operations of open-source developers.

> ## Rackspace open sources cloud platform and collaborates with NASA
>
> From a July 19, 2010 press release:
>
> *More than 25 companies, including Citrix and Dell, support open-source cloud platform to accelerate industry standards.*
>
> *Rackspace Hosting today announced the launch of OpenStack, an open-source cloud platform designed to foster the emergence of technology standards and cloud interoperability. Rackspace, the leading specialist in the hosting and cloud computing industry, is donating the code that powers its Cloud Files and Cloud Servers public-cloud offerings to the OpenStack project. The project will also incorporate technology that powers the NASA Nebula Cloud Platform. Rackspace and NASA plan to actively collaborate on joint technology development and leverage the efforts of open-source software developers worldwide.*

You don't need a crystal ball to predict that the cloud of the future will be much more open source.

9.2.7   *Pragmatic standards via Amazon's APIs*

Pragmatic standards come from market leaders; Amazon's APIs will lead the way. You can measure the maturity of an IT technology by the number, adoption rate, and depth of its standards. The cloud—at least the IaaS portion of the cloud—today is at the early edge of that scale, but that'll change rapidly. As you've seen, forces are in play that will make the cloud the platform shift that dwarfs all others.

As you've read earlier, a host of standards groups have formed and are starting to work on various aspects of cloud standardization and APIs. But necessity will drive some groups to create their own standards and not wait for standards bodies. For instance, Zend, Microsoft, IBM, Rackspace, Nirvanix, and GoGrid developed the open-source Simple Cloud API to interact with many different cloud providers. Initially, this was an effort to make it easy for PHP developers (PHP is a common workload in IaaS clouds) to access services on many clouds. Early adapters will be for file-storage services, document-storage services (initially to include Windows Azure table and Amazon SimpleDB support), and simple queue services (initially including Azure queues and Amazon SQS).

Other vendors' clouds will co-opt and retarget Amazon's APIs as fast as Amazon comes out with them. Amazon uses both a RESTful API and a SOAP API for most of its services. Usually, the RESTful will be the one most copied and used elsewhere. It's simple and easy to use and works with any application framework.

In the last decade, the IT community has discovered that it works best to take something that one vendor—the leading vendor in a category—has developed and proven, and turn that into a standard as opposed to creating a study group and a standards committee and go through the long process of releasing an international standard. You can expect a lot of standards to begin as proprietary cloud APIs and evolve into industry-wide standards over a period of time.

As in any major industry transformation, the leader gets to call the shots or, in this case, establish the initial standards. Amazon is that leader.

9.2.8 Ultimate ISO cloud standard

An ultimate ISO cloud standard is coming. Due to the hype, it's easy to forget that the cloud is new. New things don't have standards. Many people say they're sitting on the sidelines because there are no standards yet. But we can't have standards too early, because we don't know enough about usage patterns to get them right. Having said that, standards are critical, and they're coming. Standards drive choice, and choice drives market expansion. These forces are too strong for standards not to come quickly.

The Open Cloud Consortium (OCC) is already working on interoperation of different clouds. The Cloud Security Alliance (CSA) is actively urging common best practices. The (controversial) Open Cloud Manifesto urges vendors to agree on basic principles and interoperability. The few strongly pro vendors are AMD, IBM, Rackspace, Sun, and VMware. But the most important players are against the idea, including Microsoft, Google, and Amazon. They think interoperability at this early stage will hurt them the most. That's a problem and probably spells doom for this particular standards effort.

The group of standards bodies called the Cloud Standards Coordination Working Group includes the Organization for the Advancement of Structured Information Standards (OASIS), Object Management Group (OMG), Distributed Management Task Force (DMTF), Storage and Network Industry Association (SNIA), Open Grid Forum (OGF), CSA, OCC, Cloud Computing Interoperability Forum (CCIF), and the TM Forum. This group is looking at standardization in a number of specific areas, including security; interfaces to IaaS; information about deployment, such as resource and component descriptions; management frameworks; data-exchange formats and cloud taxonomies; and reference models.

ISO formed a subcommittee for SOA and web services and a study group for cloud computing called SC38, "Distributed application platforms and services (DAPS)" (www.iso.org/iso/standards_development/technical_committees/other_bodies/iso_technical_committee.htm?commid=601355). It addresses the following 10 things:

- *The end user is the primary stakeholder in cloud computing.* User-centric systems enrich the lives of individuals, education, communication, collaboration, business, entertainment, and society as a whole.

- *Philanthropic initiatives can greatly increase the wellbeing of mankind.* Enable or enhance cloud computing where possible.

- *Openness of standards, systems, and software empowers and protects users.* Adopt existing standards where possible for the benefit of all stakeholders.

- *Transparency fosters trust and accountability.* Decisions should be open to public collaboration and scrutiny and never be made behind closed doors.

- *Interoperability ensures effectiveness of cloud computing as a public resource.* Systems must be interoperable over a minimal set of community defined standards and avoid vendor lock-in.
- *Representation of all stakeholders is essential.* Vendor(s) shouldn't dominate interoperability and standards efforts.
- *Discrimination against any party for any reason is unacceptable.* Minimize barriers to entry.
- *Evolution is an ongoing process in an immature market.* Standards may take some time to develop and coalesce, but activities should be coordinated and collaborative.
- *Balance of commercial and consumer interests is paramount.* If in doubt, consumer interests prevail.
- *Security is fundamental, not optional.* Lack of security would kill cloud adoption.

ISO takes a long time for a new international standard to come out. But its involvement shows the cloud is now a serious and permanent part of the IT constellation. The ultimate ISO standard that results will have widespread and dominating influence on the industry.

9.2.9 Government leadership in cloud adoption

Government will lead enterprises in cloud adoption. Cloud computing is currently playing a big role in the federal government because the current U.S. CIO is a strong proponent of the economic benefits of the cloud for government computing and also because the U.S. government IT budget is $76 billion. NASA is using cloud computing and social media to become more efficient and to lower costs. The City of Los Angeles is an early local government entity to fully embrace the cloud. Other major government cloud projects include the U.S. Army; Department of the Treasury; Bureau of Alcohol, Tobacco, Firearms, and Explosives; and many others.

The biggest move may be that of the General Services Administration (GSA). It has decided to prebid cloud services so that all federal agencies can select and deploy cloud-based data and applications on the fly at predetermined rates and feature sets. Further, the GSA has created the Federal Risk and Authorization Management Program (FedRAMP), made up of members of the Department of Defense (DoD), the Department of Homeland Security, and the GSA, that'll inspect cloud providers for security, privacy, and other best practices. This will keep the heat on providers to stay current with best practices in order to remain on the approved list. The incentives are highest for the federal government because the scale of these agencies is so large that their cost savings dwarf what even large enterprises will see.

Even though, historically, government hasn't been a leader in use of IT technology, this time is different. Enterprises will find themselves in the unusual position of trying to catch up to the government.

9.2.10 SaaS use of basic web standards

SaaS will grow and stay current by using the basic web standards that will themselves continue to advance. SaaS, as exemplified by Facebook, Gmail, Flickr, Salesforce.com, and hundreds of other applications, is the cloud paradigm most strongly in play. Gartner estimates the size of the SaaS market will be $16 billion by 2013. IDC continues to report 40% annual growth rate for the category. More than 76% of U.S. corporations use at least one SaaS application. Some 45% of companies spend at least 25% of their IT budgets on SaaS. These companies are already shifting their users to the cloud even if they're not yet fully ready to shift their own infrastructure to the cloud.

SaaS is easy for corporations to adopt from a technology standpoint. The point of SaaS is that all you need to have to use an application is a browser. It needs no additional standards: SaaS exists because of and will continue to use the same standards on which all basic websites and web applications are built. As HTML 5 becomes broadly supported in browsers, SaaS applications will take advantage of its features, bringing a more interactive experience to users and further removing any complaints users may have when transitioning from fat clients to SaaS applications.

9.3   Ten predictions about how application development will evolve

This section focuses on how application development evolves. In short form, the list of 10 predictions about application development evolution is as follows:

- Application frameworks will have a significant role in the growth and evolution of cloud computing.
- The second or middle (application logic) tier and the third tier (storage) will more often run in the cloud.
- Rapid evolution will occur for different storage mechanisms, particularly for unstructured data and database scaling strategies such as sharding.
- Security services will include more and stronger options to protect sensitive data.
- Over the next decade, companies with valuable data repositories will offer higher-level services hosted on existing clouds, each with a unique API.
- Adoption and growth of mashups will fuel the further growth of the cloud.
- What most call PaaS (for example, Google's App Engine) and its natural extension—Framework as a Service—will become the predominant way applications are constructed in 10 years.
- More powerful development tools will quickly evolve to make it easy to build mashups.
- Developers outside the U.S. and Europe will leapfrog the West because they're not encumbered by legacy IT infrastructure.
- The cost of creating an application will become so low that it will cease to be a barrier.

Let's begin with the first prediction about application frameworks.

9.3.1   Role of application frameworks

Application frameworks will have a significant role in the growth and evolution of cloud computing. In addition to the base platform we've been discussing, a large and growing list of open-source application frameworks are coming online. These application frameworks are used broadly for building a wide variety of web applications. As such, they'll have a significant role in the growth and evolution of cloud computing as well. You can see a few of the more common and heavily used frameworks for building web (and therefore including cloud-based) applications in table 9.1.

Application frameworks are always an important accelerator for development because they provide developers with much of the foundational material of an application. In cloud-based applications, this will be more important than ever.

Table 9.1 Popular application frameworks

Framework	Characteristics
Ruby on Rails	Ruby is a dynamic, reflective, general-purpose, object-oriented programming language that combines syntax inspired by Perl with Smalltalk-like features. Ruby originated in Japan during the mid-1990s. It's based on Perl, Smalltalk, Eiffel, Ada, and Lisp.
Apache Struts	Apache Struts is an open-source web application framework for developing Java EE web applications. It uses and extends the Java Servlet API to encourage developers to adopt a model-view-controller (MVC) architecture. It was donated to the Apache Foundation in 2000. Formerly known as Jakarta Struts, it became a top-level Apache project in 2005.
Adobe Flex	Adobe Flex is a software development kit released by Adobe Systems for the development and deployment of cross-platform rich internet applications based on the Adobe Flash platform. You can write Flex applications using Adobe Flex Builder or by using the freely available Flex compiler from Adobe. It was open sourced in 2008.
PHP	PHP stands for PHP: Hypertext Preprocessor (like GNU, the name is recursive). It's a widely used, general-purpose scripting language originally designed for web development to produce dynamic web pages. For this purpose, PHP code is embedded into the HTML source document and interpreted by a web server with a PHP processor module that generates the web page document.
Python	Python is a general-purpose high-level programming language. Its design philosophy emphasizes code readability. Python claims to "[combine] remarkable power with very clear syntax," and its standard library is large and comprehensive. Python supports multiple programming paradigms (primarily object-oriented, imperative, and functional) and features a fully dynamic type system and automatic memory management, similar to that of Perl, Ruby, Scheme, and Tcl. Python is often used as a scripting language. It's the basis for Google's AppEngine PaaS cloud offering.

9.3.2 Second and third tiers running in the cloud

The second or middle (application logic) tier and the third tier (storage) will more often run in the cloud. A *web application* is an application accessed via a web browser over a network, such as the internet or an intranet. The term may also mean a computer software application hosted in a browser-controlled environment (such as a Java applet) or coded in a browser-supported language (such as JavaScript, combined with a browser-rendered markup language, such as HTML) and reliant on a common web browser to render the application executable.

As you read in the earlier section about browsers, it was Netscape's 1995 introduction of JavaScript that allowed programmers to add dynamic elements to the user interface that ran on the client side. Earlier, you had to send all the data to the server for processing, and the results were delivered through static HTML pages sent back to the client. You probably remember (and may occasionally run across) these kinds of pages. They now look downright archaic.

Flash was equally transformative for rich web applications. Macromedia (now part of Adobe) introduced Flash in 1996. Now, applications full of direct-manipulation features, drag-and-drop, floating menus, and all the other concepts that fat clients running on our PCs have had for years, are possible in web applications.

Multitier (or *N*-tier) applications have been the standard for many years and will be for many more to come, because this type of application architecture provides a loosely coupled model for developers to create flexible and reusable applications. By breaking an application into tiers, developers only have to modify or add a specific layer, instead of rewriting the entire application over. The change brought by the cloud is in the operation of those different tiers. Instead of a heavyweight PC operating system running a windowing system, the first (presentation) tier is a web browser. The second or middle (application logic) tier is an engine using some dynamic web content technology (such as ASP, ASP.NET, CGI, ColdFusion, JSP/Java, PHP, Perl, Python, Ruby on Rails, or Struts2), and a database is the third tier (storage). The second or third tiers, as you may have guessed, will more often run in the cloud.

Web applications are by definition multitier. More powerful enterprise web applications typically have powerful application and storage tiers, and those will run in the cloud.

9.3.3 *Rapid evolution for different storage mechanisms*

Rapid evolution will occur for different storage mechanisms, particularly for unstructured data and database-scaling strategies, such as sharding. At an accelerating pace, new services will be rolled out by both IaaS and the PaaS vendors. Amazon rolled out EBS, Virtual Private Cloud, a hosted MySQL service, and additions to its existing services within a period of 12 months.

Areas that will see rapid evolution of services will be around different storage mechanisms, particularly for unstructured data, scaling strategies, and support for sharding. You'll also see a large number of services built on top of the IaaS systems such as we have already seen with Ruby on Rails, Hadoop, and many data access services.

9.3.4 *Stronger options to protect sensitive data*

Security services will include more and stronger options to protect sensitive data. All of the major cloud providers will continue to push physical security to the levels of Fort Knox. They'll have enough mantraps, razor wire, multifactor authentication, biometric scanners, and surveillance to make the spy agencies jealous. Network and infrastructure security, already as strong as in any financial services enterprise, will grow and expand such that they continuously scan every port; signature-based intrusion detection will instantly detect any known attacks; anomaly detection will detect zero-day attacks; and excess bandwidth that can never be accessed by applications will thwart DDoS attacks.

Providers will hash and encrypt all files stored in the cloud and keep the data encrypted until the moment it's processed in a CPU. So-called Chinese walls will keep data from one cloud customer cordoned off from all other customers. All users will have to use multifactor authentication for access control and will have good key management to ensure the authentication and encryption of all APIs. All data in flight will be encrypted at all times. The only time the data will be decrypted is when it's in the CPU being processed. Even the cloud provider won't be able to decrypt such data, much less a hacker.

Hardware, hypervisors, and operating systems will move to a system of deep security at all levels where it will become virtually impossible for things such as buffer-overflow attacks to gain control of a CPU. Finally, because of the large number of virtual machines available to all cloud users at all times, it will become routine to use some of those machines to constantly do penetration and vulnerability testing both at the cloud user's level as well as at the cloud-provider-management level (the cloud *backplane*).

Security in the cloud—a hot topic now—is getting such scrutiny that in only a few years, it will set the standard for securing information. All data will be private and secure except at the precise moment when the CPU operates on it, making clouds the most secure places to operate.

9.3.5   *Higher-level services with unique APIs*

Over the next decade, companies with valuable data repositories will offer higher-level services hosted on existing clouds, each with a unique API. What will be interesting over the next decade will be the higher-level services that companies with valuable data repositories will be able to offer on top of existing clouds. Each will have a unique API. Think about a credit bureau turned into a cloud service. Drivers license databases, a variety of databases to authenticate consumer identity, real estate, mapping, and product databases as well as many other types of data will soon have powerful APIs to a cloud-hosted service. All these valuable data repositories will be easily accessible to developers and consumers. This model will also work extremely well for compute-intensive tasks, such as mapping, transformations, video and photo processing, and a myriad of scientific computations. All this will make it immensely lucrative for the data owner.

When you host a capability in the cloud with an API to access it, you can turn it into a consumable component to be used in a new type of application. That will change the way all of us think about applications. This approach is called a *mashup* or a composite application.

9.3.6   *Adoption and growth of mashups*

Adoption and growth of mashups will increase the growth of the cloud. In web development, a *mashup* is a web page or application that combines data or functionality from two or more external sources to create a new service. The term *mashup* implies easy, fast integration, frequently using open APIs and data sources to produce results that weren't the original reason for producing the raw source data.

Mashups are possible only because of the cloud. Their rapid adoption and growth will fuel the further growth of the cloud, and the reverse is true as well. Yet again, we'll see a self-reinforcing Krebs-like cycle where cloud enables mashups, and mashups promote much more use of the cloud. The clouds enabled mashups, but the ease of creating new applications through mashups will in turn make cloud growth literally explode.

An example of a mashup is the use of cartographic data to add location information to real estate data. It creates a new and distinct web API not originally provided by either source. Google Maps are probably the most common component used in mashups (see figure 9.8). You'll see Google Maps with all kinds of different data merged to create a simple but useful kind of mashup.

Similar to the concept of a portal,[1] mashups involve content aggregation loosely defined to be based on Web 2.0 (think social networks) types of techniques. A lot of people will wake up and realize they're sitting on extremely desirable data that they never before had a way to monetize. They'll host it in the cloud and provide an API to it, and suddenly the data will be accessible to the world of mashups.

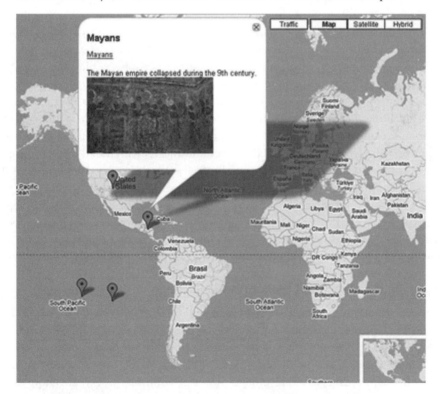

Figure 9.8 A mashup using Google Maps combined with data about collapsed civilizations. Google Maps merge together all kinds of data, creating a simple but useful kind of mashup. Source: University of Florida.

---

[1] See *Portlets in Action* by Ashish Sharin (Manning, estimated print date December 2010).

Mashups don't yet have a formal standard per se. Typically, they're based on REST (defined in chapter 2) architectural principles for create, read, update, and delete operations on some repository. The base standards on which mashups are based include XML, which is interchanged as REST or web services. Groups have already formed to fashion mashup standards. The Open Mashup Alliance (OMA) has proposed the Enterprise Mashup Markup Language (EMML). A proposed query language called MashQL is for queries against metadata models.

Analysts such as Business Insights are predicting mashup usage to grow an order of magnitude in the next five years. Just as the cloud represents a platform transformation that will cause fundamental changes in the building of IT infrastructure, mashups represent a radical change in the how and who of application construction.

9.3.7   PaaS and FaaS as predominant tools

PaaS (for example, Google's AppEngine) and its natural extension—Framework as a Service— will become the predominant way of constructing applications in 10 years. FaaS, which both AppEngine and Salesforce.com's Force.com are evolving into, is PaaS with the addition of powerful mashup construction tools, APIs, licensing, packaging, billing and ancillary tools, and services aimed at building mashups.

The ecosystem that will evolve to support mashups will include a mashup component exchange. This will be a place on the internet accessible as a SaaS application that will allow developers to find components similar to iPhone applications today. These components won't be standalone applications but instead will be components that can be mashed together with other components to create mashups. The exchange will not only allow the components to be found but will also provide a means to license components and wrap them with a billing layer such that providers have a way to monetize their use. Sample code, tests, and documentation will be included with components as well. It will be an interactive "TTL Data Book" for mashup construction much the way Texas Instruments produced the "bible" for hardware design for decades.

In some ways, we're seeing software follow a generation behind the way hardware construction evolved. Virtually all but the highest-volume parts are constructed out of standard cell libraries. Following this analogy, you can think of most hardware as being mashups of a collection of standard cells.

9.3.8   Evolution of development tools to build mashups

More powerful development tools will quickly evolve to make it easy to build mashups. In addition to and in support of a mashup component exchange, more powerful development tools will quickly evolve to make it easy to build mashups. In particular, because of so much pent-up demand to have end users build their own applications, a class of tools will evolve that allows this. An old-fashioned power programmer will create a tool tuned to a specific application domain. This domain might be some aspect of a business process, or it might be for social scheduling or anything in between. Then, a non-programmer—an end user—with initiative will effectively use such a tool. They'll quickly use the set of components laid down by the power programmer relative to the domain into which the user wants to insert a new application to create the application they and their friends or associates want to use.

Because they're well-constructed application components, and because the tool to create a final application will be careful in what it allows users to do, the resulting application will be robust. It will run in the cloud as its piece parts do. This will allow the most exposure to the tools, the applications, and the components used in those applications to use the network effect to virally spread what is good and what isn't. Thousands of simple applications will be created this way. We're seeing a preview of this with iPhone and Facebook applications. But what is changing is the nature of the individual creating the application.

It's informative to see the high-level categorization of the more than 2,000 mashup components currently listed at ProgrammableWeb.com. Table 9.2 shows the categorization of what ProgrammableWeb calls Mashup APIs. In parentheses with each category is the number of APIs supporting that category, which gives an indication of the richness of each area listed.

Table 9.2 Categorization of the Mashup API categories listed on ProgrammableWeb.com as of this writing, with the corresponding number of supporting APIs

Advertising (18)	Games (26)	Reference (78)	Answers (5)
Government (43)	Search (56)	Blog Search (8)	Internet (120)
Security (26)	Blogging (23)	Job Search (16)	Shipping (8)
Bookmarks (17)	Mapping (102)	Shopping (60)	Calendar (5)
Media Management (9)	Social (104)	Chat (13)	Medical (14)
Sports (13)	Database (19)	Messaging (61)	Storage (19)
Dictionary (1)	Music (68)	Tagging (9)	Email (35)
News (22)	Telephony (54)	Enterprise (50)	Office (22)
Tools (48)	Events (17)	Other (101)	Travel (33)
Fax (3)	Payments (14)	Utilities (29)	Feeds (14)
Photos (49)	Videos (65)	File Sharing (10)	PIM (10)
Weather (9)	Financial (87)	Project Management (20)	Widgets (17)
Food (6)	Real Estate (16)	Wiki (9)	Games (26)

With this many categories, and more being added all the time, combined with powerful but simple-to-use tools highly targeted at specific domains, the concept of developing an application has radically changed forever. We're not saying that you won't need powerful business applications. But in terms of the sheer number of applications created, the tide will turn toward individuals creating the applications they need and want for their little groups.

9.3.9   *Success of non-Western developers*

Developers outside the U.S. and Europe will leapfrog the West because they're not encumbered by legacy IT infrastructure. They'll build and sell mashup components and the tools to develop them, or they'll build more sophisticated applications that run in the cloud. And they can do so much more cheaply because they don't have to buy expensive IT infrastructure.

9.3.10 *Development cost no longer a barrier*

The cost of creating an application will become so low that it will cease to be a barrier. Many forces will act to make the pool of application developers expand greatly. You won't need to purchase equipment. You won't need to hire computer scientists. Even the nature of outsourced development will change.

Today, when you need information, you search for it on Google. What you see is a web page or a document of some sort. But what if that page was active and had the ability to take inputs and produce outputs? Some of those outputs might be visible on your mobile computing device. You'd be able to take the inputs from one such object and connect them to the outputs of another. And you'd be able to customize the behavior of the overall collection of communicating objects (will it still be called a *mashup*?). Some or all of the objects may charge for their usage. A mashup object will be able to charge you directly by directing one of its inputs to your bank account object, itself a mashup component with inputs and outputs of its own.

You'll be able to do all your computing in the cloud, similar to how the power company and the phone company provide electricity and communications today. Everything will be objects strung together the way we learned to do with the Unix `pipe` command in the early 1980s.

Today's developers will become the creators of flexible and sophisticated mashup components, but the rest of the world will be the application creators who put these objects together into new and interesting ways that suit their needs. Society will change as a result of everyone constructing applications to suit their needs. This is a bold vision, and it's only possible because the cloud is providing the backbone and the mobile revolution; the social aspects of Web 2.0 provide the other component of a perfect storm to finally bring us computing as a utility.

9.4   Summary

This last section of the final chapter offers a brief summary of the entire book.

9.4.1   *Five main principles of cloud computing*

In chapter 1, we summarized the five main principles of cloud computing as a pool of off-premises computing resources available for use when needed, built from virtualized computing resources to maximize hardware utilization, scalable elastically up or down according to need, and controlled through the automated creation of new virtual machines or deletion of existing ones, where all resource usage is billed only as used.

9.4.2 Significant benefits of adopting the cloud

The most significant benefit of cloud adoption is economic viability: converting CAPEX to OPEX means less up-front cash outlay as well as finer-grained control over dollars spent for IT. This has a real impact, particularly on smaller companies, but will increasingly affect the bottom lines of even large enterprises.

Agility is another potential benefit. Almost zero time for procurement means faster time to working systems where development occurs and, therefore, faster time to market.

These two benefits combine to make companies more efficient and more competitive. Another benefit is, somewhat surprisingly, increased security. This counterintuitive observation is because cloud providers specialize in and are dedicated to maintaining state-of-the-art security, and this will make them better at it than everyone else.

9.4.3 Reaching the cloud through an evolutionary process

Paradigm shifts in computing come in generations and proceed to transform IT: client-server replaced mainframe time-sharing, and from there we went to Grid and SaaS (with its variety of early names). Meanwhile, data centers evolved equally fast. Costs decreased, and scale increased. We got cheaper but faster computing, cheaper but denser storage, faster networks, and commodity hardware, all of which lowered costs for data centers. This enabled a dramatic increase in the scale of data centers, which now cost over $500 million to build.

On the software side, software componentization went through several generations, each with a different set of terms, such as distributed computing, object orientation, components, software services, and service-oriented architectures. Virtualization was a vital step in cloud evolution because it solved the utilization problem plaguing large data centers.

The internet was the original cloud metaphor. In the early days of describing an architecture that interacted with the internet, a cloud was used to represent the internet.

The cloud can't be classified under a single head; and to avoid comparing apples to oranges, classifying the different types of clouds is important.

9.4.4 Cloud classifications from IaaS to SaaS

Chapter 2 took on the task of breaking down all the cloud types and labeling them. IaaS is Infrastructure as a Service, where providers sell virtualized servers with a full application stack by the hour; examples include Amazon EC2, Terremark, and part of Microsoft Azure.

PaaS is Platform as a Service: a programming interface with a powerful operating environment replaces the bare-bones but infinitely controllable virtual servers of IaaS. Automatic scaling is one benefit of this approach. Loss of control and customization in addition to vendor lock-in are the price. Examples include Google App Engine, Ruby on Rails running on Amazon, and part of Microsoft Azure.

FaaS is Framework as a Service, which is typically offered as a programming framework adjunct to a SaaS product you already use.

You can program and access the data you already own through use of an SaaS application, as in Force.com. SaaS is Software as a Service, and it's the oldest incarnation of the cloud. You'll find hundreds if not thousands of SaaS applications, including Salesforce.com, Google Docs, Intuit and many more.

Finally, there is some talk of DaaS, or Datacenter as a Service, which is a euphemism for private clouds.

9.4.5   *Technological underpinnings*

When you understand what a cloud is, where it came from, and its various flavors, the next most important thing to understand is how it works. It starts with a powerful, cost-efficient data center. Cloud data centers are becoming large so they can drive down costs through efficiency. They expand that efficiency manifold through virtualization.

Users need to access the virtual servers they agree to pay for; the cloud needs an API to provide that control. Data such as applications needs to be stored close to the computing environment; clouds provide persistent storage. Many applications need structured data while running; clouds also provide various flavors of databases. Finally, we need a way to have an application running in the cloud scale up (add more servers and storage) and scale back down as demand ebbs and flows. We can render this elasticity either automatically (as in PaaS) or manually (as in IaaS).

9.4.6   *Paying only for what you use*

In chapter 3, we examined the business case for cloud computing. What all the cloud classes have in common is a completely different economic model than purchased software or hardware. The cloud uses a pure rental model like a managed service, but it's virtual capacity, not physical. No matter what your need, you only pay for what you use. Among other things, this makes expansion for development, testing, or scale doable.

The cloud makes great business sense right away when you have a short-term need, an application with volatile scale, or nonstrategic applications. But it's not a panacea, and it may not make sense for legacy systems, real-time applications, or highly confidential data.

The world has changed for startups, and the zero-capital startup is now commonplace. Medium-sized businesses are heavy cloud users for corporate websites, backups and file storage, and new product development. And a few bolder enterprises find the cloud to be a solution for heavy compute tasks, deadline-driven needs, and their online web presence.

9.4.7   *Overblown security concerns*

In chapter 4, we explored the number-one issue slowing adoption: security. Cloud providers are the operators of the largest data centers and are experts at security. They employ state-of-the-art physical security, they all get SAS 70 certification, and they use strong access-control mechanisms, including issuing customers public keys for access and encryption.

Their network and data security is best-of-breed as well. This includes operating system security, network security, control over comingling, and data-storage security. For those that have significant excess capacity or have uncompromising data security issues, there is the private cloud model.

9.4.8 *Private clouds as a temporary phenomenon*

When you drop the off-premises and metered-billing components of the cloud computing definition, you end up with private clouds that are also called internal or corporate clouds. But be careful, because this may leave you with resource scarcity, and you may not be able to participate in the economies of scale that the huge data centers enjoy.

You have many options when going the build-your-own private cloud route, including open-source vendors Eucalyptus and Open Nebula. For-profit vendors VMware and Enomaly will build it for you. Savvis and SunGard will host it in their facility for you but cordon off what is yours. Finally, a hybrid option called a virtual private cloud (VPC) tries to offer the best of both worlds. A VPC is a secure and seamless bridge between an organization's existing IT infrastructure and a provider's public cloud. This allows a corporation to expand certain applications into the cloud, to elastically scale a website as it gains popularity, and to set up a disaster-recovery scenario.

9.4.9 *Designing for scale and sharding*

Chapter 5 focused on designing applications that fully utilize the potential scale on the internet as well as applications that suddenly exceed local capacity and those that need sudden expanding storage. The main issue with applications that need to handle scale is that database bottlenecks hinder expansion. The solution is a database-partitioning scheme called *sharding*. Sharding is a decomposition of a database into multiple smaller units (called *shards*) that can handle requests individually.

When you want the best of both worlds—an internal data center that can expand out to the cloud as needed—you can use another type of scaling called *cloudbursting*; it allows the data center not to be overprovisioned and still handle rapid increases in demand. Scale can also apply to storage, and cloud storage with its pay-for-what-you-use model is an ideal way to handle storage capacity that needs to expand and contract over time.

9.4.10 *Designing for reliability and MapReduce*

Chapter 6 shifted to the issue of reliability. Distributed computing and loose coupling can lead to more reliable systems because they avoid single points of failure. A type of distributed computing used heavily by businesses, which was a precursor to the cloud, is SOA. Much of the cloud is built out of and uses SOA as its fundamental underpinning.

As the cloud providers discovered the economic benefits of building large data centers out of commodity hardware, they also increased the challenges to reliability.

The solution is redundancy. The developer who expects an application to expand to many servers has to plan for reliability. One tool for doing so is MapReduce. As the name implies, the keys are the map and reduce functions. A map takes as input a function and a sequence of values. It then applies the function to each value in the sequence. A reduce combines all the elements of a sequence using a binary operation. This achieves reliability by parceling out operations on the data set to each node in a network. Each node reports back periodically with results and status updates. Obviously, a failed node will remain silent. That node's master notes the dead worker node and sends its work out again.

Hadoop is an open-source MapReduce. It's available on Amazon AWS and is used by Amazon A9, Adobe, Baidu, Facebook, Hulu, IBM, Netseer, the *New York Times*, Rackspace, and Yahoo!.

9.4.11 Better testing, deployment, and operations in the cloud

Chapter 7 got pragmatic and delved into how you can use the cloud in testing, deployment, and operations. In traditional data centers, development, test, and staging machines drive overprovisioning and low server utilization. A single application may have quadruple the number of servers it needs in production. The cloud is a natural way to avoid these costs and waste.

Additionally, the cloud speeds up test automation and even manual testing. You can use it to employ parallelism in testing. Load testing takes advantage of the commodity flavor of virtual servers. Even browser-based load testing becomes simpler due to easy access to limitless server resources.

Most important, the cloud can fundamentally change application development. By using both the cloud and the crowd, we get close to a model of *continuous deployment*. In this model, the time between changes to the software by developers and end-to-end quality assurance shrinks to the point that it isn't unreasonable to push new releases every day while maintaining complete confidence in the quality of those releases.

9.4.12 Choosing a cloud vendor

In chapter 8, we discussed practical considerations, such as how to choose a cloud vendor. Choosing a cloud vendor is important because lock-in is a real danger for a few years. You need to consider business viability: financial, operational, and contractual. On the technical side, you need to assess availability and performance, elasticity and scale, security and compliance, and interoperability and compatibility.

9.4.13 Monitoring public clouds and SLAs

"Trust but verify" applies not only to nuclear disarmament but also to cloud SLAs. You'll need the necessary data to measure the cloud provider's compliance to the committed service levels. A practical strategy for maintaining good performance starts by assessing availability and performance as experienced by end users through continuous monitoring of the deployed application.

9.4.14 *The future of cloud computing*

The cloud will morph into utility computing: normal companies will no more have their own data centers than they would generate their own electricity. This won't happen overnight but will happen within the next 20 years.

Surprisingly, in the U.S., government will be a more aggressive adopter of cloud computing than enterprises because of the huge cost savings. And not surprisingly, when such a dramatic technological or social transformation takes place, the groups with less legacy build-out can move faster, and this will enable the non-Western world countries to leapfrog as they use the cloud to advance their participation in IT markets.

Alongside this transformation will be the mobile device revolution that we're seeing the beginning of now. One transformation is helping the other move even faster. The cloud is a must-have when the end-user device is small, is mobile, and has limited capabilities. But these devices generate and consume vast quantities of data and computing, driving the need for the cloud. Ultimately, we'll see computing devices built into everyday devices and almost every surface. We'll take them for granted. For that to happen, they'll need to be interconnected through—well, a giant cloud.

appendix:
Information security refresher

In this appendix, we'll review the basics of information security that will help you understand how security in the cloud works. We'll cover six topics:

- Secret communications
- Keys
- Shared-key cryptography
- Public-key cryptography
- XML Signature
- XML Encryption

These topics are relevant because cloud providers, having based their services on web services, all use these security technologies in their everyday operations. As you'll see, keys are issued the moment you sign up for cloud services. The APIs used to create and control machine instances all use one or more of these means to keep your operations secret and secure. Let's begin with the concept of secret communications.

Secret communications

Keeping communication secret is the heart of security. The science of keeping messages secret is called *cryptography*. You may think of cryptography as being used to scramble and unscramble messages to keep prying eyes from seeing your secrets. But that is never enough: you also need to know who is sending and receiving the message and whether they're authorized to do so.

Binding a known *identity* to a message you can see, interpret, and trust across a network also uses cryptography. That identity, asserting itself, must be *authenticated* by a trusted agent for the binding to be valid. That agent may be the cloud provider or a higher authority that both you and the cloud provider agree to trust. After you know the identity, *authorization* allows the communicating parties to specify what the individual with that identity is allowed to do.

When someone receives a secret message, they need to know that nothing in the message has been changed in any way since it was published—an attribute called *integrity*. When cryptography successfully keeps a message secret, it has satisfied the requirement for *confidentiality*. At times, you may want to know that someone who received confidential information can't deny that they received it, an important security concept called *nonrepudiation*.

Note these descriptions are brief; it takes an entire book to cover these concepts in depth.[1] But you need to know about these concepts to begin to appreciate information security and how it applies to cloud computing. And the key to all of cryptography is the keys.

Keys

A *key* is a set of bits that acts as an input parameter to a crypto-algorithm. Think of the crypto-algorithm as the lock on your front door. That lock is standard, as is the door. Lots of other people have doors and locks that are outwardly identical. But inside the lock are some unique (or almost unique) settings of tumblers that exactly match individual keys.

Uniqueness of keys

Keys used in cryptography are "almost unique" because, like door locks, there is no absolute certainty that two keys are unique. But the chances of two keys being the same are infinitesimally small, as is the chance of your key opening a neighbor's lock.

Algorithms for encryption and decryption do not need to be and normally are not kept secret. It is the key that is kept secret. It is an important fundamental principle of cryptography that the algorithms be public, standard, widely distributed, and carefully scrutinized. This principle ensures that all the world's cryptographers fully shake out the algorithms for any security flaws.[2]

The key is the variable that makes the algorithm result unique and secret. For some crypto-algorithms, the key may be a random number. For others, such as public-key algorithms, you (or rather, an application on your computer) must carefully choose matched keys—a complex, time-consuming mathematical operation by itself. The key space needs to be large. A huge number of possible keys helps prevent guessing attacks. Different algorithms require different key lengths for good security. Most keys today are typically 256 bits or larger.

---

[1] See *Applied Cryptography* by Bruce Schneier (Wiley, 1996).
[2] This wasn't the case earlier. Even post World War II, it was thought that the algorithms needed to be top secret. But after those algorithms fell to hackers one after the other, it was determined that the openness policy worked much better.

Shared key cryptography

Shared-key cryptography uses the same key to encrypt and decrypt a message. This requires that both communicating parties share the same key and, vitally important, keep it secret from the rest of the world. In the shared-key cryptography process, the sender, using the shared secret key, encrypts plaintext into ciphertext. Then, on the receiving end, the recipient decrypts the ciphertext using the same (shared) secret key to read the plaintext originally sent. See figure A.1.

As long as you keep the shared key secret, use a reasonably long key, and employ an approved modern crypto-algorithm, there is no way anyone can decipher the ciphertext and get at the data in the message. Your data is safe from prying eyes and attackers.

The advantage of shared-key encryption/decryption is that the algorithms are fast and can operate on arbitrarily sized messages. The disadvantage is that this approach creates great difficulties managing a shared key that must be kept secret across a network between message senders and recipients. Still, this is a form of cryptography you run into frequently, because it's the basis of Secure Socket Layer (SSL) security and is the foundation for XML Encryption, which is used heavily in web services and cloud computing security. The next type of cryptography solves the problem of keeping a single shared key secret.

Public-key cryptography

Public-key cryptography uses a key pair called a *private and public key*. Because the keys are different, this type of encryption is called asymmetric. You use one from the pair of

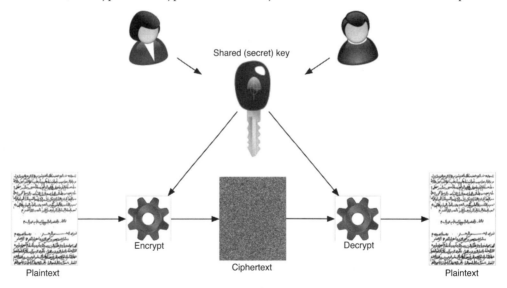

Figure A.1   The shared-key (symmetric) encryption process. Plaintext is encrypted by the sender using the shared (secret) key with a symmetric cryptography algorithm, turning it into ciphertext. The recipient, using the same key and the inverse decryption algorithm, turns the ciphertext back into the original plaintext.

keys to encrypt the data; only the other half of the pair can decrypt the data. Of vital importance is that you can't share the private half of the key pair. Only the public key can be shared; in fact, it can be widely distributed to others. It is an absolute tenet of public-key cryptography that each subject keeps their private key confidential, never sharing it with anyone.

You can choose to use either key to encrypt, but only the matching key from the pair will decrypt. In figure A.2, Alice uses the recipient's public key to encrypt her plaintext message into ciphertext. Bob uses his private key to decrypt the ciphertext back into the original plaintext message.

If you want to make sure only the recipient can read your message, use that person's public key to encrypt, and then they and only they using their private key can decrypt. This is *encryption* to send a secret message to only the intended recipient. If you want everyone who gets your message to know it came from you and only you, use your private key to encrypt; then, the recipients can use your public key to decrypt. This is using a *digital signature* to prove that you and only you could have sent the message.

Whichever way asymmetric encryption is used, it's limited to relatively small messages. A frequent pattern is to use asymmetric encryption to encrypt and exchange a shared key but then to use shared-key encryption for large messages that are being exchanged. The ubiquitous and highly successful SSL technology uses this pattern for virtually all web sites doing secure transactions: it uses asymmetric encryption for the initial authentication and to exchange a shared secret key; then, using the shared key, all the data transmitted across the SSL channel is encrypted using a symmetric algorithm.

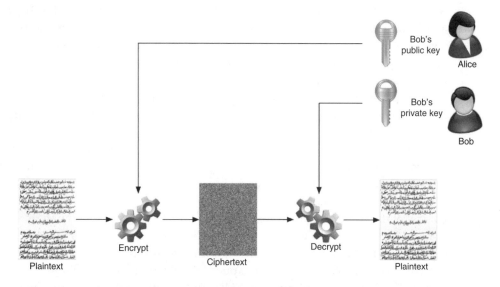

Figure A.2 **The public-key (asymmetric) encryption process. Alice uses Bob's public key to encrypt plaintext into ciphertext using an asymmetric (public-key cryptography) algorithm. Bob uses his private key from the same key pair to decrypt the ciphertext into the original plaintext. This message is completely unreadable by anyone without Bob's private key.**

For web services and cloud computing (which is based on and uses web services), digital signatures and encryption are typically applied to XML streams of data (or used inside SOAP envelopes). The standards formed for this purpose are called, not surprisingly, XML Signature and XML Encryption.

XML Signature

XML Signature is a foundational technology for web services security in general and its use in cloud computing security. XML Signature is built on top of mature digital signature technology. The purpose of digital signatures is to provide a mechanism for message integrity (no one has changed the message since it was created) and nonrepudiation (you can't refute this message exchange). XML Signature was created to encode digital signatures into XML.

Congress approved electronic signatures in June 2000. This approval gave legitimacy to electronic signatures. It prevents the contesting of a signed contract solely because it is signed electronically. This event set the stage for digital signature standards. XML Signature came out of an IETF/W3C working group called XML-DSig that was established to create a highly extensible signature syntax tightly integrated with existing XML technologies, but one that could also handle composite documents from diverse application domains as well.

XML Encryption

Similar to XML Signature, XML Encryption is built on top of mature cryptographic technology—in this case, shared-key encryption technology. Core requirements for XML Encryption are that it must be able to encrypt an arbitrarily sized XML message, and it must do so efficiently. Those two factors led its creators to choose shared-key (symmetric) encryption as the foundation for XML Encryption (remember, shared-key encryption can handle arbitrary-sized messages, whereas asymmetric key encryption is limited to small messages).

Encryption provides for message confidentiality (the message is secret from all but the intended recipient). You need XML Encryption over and above transport-level encryption, such as SSL, because you want to control message-level security at the application level and not leave it to the underlying infrastructure (which you don't control) to provide it. With XML Encryption, you can maintain confidentiality of messages in the face of the message taking multiple hops on its way to its destination, which can compromise end-to-end security. At SSL termination points, you lose control of the security of your data. This is common when you use shared services. You also need confidentiality when storing the XML message, even after it reaches its final destination. This requirement is called *persistent confidentiality*.

Like XML Signature, XML Encryption applies standard algorithms to data and then stores that encrypted result in XML. And as with XML Signature, you can apply encryption selectively to portions of a document.

XML Encryption builds on and shares several concepts with XML Signature. Like XML Signature, it's a W3C standard. It's a vitally important second foundation to web services security because it's the way to achieve confidentiality in XML messages used to control and manage cloud-based services.

With that refresher on information security as a backdrop, you're well equipped to fully understand the discussions of cloud security in chapter 4.

index

RELATED MANNING TITLES

Azure in Action
by Chris Hay and Brian H. Prince

   ISBN: 978-1-935182-48-1
   488 pages, $44.99
   October 2010

jQuery in Action, Second Edition
by Bear Bibeault and Yehuda Katz

   ISBN: 978-1-935182-32-0
   488 pages, $44.99
   June 2010

Website Owner's Manual
by Paul A. Boag

   ISBN: 978-1-933988-45-0
   296 pages, $34.99
   November 2009

Understanding Enterprise SOA
by Eric Pulier and Hugh Taylor
  with foreword by Paul Gaffney

   ISBN: 978-1-932394-59-7
   280 pages, $39.95
   November 2005

For ordering information go to www.manning.com